I DID IT MY WAY

Memoirs of a Maverick

Crawford 'Scotty' Kemp

HOLOROSE PUBLISHING

Published by

HOLOROSE PUBLISHING

6 Glebe Road, Kinloss, Forres,
Moray, IV36 3TU, Scotland.

ISBN 978-0-9573188-0-9

Printed and bound in the UK by Biddles, part of the MPG Books
Group, Bodmin and King's Lynn

Interior design and Cover Design by Susan Kemp.
Illustrations by Crawford Kemp,
Copyright © Crawford Kemp 2012.
Photographs Copyright © Crawford Kemp 2012.

First Edition

Disclaimer

I have at times invented a few names, dates and places without actually losing the gist of the story to protect both others and myself. In addition, this occasionally allows my sometimes-reluctant memory some leeway when dealing with long forgotten dates and details.

The Title of this Book

I was told that writing a book is a journey, but I soon learned when writing a book that requires reflection on one's own life, the journey doesn't end with the completion of the book. So it was only after I had finished the writing that I felt that I had to change the title from the original *Half the Lies you Hear Aren't True (Unless They Are)* to something more in keeping with what the completed book had engendered. The new message was *I Did It My Way*.

However, I would like to explain the reasoning behind the original title, which I may use in a future book. My father was a quiet man, neither philosopher nor advisor, but one light-hearted comment always stayed with me when, with a sidelong glance in my direction, he said, "Don't forget laddie that half the lies you hear aren't true." For some reason this seemingly flippant observation went deep into my awareness and I eventually interpreted it as a reminder that the best things in life are usually achieved in a light heart, and to accept nothing for its face value but always to seek wisdom in the not so obvious. At the same time I am not oblivious to the hint of cynicism contained in his observation, something, which I feel should be applied very sparingly, if at all. Hence the original title of this book.

So I want to thank you dad, and I know that you won't be surprised that, once again, I did it my way.

To Carolan

With best wishes

[signature]

I dedicate this book to all those who have suffered injustice with quiet dignity.

I DID IT MY WAY

About the author

Born in January 1929 in a council house in Greenock, Scotland Crawford Kemp attended school in Glasgow, Port Glasgow and finally in Yorkshire, when his father, a shipbuilder, was sent to work during the war. On leaving school, Crawford became an apprentice compass adjuster sailing out of Hull and Grimsby while attending technical college evening classes. After the Second World War, he worked for the shipbuilders Yarrows of Glasgow in Montevideo, Uruguay, until this company went bankrupt.

After some years cattle ranching in the land of the gaucho, Crawford moved into the industrial side of the beef industry and the food industry in general, where he held executive posts in Buenos Aires for many years, requiring extensive travelling to other countries.

He later worked in Egypt and Saudi Arabia and the UK as project manager for different organisations as well as chief executive for a company in Shetland, before leaving big business and setting up a successful natural health practice in Brighton in the 1980s.

Crawford has never fully retired and after providing for himself as a watercolour artist for several years he took up adult education, teaching holism, English and Spanish.

Now living - once again in a council house - on the Moray coast of Scotland, Crawford likes to spend his time exploring leading edge science ideas, cutting edge healing modalities and personal development methods, as well as reading, writing, rowing, walking, cycling and spending time in nature.

Contents

I DID IT MY WAY

I DID IT MY WAY

In the Beginning

Between Two Wars

First of all let me explain that almost every man that I encountered in my formative years was a survivor from that most horrendous human slaughterhouse ever created by human beings. Those who had created this war (and no doubt those who had profited by it) chose to call it 'great' and so the first misleading euphemism amongst so many more that would affect my thinking was planted in my young mind. At the same time that smidgeon of thought conditioning or autosuggestion was inviting all and sundry to accept this unspeakable human indecency as a Great War. What a 'great' way to surreptitiously plant an attitude into the unsuspecting human psyche when the very last thing that the sane amongst us are looking for is more war.

Already at a very young age I had an instinctive awareness that I might find it difficult to accept the rules that I was being told we must all obey, or that I would follow the road that was expected of me. I sensed a quite enjoyable, if controversial, road ahead.

More than ten years had gone by since the signing of the armistice and 'the war to end all wars' had passed into the history books. Meanwhile the future, personified in our family by the birth of a baby boy, was taking place in a small council house on the river Clyde in Scotland while mother, father and baby sister were doing their best to survive the 'great' depression (which in some towns and cities caused unemployment to reach 70% as ship building fell by 90%).

The way my working class community handled this was to develop an incredibly infectious sense of humour that permeated life and had a lasting effect on the Clydeside character. Stand-up comics could be found at every street corner and today still produce characters like Billy Connoly.

So it was that at the end of that particularly cold month of January 1929 that I came into this world and commenced this rich, scary, interesting and varied adventure.

Both of my grandfathers, my father and all of my uncles who had come home from the war worked in the shipyards, the only exception was my uncle Willy who had been to university and was well on his way to a brilliant future in the academic world. Having a university degree he had been given a commission in the infantry, only to be blown up by a German shell while leading his kilted platoon across no man's land. Ah well, king, country, GREAT Britain and all that you know. Amongst others, Queen Victoria is quoted as confirming that "there is no finer death for a man than on the battlefield", thus inviting us to acknowledge that fighting each other, killing other young men and being killed has become deeply engraved in our collective psyche as something 'good' and is actually accepted as 'good' by otherwise apparently sane human beings.

I say apparently sane because, can you imagine coming from some well-balanced, peace-loving civilisation and meeting people like you and I who accept, support, and practice such depraved and revolting activities while suggesting that we are sane? Yes it's us I'm talking about, you and me, not them, whoever 'them' might be.

Before I launch into my anecdotes I invite you to stand back for a moment and contemplate these depraved practices, which are of our very own creation, yours and mine! We created them and we support them. We finance them with our taxes and we encourage our young children to put on these same military uniforms and become cadets, thus preparing them to continue this gross indecency into their future, as we supply them with ever more and more ingenious and diabolical horror weapons of mass destruction. Are you creating this horrendous future for these babies you see in prams on the high street, in the park or in the supermarket, and still claiming to be sane? I would suggest that you might follow my example and admit that you are really not fit to be let out alone. Know the truth and the truth will set you free; it's a great feeling.

I would ask you to please guard against taking this personally since I confess that I most decidedly did not always take this point of view because, like so many youngsters of my generation, I was not only expected to accept this preparation for conflict as I grew up, but was actually to spend the first seventeen years of my life having it reinforced, nurtured and hard-wired into my subconscious, to the point where all I wanted to do was to put on a uniform and kill people, preferably Germans, or even the IRA. But let me introduce you to these first seventeen, vulnerable, unsuspecting, innocent and formative years.

As a small child, and as I grew up, I would be taken on Sundays to visit my grandparents. My maternal grandfather was a cabinetmaker working in the shipyards. His was a churchgoing family and they had their own church pew, which accommodated all eleven of them. He was also very involved in freemasonry, which was to raise its controversial head and challenge me for years to come.

If given a choice I preferred the visits to my paternal grandparents where my two aunts, two uncles and my father had been born and brought up in two rooms on the third floor of a tenement. It was heated by a coal burning range and lit by gas but did not have electricity. My magical diminutive granny, Annie McDonald Kemp by name, would be busy preparing a meal at the black range while my father, grandfather and uncles would gather around the wireless and then discuss the news items, politics and the world situation. I always loved to listen both to the wireless, then the views and opinions expressed, which I accepted as the last word in worldly truth and wisdom. I can remember being warned that the glass accumulator (which powered the wireless) cost money to recharge and it was also full of dangerous acid, so the wireless was a 'no-go' area for all except my grandpa.

He was tall, a professional footballer of athletic build by the name of Peter Crawford Kemp and he had piercing blue eyes, so that when he looked at you, you knew that you were being looked at (or into). I never found out much about my granny who was, I believe, unable to speak any other language apart from her native Gaelic until she was grown up. I also have a strong conviction that she was what we call a tinker. Tinkers were very common when I was growing up and they were mainly the crofters and farmers who had been turned off their land by the triumphant Hanoverians following the battle of Culloden. These pitiful families tried to survive as tinkers (the origin of the word tinker is the Gaelic *tinceard*, meaning 'tinsmith' or 'black tinker'). The use of Scotland's rightful language was no longer punishable by death when I was growing up but was still a severely suppressed tongue. On one occasion, after discovering this 'secret' tongue, I did the unmentionable. In my eight-year-old childish innocence I asked my granny if she spoke Gaelic. My gentle loving sweet wee granny was instantly transformed into a fiend, shouting at me that she would not have any such talk in her house and never to mention it again. Although I left the kitchen in tears I had been given a frightening and alarming insight into the terrible deep wounds left in those who had dared to speak their own native tongue belonging to the country of their birth. I still hold deep emotional feelings when it comes to this subject and so rather than indulging my emotions I would like to quote John O'Donohue, who expresses such things so very clearly in his magical book *Anam Cara*, when he talks about the destruction of language in Ireland.

"Yet the attempt to destroy Gaelic was one of the most destructive acts of violence of our colonization by England. Gaelic is such a poetic and powerful language, it carries the Irish memory. When you steal a people's language, you leave their soul bewildered."

I must conclude that the unexpected outburst from my normally gentle granny had its origins in her soul's bewilderment.

The magical conversations around the wireless (during which I seemed to be invisible) taught me about politicians and politics and especially that the "only good Germans were dead Germans" (this view was also taken of the Irish Catholics sometimes, who wanted freedom from London's rule) but it was this hate for all things German that dominated. On reflection it has to be said that there was a total absence of anything that could be classed as particularly enlightening or mind expanding in these conversations and most things that were discussed were strictly part of that material world as dictated by London. It has also to be acknowledged of course that these close relations of mine were all 'survivors' who, having experienced trench warfare, would today be classed as suffering from post-traumatic stress or something worse. In those days, however, anyone showing signs of shell shock or trauma ran the risk of being forced to stand on top of a barrel, accused of being a coward, and then shot.

But for me this perhaps bigoted, non-spiritual 'man's talk' was gospel truth, so by the time I reached the age of twelve I had become totally mind conditioned. I needed no further convincing; however just to make sure that I, and my generation, really got the message my country went to war once again with these same nasty Germans. This was of course not any kind of deliberate brainwashing but it was however perhaps conditioned thinking at it's most effective.

In spite of all this, or perhaps because of it, I really still preferred to avoid conflict.

I did not like the fist fights that were very much a part of life at school and I always felt uncomfortable when the men in my little world would ask me about my fights at school or in the street, since I dared not say that I did not enjoy them.

My father harboured dreams of me becoming a professional football player like his father had been, or even a boxer but although I enjoyed sport and outdoor activities I was not competitive by nature. It is interesting to note that my grandfather would go to these professional matches on foot with his boots tied together and hanging round his neck and that he was paid five pounds a year as a professional playing for Greenock Morton. He kept his family by working as a brass worker in the shipyards and played football on weekends.

For a number of years we lived in Port Glasgow and our schoolboy fun consisted largely of exploring an area above the town known as the piggery, not that there were any pigs to be seen, but it was an area that provided us with steep slopes, small ravines and places where we could dare each other to do dangerous things. It also supplied me with an occasional escape into nature on my own, where I secretly enjoyed the smell of the grass and earth, the roughness of tree bark and, above all, freedom from people and being told what to do all of the time.

We fought real battles from time to time with the Catholics - who were referred to as Fenians - using sticks, stones, catapults and fists but nobody ever seemed to get very badly hurt. When the police became involved I always seemed to escape with a telling off or a visit by the sergeant to my house, where I was given a serious telling off in front of my parents. It took me years to understand that the policemen were what some people in England might call WASPS (White Anglo Saxon Protestants). So my family and most of my friends, as Establishment-supporting Presbyterians were the Scottish equivalent of WASPS, and this meant if anyone was going to be taken to court it would probably not be one of us. Many of the police were also freemasons like my father, grandfather and my uncles, but I knew nothing of such things at this stage although I cringe all these years later as I write this.

Then there were the weddings and, in my tenement life, money would be thrown out of the departing car or carriage window and all we street urchins would scramble for the coins. I think that this took place as the bride and groom drove away but I really cannot remember since I was usually on my hands and knees trying to pick up the pennies. When you consider that the lucky ones amongst us were given a penny a week as pocket money, then several weeks' income lying on the road was perhaps worth scrambling for, although the fact is that I had a secret aversion to scrambling and fighting for these coins (another aspect of my secret life). I never thought about this custom until many years later when, as an adult living in Cairo, I happened to be present in the Cairo Hilton Hotel while a very expensive looking wedding was taking place. Suddenly a large group of ladies all dressed in their finery and dripping with gold started to ululate like desert Bedouins while hundreds of small coins were thrown from the mezzanine floor down onto the floor below. I happened at the time to be with a Cockney engineer who waded in and retrieved a few pieces of 'gold' only to find that they were very shiny and very thin copper discs worth nothing. One thing I do remember from my boyhood days is that if we followed a wedding and no money was forthcoming we would chase the car shouting, "Hairy weddin'! Hairy weddin'!" at the top of our voices. Again I have no idea why this was done but it probably guaranteed that we would always profit on such occasions.

It was at about this time that I heard on the wireless that some scientists were trying to split the atom (whatever that meant) and that, if successful, we would be able to heat the average three-bedroomed house for half of one (old) penny per year. Seventy years later I am having difficulties keeping warm on more than a thousand pounds a year, which is below the average heating bill, and of course, at the time nobody suggested that this new invention would actually be used to fry 250,000 human beings alive. So you see, half the lies you hear really aren't true.

Temptation

On Sundays our family, consisting of my mother and father, my sister and myself, would go to church. This was the Kirk, or Scottish Presbyterian Church. There would be the usual boring service and occasionally the Sunday school children would attend the service as a group. On these occasions the minister would speak specifically to the children. I remember this rather terrifying man with red hair looking down on us from the pulpit and telling us about the danger of misbehaving. He addressed the boys in particular one Sunday when he warned us against the temptation that might make us want to touch the girls, or perhaps do things which would guarantee that we would burn in hell. At the time I must have been ten or eleven years of age and I remember thinking that I certainly had nothing to worry about since girls were boring and silly. As time went by I often thought about these periodical warnings and although I had no desire to make contact with girls I did begin to think about the suggestions made by the minister and eventually I began occasionally to secretly fantasise about what it was that was so wicked and prohibited. This was my secret and I was totally safe from ever being burned alive because I could think of nothing more pointless than getting even close to a girl. Some time later the minister decided to talk to us about of the evils of thought, and in this talk he made it clear that thinking about girls was even worse than touching them.

Since I had been increasingly thinking more about girls it came as quite a shock, at this tender age, that I was damned to hell for all eternity. I was heading for that everlasting fire that never went out and there was no escape. When, over the next few weeks, my mother asked me why I was so quiet and down at the mouth I simply dared not mention the unmentionable. This was just one more example of another bigoted, poorly educated minister of the church doing his job and doing it well. Sow fear and dread amongst the people and you will increase the power of the few over the many, and if you get them young you'll have them forever. This, by the way, was as close as I ever got in my life to being instructed or taught about love, relationships or sex. What it did do was to invite me to question these men in black wearing dog collars and spouting venom and ill-conceived messages to the vulnerable. This questioning, however, would require the courage to take back my power and think for myself; something that seemed, at the time, to be akin to committing suicide.

Special Sunday

Another special Sunday in my young life stands out and, although more than seventy years have passed, I still remember it clearly. It was 1939 and, as was the custom, I had gone to church with my mother, father and sister. Usually the service was a combination of bible readings, intermingled with veiled threats of hellfire and damnation, all punctuated by hearty singing, which made everyone feel warm and ever so good. It also helped to create and nurture that indulgent self-righteousness that was part of belonging to the dominant Protestant faction who ran things, all the way from Buckingham Palace right down to the man and woman in the street.

This Sunday, however, turned out to be very different! The Reverend Whitley (who later became the high priest of our particular brand of Christianity, of which I am told there are now twenty-two thousand varieties) climbed into the pulpit and looked around in silence. For once, he did not bother to threaten or rebuke. For once, he did not fill me with fear and dreading, which in itself was a pleasant change and a new experience. Instead, after his silent look around the congregation he said something that had a much more electrifying effect on the grown ups than any of his hellfire and threats of eternal damnation. What he said caused the congregation to actually talk to each other across the aisles, the men no longer whispering, but not talking too loudly either, while some women were openly crying. This felt great, not like church at all, and I felt kind of liberated and confused at the same time but I really enjoyed this new feeling. Could this thing be worse than being burned alive forever and ever by that wee chap with the tail using his pitchfork to stick holes in my flesh? I looked at the expressions on the faces around me, and I waited for something terrible to happen.

I waited for days, and weeks, and finally I decided that a declaration of war was just another one of those inexplicable things that adults exaggerated. The adults were apparently scared of this war thing, but I still felt that the wee man in my Sunday school book with the red suit, horns and tail with the arrowhead on the end was much more of a worry than Mr Hitler. My young vulnerable mind could think of nothing and nobody more fearful or more impressive than this all-powerful Christian god that they called The Devil.

Yards of black paper to cover the windows, gas masks, air raid drills, air raid shelters and sandbags were all a short-lived novelty. An increasing number of uniformed men and woman appeared on the buses and in the streets, but nothing had really changed.

Junior School

I attended Jean Street School, an old Victorian building complete with its tall iron railings and a tarmacadam playground. Mainly poor, hardened, dirty children attended it and they suffered from head lice, fleas, dirt and some from a lack of food. Most of the boys wore short trousers and woollen jerseys that came up to the neck and had collars, just like a woollen shirt. Some of these jerseys were quite dirty and smelled badly, as did the bodies inside of them; not all enjoyed a Friday night bath as I did.

Every day there were organised fights outside the school at four o'clock, where badly cut and bruised faces were accepted as being normal and the failure to win a fight could often mean trouble at home.

Schooling was a strict, no-nonsense experience where you did as you were told or you got punished. We wrote on wooden framed slates and we were not encouraged to question things. For some reason, I seemed to experience more than my share of punishment. This tended to make me both afraid and secretly angry at the same time.

The pain from being 'strapped' on the hand was no novelty to me, partly because I was not a very good student, but also because I occasionally challenged the status quo. So when, at the age of eleven, I was sent to the headmaster to be strapped yet again, this time for having dirt on the back of my hands (which I claimed were chapped from the cold) I thought little of it. I presented myself at his door thinking of the strap cutting into my sore hands, and the trouble I would be in when my father found out.

"Come in and put yer hand out!" The cadaverous head stared down at me, "Put yer hand out!" I stood my ground and refused to move. "Put yer hand out when yer told." The voice sounded less sure of itself. I put my hand out and as the strap hit I grabbed it and wrenched it from the headmaster's hand. I had no prior intention of behaving like this and it felt as though someone else was doing these things, but I set about the skinny old man, swinging the hard 'handle' end of the strap at his now retreating body. I was detained in the office and my parents were summoned.

For some mysterious reason I was allowed to leave the school without being expelled and the police were not informed. I was still to learn about being well connected through the church and being the son and grandson of a freemason. At this early stage of my life I still had no idea how things worked in the adult world, but I knew that this incident was to close one chapter and invite the next one to unfold.

A Taste of War

One unexpected early introduction to the realities of this new war happened when a French ammunition ship blew up out on the river Clyde right in front of our town and the whole population was witness to some shocking and distressing scenes as the poor wretches who survived were brought ashore to be transported to hospital in any way possible. This included in carts, wheelbarrows or simply being physically carried by willing volunteers. In spite of my parents efforts to hide us from the nasty things going on, the realities of war were soon to become commonplace as my maternal grandparent's house was obliterated by a German bomb, forcing my two very genteel maiden aunts to live under a railway bridge for a time.

As a schoolboy and young adult I experienced the almost daily air raids and dog fights over Hull, where my father had been sent to work, and then in 1941 for several unreal days and nights these Germans decided to blitzkrieg the city. The wireless reports on the bombing always referred to 'a northern town' for security reasons, but Hull was actually the most bombed city in the UK after London. Ninety per cent of all houses were damaged and the numbers of dead and injured bore this out. Later when I was sent to train on the SS Discovery tied up on the

Thames Embankment I saw for myself what was happening to London. So my mind conditioning, having travelled through the philosophical into the hands-on and practical, should have, in theory, produced some wisdom. What I think it tended to do in the longer term was to turn me from a potential Establishment gun fodder, toe-the-line zombie into a kind of anti-war peacenik and oddball, a conscious 'traitor' to the Establishment and a bit of an embarrassment to my friends and relatives. In addition to this I was always very aware of an unspoken dimension to life. I had a knowingness and awareness that we were much more than our society acknowledged or allowed to surface. I was aware at an early age of a presence of a something or someone outside of myself, but had no one with whom I could share such thoughts or from whom I could learn. I felt protected and looked after at one level, but I was sure that to broach this kind of subject would bring ridicule, and distance me even more from other 'normal' people. This was another deep, if undefined secret, which I was obliged to keep totally to myself, all bottled up but wanting to escape.

I know now that this 'something', was simply my knowingness that I was more than what was being acknowledged, and that life was more than what I was being told by those who invent and run religions and philosophies to feed their own hungry egos and bank balances. I had always been a bit of a cuckoo in the nest at home and a challenge to my parents, but I think that this had more to do with what was not being said rather than what was openly spoken about.

I enjoyed life in my own way though, especially out in nature or on the water. I quite definitely did not enjoy school in England where I was singled out, not only by my class mates for having a Scottish accent but also by one teacher who would ask the class a question and then explain to the class that I, being Scottish, would have the answer because everybody knew that Scottish education was superior to that taught in

England. This speech was always accompanied by pulling the hair above my ear. I developed an aversion to schools, classrooms and teachers in general. My parents who had little time for, or interest in, academia supported my aversion to some degree.

I still watched with envy as the older boys left school and then reappeared in uniform, some as officers sporting swagger sticks, some with medal ribbons.

I moved up one class at a time and the war continued one year at a time. In spite of some terrible things (German again) that I was experiencing from time to time, I still wanted to leave school and get into a uniform.

Lost Friends

One of my friends, who I had originally met as a Sea Scout, was only a couple of years older than I was and after joining the RAF he flew a number of missions over Germany, bombing industrial complexes and other targets. He was the rear gunner in a Lancaster bomber, which meant that he was separated from the rest of the crew and spent many cold, lonely and terrifying hours at the tail end of the plane with German fighters trying to shoot them down, watching other planes being shot down or just scanning the sky anticipating the next attack. When he had time off we would go walking or camping since we both enjoyed being out in nature.

Early one morning he walked into our house in full sheepskin flying gear, complete with parachute and said his plane had crash-landed close by and we were the nearest people that he knew so he had come to us for help. My mother got him into a taxi and sent him to his home, about four miles away. He was eventually certified insane and was locked away at the age of twenty for the rest of his life. His name was Keith Holmes but we called him Sherlock.

Another friend, James Parker by name, known to one and all as Spud, managed to join the Navy straight after our training on board the SS Discovery. On his very first trip to Murmansk he drowned in the icy northern waters, as many hundreds of others had, trying to supply our (then) Russian allies. Yet even as I heard the news about these two close friends, Spud Parker and Sherlock Holmes, I still felt a compulsion that I had to become part of this mind-boggling madness. I suppose that that is how overwhelmed the conditioned mind can become. Later I read somewhere that Winston Churchill, as a twenty-something year old officer had walked into a prison camp, taken out his brand new Luger pistol and shot dead a number of unarmed prisoners, reloaded and then murdered a few more. This was a very wealthy young aristocrat who had been to the most expensive English public school followed by military training at the Royal Military College. While I was growing up I was being taught to look up to these 'ruling classes' while at the same time the legal system sent murderers and serial killers to be 'hanged by the neck until dead'. The more I tried to reconcile such conflicting events, the more isolated I felt. I suppose in a way that soldier with his Luger pistol, who was part of the English 'officer class' is simply you or I, differently conditioned. Nevertheless, how to reconcile these disparities kept my active and enquiring mind in a spin.

In my particular case it would seem that someone, somewhere was looking after me for I did not do that which I was conditioned to do during those seventeen years. This was not because I had changed my mind but because the war came to an end in 1946 just when it was my turn to get into that long-awaited uniform.

Of course at the time it seemed so very unfair that I had been cheated by such an untimely end to the war but I now thank God that I never became part of our frighteningly dominant and indecently expensive military establishment. The foregoing also serves to remind me that when I feel frustrated at young men and women joining the military today; and much as I dislike the whole outrageously mad and expensive, establishment-backed, military culture, I have to say 'judge not' because but for the grace of God I would have been fed, clothed, trained, mind-conditioned and nicely packaged as 'one of our boys', a hero fighting for democracy and the English Establishment.

I could have been one more unsuspecting, performing monkey who has given his power away, and in order to avoid seeing reality has stuck his head where the sun never shines. If you feel offended by that then maybe you will appreciate my feelings when I contemplate the money and effort that has gone into persuading my generation to join this collective indecency which, I believe will eventually wipe us off the face of the earth unless we wake up and take our power back and refuse to support the establishment.

Adult World and a Fishy Story

During the six years between almost being expelled from school and starting my apprenticeship Europe had been at war, while I had been mostly at school.

Now it was 1946, the war in Europe had come to an end and I had got out of school and become an apprentice compass adjuster and fine instrument maker sailing out of Hull and Grimsby on the east coast of England. This meant that the time that I went to work was largely governed by the tides, since it was at high tide that the minesweepers, sea-going tugs and trawlers set sail, and we had to fit in the compass adjusting as they went to sea. When we were not on board a ship we worked in what was an old Victorian workshop, which smelled of special paints, brass cleaning liquids and alcohol to mix with the water used to fill the compasses. There were benches and lathes, rolls of copper and sheets of brass, as well as special paints and hundreds of magnets of varying sizes. There were dry compasses from a bygone era, and Walker's logs as well as barometers, clocks and thermometers all living side by side with items long since brought ashore from ships which no longer sailed the seven seas; a veritable Aladdin's cave of things nautical. I learned about bezels and gimbals, and how to turn brass rods into connectors, handles and holders for the compass needles. Mr Hooper, who had been in this workshop for over thirty years, refused to work with the electrically powered lathes and opted for a lathe powered by a foot treadle on which he turned out beautiful work. Sid Brown, who had finished his apprenticeship, was my best friend and always had something good to say about my creations and was always ready to give me a hand. New apprentices were traditionally the butt of jokes and leg pulling, and the only way to avoid them was to have another new apprentice under you. One standard joke was to send the unsuspecting victim to the basket-making loft to ask for a long stand. You could be left standing for an hour or more before someone asked you if that was a long enough stand. These were all good-humoured innocent pranks and a requirement in all apprenticeships. There were also some other pranks not so innocent but I'll not go into that.

There are many stories linked to this time in my life when the food shortage was more serious than it had been during the war. I sometimes sailed on American sea-going tugs that after years of food shortages, seemed to me to be awash with exotic edibles, some of which, thanks to the Americans' generosity, often ended up in my instrument bag. In addition to this, sailing from the fish docks always presented the chance to acquire fresh fish, so that apart from bringing some money home I also managed to help with the dire food situation.

On one occasion we were well out to sea when I was asked by an American skipper if there was anything he could offer me, to which I replied that a little bag of sugar would be like gold dust since there had been none in the shops for a while. Time came to clamber over the side and down the rope ladder into the launch that would take us back to land while the tug continued on its way. I, disappointed that my promised treat of some sugar had not materialised, was just throwing my leg over the gunwale when a shout came from the bridge, "Don't forget your sugar". I looked along the deck and there it was, a 56-pound hessian bag of sugar. The launch was rising and falling from about eight feet up on each crest to away down in the trough of each wave. I looked at the bag and then down at the launch. What now? Well we did eventually get the bag down into the launch, but Charlie, the owner of the launch, was not at all happy with 56 pounds of saltwater-soaked sugar threatening to turn his immaculate varnished boat into a sticky sweet shop. We all carried little bags of gratefully accepted sugar home to our respective homes for weeks to come, but Charlie never quite forgave me for the sticky situation I had got him into.

At times we had to endure rough weather and at times some rough seafarers (especially some of the fishermen) but by far my greatest terror was when I had to deliver a compass, a Walker's log, or a barometer to a ship anywhere near the fish dock during the herring season. The herring lassies took great pleasure in waylaying any young lad wandering on his own, especially one like me dressed in a white boiler suit with Brylcreamed hair. The unfortunate victim would become the target of some very personal and sexual observations and suggestions. Then, if they could catch him they would fondle, hug, expose their bodies to, and then take handfuls of fish gut and stuff it down the victim's trousers, all this accompanied by hoots of laughter and screaming encouragement.

Latin America

Apart from the herring lassies I found this life much better than school.

I enjoyed the work, the time on board the ships and the chance to see another side of life, but in spite of all these things I longed for  something else. I was not only an oddball in my own family; I was also a 'bloody Jock', as some people see anyone from Scotland and are not shy to verbalise. So all these factors probably helped me to feel a bit of an outsider wherever I lived. I know that I was a bit of a trial for my parents as I constantly talked about leaving home and going abroad, although I could not define where or what I really wanted. Because of my inability to settle and largely thanks to my father's contacts I ended up with a ticket on a converted bomber belonging to the British South American Airways bound for South America.

For four bumpy interesting days we flew over land and sea at a height of a few thousand feet, where everything down below, from towns, mountains, ships at sea and jungle could be seen quite clearly. We were twenty-five passengers in total and we had five airhostesses to look after us. The seats could be turned into beds and the excellent food was served on fine china plates. The constant noise from the engines and the never-ending bumps and jolts slowly became part of this new experience called flying. I had once visited a grey wartime London, and that was about it as far as my travelling had taken me, so after four head-spinning days visiting Portugal, North Africa, Northern Brazil and then following hours of flying over the Brazilian jungle, breathtaking Rio came into view. The never ending green of jungle was abruptly replaced by a scene beyond the limited descriptive capabilities of someone brought up in a hard-pressed, war-ravaged Britain and then suddenly exposed to what I saw below me. The bright colours, blue sea, sunshine and golden beaches all conspired to scramble my senses and render description impossible. Of course this was Rio from the air, I still had to walk along the Copacabana promenade bordering the famous beaches with the bathing beauties, not in their dozens but in their thousands. The aeroplane suffered some kind of mechanical problem and we were put into a very posh hotel overlooking Rio Bay for two relaxing, sightseeing days. By the time we arrived at Carrasco airport, near Montevideo in Uruguay I was suffering from a serious bout of culture shock.

It took me some time to get settled in Uruguay. The sunshine, the golden beaches, the shiny American cars, beautiful suntanned girls and lots and lots of food, to say nothing of the language, all conspired to delay adjustment to this new reality for which, I have to acknowledge, I was totally ill prepared.

I DID IT MY WAY

A Little Piece of
Patagonian History

Scottish Cowboy

Allow me take you forward a few years to when I was ranching in the early '50s in the north of Patagonia. I would ride out at times with anything up to sixty or eighty men and depending on the job in hand we would stay out for a week, two weeks or, as was the case during lamb marking, up to a month.

We carried no food, no tents and very little by way of cooking utensils. In this man's world you did not ask too many questions so that young *ayudantes de campo* or *mayordomos,* as aspiring young ranch managers were called, would be totally mystified as to how we were all going to survive.

In fact there was a small mule cart, which at times was used to transport mobile corrals and the cook would be allowed to transport a very large iron pot, a number of iron staves two inches wide and three feet long, and a bag of *'mate'* tea, salt, and hard tack bread, known as *galletas de campo.* The diet, year in and year out, consisted of meat, hard biscuit and *mate* tea. When we lived outdoors for extended periods the horse boy and cook would ride ahead and make camp. After settling the horses down they would catch ten or fifteen sheep. These were killed, gutted and skinned. The practical way to cook these was to take the legs off, then separate the ribs from the backbone. A large fire was allowed to burn down until it had produced a large quantity of hot embers. The ribs were stuck on a stick or metal rod and planted in the ground near the embers. No smoke or flame was allowed to come into contact with the meat. The legs were cut round and round in a spiral, rather like unrolling a roly-poly pudding so that one ends up with a strip of meat with a bone at one end. This again is speared with a metal stave and cooked near the fire thus making it easy to cook and also to cut. At times the whole carcass would be cooked but usually for expediency this 'quick' way would be adopted.

Eating Out

One of the few pieces of equipment carried by the cook was his large iron pot. The purpose of this was to cook the backbones and any bits that had not been big enough to roast on the iron staves. This stewed meat was not so popular but eaten once or twice a week when the pot became full. I personally enjoyed every meal and never tired of it. I understand however that the people who live on this diet, of whom there are a great number, suffer more from stomach cancer than other groups. If a lamb was cooked, it was usually cooked whole. When the meat was ready the men would collect a piece of biscuit or 'hard tack' from the cook; some would put the 'hard tack' biscuit under the meat to collect the fat and juices, some would toast it. When the cook gave the okay, the system was to hold the bread in the left hand, leaving the thumb and fingers free to get hold of the meat. Drawing the knife with the right hand one carves off a large piece of the cooked meat, then gripping it with the your teeth, the knife cuts upwards, being careful to avoid the point of your nose. The men, and the dogs, usually ate everything, unless a piece of meat might be kept for a snack at a later opportunity. It was traditional that nobody had less than their fill on these large *estancias*, or ranches and, as already mentioned, I always enjoyed these meals, which were the same three or four times a day.

There had been attempts during the Peron regime to legislate that all the men had to get vegetables and a varied diet but it failed completely since no one would conform to the new rules. Even back at the *estancias* there was very little deviation from this all meat diet. I remember trying to serve a diet of meat and vegetables at Pilcaniyeu Estancia then watching as the men walked to their place at the table, picked a piece of meat from the plate and then walked away, drawing their knives to eat it in their traditional way, totally ignoring the vegetables.

The typical bunkhouse kitchen was usually a long room with a large built-in fireplace in which one could actually sit; the rest of the kitchen had benches and tables where the men would eat, play cards, sew and repair their gear or go over what had happened during the day's work. This continual reminiscing was very common and some incidents would be gone over time and again especially if they were entertaining or funny in any way. Large quantities of hot water were consumed with *mate*, or green tea, which probably made up for the lack of any greens or fruit in their diet. *Yerba mate* is very popular in southern South America and while having many health-enhancing properties is also a light narcotic and therefore addictive. This is a sore subject in some places where people see it as traditional, health giving and beyond any kind of questioning. The mystery of how a large group of men were to heat the water for their *mate* (pronounced MAH-tey) when working away from the home farm was revealed to me shortly after arriving. Each man carries a *mate* pot or gourd, or just a tin cup and a metal straw or *bombilla*. The first night out, following the arrival at the campsite, empty wine bottles appeared from under the rocks, beside fence posts or from the middle of nowhere. These were previously tucked away at the different campsites and returned to their secret hiding places when camp was broken. By filling these bottles with water and turning them constantly in the hot embers the water would come to the boil very quickly without the glass cracking. The rivers were totally unpolluted and nobody questioned the wisdom of drinking the water, boiled or not.

The men, mostly indigenous to the region, with some Spanish and Italian blood mixed in, would carry things of their own choice such as a small bag of sugar to sweeten the *mate*, or to mix into an ostrich egg as a bit of a treat, but apart from something to sleep on, a metal mug and a *bombilla* (metal straw) plus tobacco and a large knife, nothing else was carried. I should perhaps add that some carried a small mirror, which would be produced during leisure time to look into as the sparse facial hair of the indigenous locals was carefully plucked one hair at a time.

The Horse Boy

It was the job of the *tropero* (horse boy) to look after the troop of horses, which at times could number several hundred. He would look after them, stop them from straying and keep the men supplied with fresh mounts, all in rough open country with few fences and no corrals.

At one ranch where I spent almost two years the so-called horse 'boy' was nothing short of uncanny. His name was Bernabe Carrequeo. He was very short and surprisingly agile and seemed to be quite an old man by all appearances. He was about five feet tall, bow legged and deep chested, and he waddled as much as he walked. He dressed as all the men did, in riding boots, baggy trousers, neckerchief and hat. However, his boots were made from the lower part of a horse's leg (see drawing) and were rarely seen in use any more. These were called *botas de potro* (*potro* meaning colt or filly) and apart from on this old man I have never seen them in daily use. Stuck into his belt that held up his *bombachas* or baggy trousers, he carried a very long knife. When he talked his very short worn down teeth could be seen. They were worn down to the gum rather like an old sheep that had chewed too long on hard dry grass. His cinnamon coloured face was a mass of wrinkles out of which, when spoken to, would shine two twinkling black eyes. This little old man could walk into the middle of a large, restless troop of horses all of which towered over him, put a horse collar over one, and lead it out to be saddled.

He never seemed to sit down, but chose to either squat or kneel. At mealtimes we would sit around the fire and eat the meat (which in this area was usually mutton) cooked on the open fire, eat hard tack, and drink *mate* tea. During the evening meal we would talk of the day's activities, plan the following day's work, and tell stories about who had fallen off their horse or perhaps recount an incident when a girth had broken and the rider had ended up on the ground but still holding on to the reins. Stories like this were always an important part of the evening and the men loved to laugh at everything. If the boss had had a problem it would be gone over again and again until every angle had been exhausted and every grain of mirth had been squeezed out of it.

I took advantage of these evening campfires to find out more about our horse boy, who had caught my attention. This man intrigued me and I could not help feeling curious about him. He would squat at a respectable distance as I tried to engage him in conversation, but it was apparent that this very private, mysterious little old man really did not want to talk with this *uinca* (white man) so I had to gently entice him to divulge a little of what I am sure could have filled several books had he been less reticent. I am aware that what I managed to extract from him was only a small tip of the iceberg, but since so little seems to have been written from the indigenous point of view I think it is worth relating his small contribution.

Years of ethnic cleansing, brutal mistreatment and ridicule by people like me and you who had come from Europe were mostly responsible for the reluctant or non-existent communication with most of these people. The fact that I was white and very tall compared to the locals and also ridiculously young to have such authority, made things no easier.

This old man would squat on his heels, usually holding a twig that served as a toothpick while he wafted the smoke from his face. The circle of dark faces reflected the dancing flames from the fire, and in the background giant majestic outcroppings of rock pointed at the black sky, punctured here and there by a silver star.

Bernabe's Story

BOTAS DE POTRO

My first attempt at conversation went something like this.

"Are you from Chile then?" This was followed by an uneasy silence.

After a while the old man slowly straightened his short legs and after removing his hat replied in a loud clear, almost aggressive voice, "No señor!................I was born over there," he said, pointing to the west. "We lived in the foothills............other side of the lake." He was referring to the Nahuel Huapi Lake.

The pregnant silence was accentuated by the crackling of the wood in the fire as the smoke quietly rose into the black Andean night.

"That land was all ours...............it is all ours! Although nobody could say they owned it. It was just the land where we lived and we are the people of this land."

He seemed to have finished talking but nobody, including myself, dared to invade the silence. With these few words he had cast a spell over us, and we sat there unable to move, or speak........... listening to the silence.

Then unexpectedly, "Si señor................................life was simple...........we did not have to work.............there was no such thing as money ...." His voice faded as he mumbled to himself. He was reminiscing, lost in memories of his youth and he no longer addressed anyone in particular.

The silence returned and we sat there for a long time, aware of the deeply emotive memories that my questions had stirred up. I had trespassed into sacred territory, into a place I knew nothing of, and I felt guilty and out of place. Perhaps this little piece of history should be allowed to fade away, undisturbed, unrecorded and, like most of these people's history, forgotten.

After a while a couple of young hands whispered to each other and the spell was broken. The old man turned in their direction and dismissed them with a withering stare and then, slowly replacing his hat, he squatted down with his back to the fire and seemed to be totally absorbed by the horses that were just beyond the circle of firelight.

I waited for a polite period and then said, "I'm interested in what you have to say but please do not stand up and you don't have to remove your hat. Just talk to me."

I got no reaction at all as he stared into the darkness. A breeze sprang up and rustled the grass as he sat in dignified silence with everyone watching and waiting.

Unexpectedly, his voice, now deeply touched with emotion, rang out, "We ran away to Chile but that does not make us Chileños..........we went over there and stayed behind the Volcano Lanin."

The dark faces began to look uncomfortable. His comments were moving into an area that was never mentioned in front of the *uinca*. A couple of the men quietly laughed to cover their embarrassment; another became engrossed in rolling a cigarette while others shuffled their feet and looked off into the Patagonian night.

Once again the old man's voice burst upon the silence. "We didn't have a chance, we had never harmed them yet they attacked us without pity."

He was shouting now.

"We had to run or die, they killed the children but," then throwing out his chest, he continued, "I'm not afraid, it does nothing to me to see women being…"

"¿Que mierda estas diciendo?" What the hell are you saying? One of the younger men was trying to get the old man to shut up. They all stared at him and at me, and there was a volatile feeling in the air of fear, anger and danger.

I had somehow enticed this old man to mention the unmentionable and trespass where the Mapuche would never publicly dare to go, creating a potentially dangerous situation.

As the men stared at me and back at the old man the tension became unbearable. Slowly I stood up, said thank you and good night and went off into the dark to lie on my bed of *nineo* (a kind of tumbleweed which can be piled together to make a soft bed).

Over the following weeks I managed to have several bits of conversation with this wonderful being who held so many untold stories and had captured my curiosity. I tried to stay as casual as I could, and so it was that over a period of time I was able to make a few notes and put the pieces together from which I tell this story.

I learned that Bernabe Carrequeo, was as he put it, "algo pasado los ochenta anos" (something past eighty years of age) so given that this was 1951 or 2 he certainly was alive during the wholesale slaughter of the native population, or the Conquest of the Desert as the historians euphemistically like to call it. Carrequeo had probably been born about 1870 in the foothills of the Andes in what is now part of the Argentine province of Rio Negro. He was a Mapuche and a member of the Araucana nation. He spoke Mapudungun and later would learn Spanish. 'Mapu' means land and 'dungun' is the word for speech. So their language was the language of the land. In the same way *Mapu* means land, *che* means people so they were the 'people of the land'. It is interesting to note that this word *che* is very commonly used today in the Spanish spoken in Argentina and this is why people in the rest of South America call Argentines the *Ches* and the Argentine revolutionary, Doctor Ernesto Guevara, whose family I knew well, was known as 'Che' Guevara.

El Tero

European Invasion

The area in which the Mapuche originally lived was a plentiful land. The rivers were full of salmon, trout and freshwater shellfish and wild deer were plentiful, Patagonian hare, ostrich and armadillo were in abundance, while large herds of the elegant *guanaco* grazed the hills.

They practiced different rituals and festivities to acknowledge the changing seasons, births, marriages and deaths and although they talked of spirits or creatures from the unknown who appeared from time to time they did not seem to have any religion.

Life was easy and the children were the centre of the community, although it has to be said that it was a very primitive existence.

On one particular occasion white men had apparently visited a native community only a few days walk away and wild stories circulated about men having red hair and sticks that could kill a deer at a distance. These strangers came in many forms and some had two heads and four hooves and a flowing tail, but these tales were not taken very seriously since everyone knew that the storytellers invented such monsters.

The *toldos* or tents were made from pine poles and *guanaco* skins and everyone dressed in *guanaco* skins, which were as soft as silk and kept them warm during the cold winter months.

One day there had been an argument about one family, who it was claimed had been getting more than a fair share of the meat and the Cacique, or leader, had told the hunters to go out and bring fresh supplies so that he could personally supervise the distribution of the hunt on their return.

The men collected their lances and bows and arrows and, still arguing, set off.

"Get out there and do what men are born to do!" their leader called after them. "You are like a bunch of old women who have forgotten what a man feels like." This caused some laughter and lightened the mood. They had left their *quillangos* or *guanaco* robes behind in order to travel light. They headed for the river where they crossed over by the old *Notro* tree, its bright red flowers visible for miles around.

After reaching the *mallín*, or flat valley bottom, they spread out and walked silently. They slowly advanced for almost an hour, each aware of the position of the others. The only sound was that of the breeze blowing through the long grass. Senses sharpened and differences were forgotten as they smelled the air and strained for any signs of wildlife.

Llanqehuen, a lad of sixteen, who was over on the right flank, stopped and raised his hand, which held an arrow. When he had the others' attention he pointed with his chin to a flock of *teros* (noisy birds rather like lapwings) sitting on a bare patch of ground. The whole party crouched low and moved to the left keeping well away from the birds. One mistake and these birds would to take to the air calling, "Tero! Tero! Tero!" alerting the whole countryside for miles around.

They headed for the bushes at the far side of the *mallín* where the small deer that they called *pudu pudu* liked to graze, they slowed down, smelling the air. Then suddenly Apolinario, a well seasoned hunter who had caused all the fuss back at the *toldería* (campsite), stood up straight and before the others had time to react the feared word *UINCA* (white man) came hissing across the grass. The hair stood up on the back of their necks as they sniffed the air and looked around while coming closer together. Where are the *uinca*? Apolinario pointed to the north but none of them could see anything unusual.

"You listen to too many stories." It was the young one speaking. "My father says there is no such thing as men with white skins, and all these stories are thought up by troublemakers like you."

A flight of geese flew overhead and about half a league to the east a herd of *guanaco* grazed.

The boy continued, "We could go after these *guanaco*?"

Just then there was a light away to the north but at what distance was hard to tell. A few moments later the light flashed again and this time they all saw it and they agreed that it came and went like a star reflected in the lake.

They instinctively moved to higher ground, partly for safety and partly to get a better view. Over a period of two hours they watched as the lights came gradually closer and closer until what looked like men sitting on the backs of animals could be distinguished. These strange beings carried long knives and long things like poles slung over their shoulders and our little party agreed that the lights that looked like the reflections from the lake came from these things that they carried.

They crowded together behind an outcrop of rock known as Lepa, and as the hair on their necks stood up straight they instinctively crouched lower and lower and watched in fear and astonishment.

Suddenly it was time to go.

They grabbed their belongings and they ran all the way back to tell the tribe what they had seen. However, on reaching the *tolderia* without any meat they were met first of all with anger then curiosity, followed by a mixture of fear and disbelief.

For days they talked about nothing else, while the lookouts posted around the *tolderia* scanned the countryside but had nothing to report. Soon they began to lose interest and even suggested that it was all lies anyway as they challenged those who had told the story.

Their leader, who was an intelligent individual, questioned the hunters who had reported seeing the lights and the strangers, and it was decided that since they had no meat, a hunting party would go out together with scouts and lookouts and that no risks would be taken.

They left the *tolderia* in high spirits and headed down the river towards the *mallín*.

It was thirty seven hours later that seven out of the forty eight staggered into the *tolderia*; they carried nothing, except for one who held a bunch of grass to a wound on his chest.

I will spare you the grizzly details, which I got from Bernabe regarding their encounter with the soldiers, but basically they had been chased by about eighty soldiers who wore blue uniforms and rode horses (all things the Mapuche had never seen). Once they had been surrounded the soldiers kept out of the range of the bows and arrows and then they pointed these strange things at them and CRACK, CRACK, CRACK, the Mapuche were falling down. Then the soldiers took out their long knives and had great fun finishing them off.

The survivors told how they had pretended to be dead, lying still until dark and then quietly escaping.

Bernabe told me of these things as if they had happened the day before and I half expected him to ask me for help but I think on reflection that he just wanted some kind of acknowledgement that these things had taken place and that somebody out there should be aware of them. The advent of white men and soldiers was an alarming new experience for the Mapuche. This had had no precedent and both the remains of his tribe and neighbouring tribes were thrown into complete confusion as to what to do. Their total lack of any such experience left them bewildered.

The old man said that some of the young men had wanted to fight, others thought that if they just carried on as usual the soldiers would go away and leave them alone, while the more daring wanted to go and see what these strange creatures looked like.

I do not know over what period of time all this took place but apparently in the end as they learned of more massacres taking place they decided, together with other tribes, to abandon their ancestral land. They fled over the Andes to a valley beyond the Lanin Volcano where he told me that they were forced at times to eat roots and tea made from tree bark. Many died and the old ways were gradually abandoned. As he told me his story he would fall silent as if he were transported back to the incident he was relating, his head would nod as if reliving the scene, then with a deep sigh he would talk quietly to himself.

"And now here I am working at the age of eighty-something as a horse boy and telling this young foreigner things which have been so secret and even sacred to me and my people. Ah well, it sounds as if the horses are getting restless; perhaps it is that lion that has been watching us for two days now, and yet this young boss is not even aware of it...... well I suppose I still have a few secrets left."

I DID IT MY WAY

Honky Tonk

Home Sweet Home

I was temporarily back from my travels to my place of birth, namely Greenock, but I felt out of place, standing there in the small crowded butcher's shop. For some reason a remark made to me by my good friend Dave Holsworth as I was leaving Uruguay for Scotland came into my head; it was, "If you see any of my folks over there, tell them I'm playing piano in a honky-tonk. I would not like them to think I was working for the Vesteys."

Perhaps I should have said that I worked in a honky-tonk instead of what I did say when the old butcher, who had cut me several large steaks from a loin of beef on his counter, had asked, "What kind of sheep do you run out there in South America?"

I had simply told the truth, "...most of the three million sheep are merinos with a few corriedale for home consumption." I was about to continue telling him about the thousands of cattle, horses and mules but I instinctively knew that I had put my foot in it. Everyone in the shop was looking at me as if to say, "Do you think we're daft?" The atmosphere in the small shop suddenly felt claustrophobic. "Of course they're not so well looked after as the flocks here...", I ventured, but it was too late.

I escaped out into the rain carrying my steaks and wandered down Ratho Street towards 'the' enormous crane in the James Watt dock - named after the great engineer and inventor who is claimed amongst other things to have made the industrial revolution possible - which I could remember being there when I was a small child. It still symbolised for me the shipbuilding Clydeside of my birth.

The problem was that here I was back in my native town of Greenock on Clydeside and I felt, more than ever, totally at odds with the dreary tenements, the empty shipyards, and that unique Clydeside humour all too often laced with cynicism. No wonder my relations thought me a bit strange.

As I stood there under the big crane I tried to remember an old poem:

"Oh! What a dirty rotten toon
Te swing a cat ye hanny room
Oh! Send an earthquake as a boon
Te last for years
And tumble all these shanties doon
Aboot oor ears..." etcetera etcetera.....

My memory wandered back to the wee boy standing under this very crane at the bottom of Ratho Street at this very same bus stop, which seemed like several lifetimes ago.

I must have been about eleven years of age and I stood with my father and mother, waiting for the bus to take us all home to our top floor flat in a tenement in Port Glasgow.

Across the road a group of men were emerging from what was a normal, dirty-looking and smelly pub, which had sawdust and spittoons on the floor. I had been brought up in a non-drinking, churchgoing family and I had been taught to regard those who frequented such places as a 'lesser species'. I pushed my face into my mother's fur coat and imagined far-off places where there were no miserable wet streets, no oppressive religious bigotry, no smelly pubs and, above all, there was no fear. Yes, that was the worst aspect in my view, fear, that religion-promoted fear, which seemed to permeate all aspects of daily life. Catholics and Protestants brought up to hate each other and to damage each other whenever possible, and all in the name of the same God i.e., Jehovah!

The bus brakes made a loud squeaking noise as it drew into the kerb and stopped. As the rain poured down two men stood, or rather swayed, on the bus platform. The one facing our little group had blood all over his face and his head was unconventionally bare. His mouth looked like a squashed tomato. My mother pulled me back. The first man stepped off the platform, inviting the other in slurred, abusive language to follow him. 'Bloody face', in answer, received a fist on the forehead and fell flat on his back on the wet pavement. This was not an unusual scene in pre-war Clydeside but it stayed with me for years. The rain fell on the upturned face and soaked into his shiny coat and trousers. I was always to remember this poor drunk creature lying there on his back in filthy clothes, blood smeared, and ranting on through his tomato lips about the Irish being the greatest and most God-fearing people on earth, while the rain kept pouring down on us all.

As we started to get on the bus, the conductress was telling 'Big Fist' to get off. Actually, what she was saying was, "C'mon ge' aff, ge' aff the bus, 'r'll ge' the polis te' ye'", which was the way that she spoke English, the language her people had been forced to use on pain of death, and the only one she knew.

The bus got under way, and as we settled in our seats, the smell of beer filled the air; someone had been sick in the passageway, and a drunk in front of them almost fell off his seat each time the bus moved to one side or the other. Most of the women wore shawls drawn over their heads and crossed over their breasts framing grey, aggressive, tense old faces on young women.

Why did I feel like an outcast? I didn't feel I belonged to the group around me, or to the smell, the rain, and the black rows of tenements we passed, with their scraggy windows staring across the dark wet night at the cranes and derricks of the shipyards. It was difficult for me to understand or feel sorry for these fellow mortals who had no fur-coat-cum-imagination to transport them from the dismal reality of pre-war Clydeside. The men on the bus wore black greasy jackets, trousers and caps that never seemed new, nor particularly old, but never seemed to get washed. They smelled of shipyard iron, sweat and beer and in the heat of the bus smelled of wet dog. Yet this, I was told, was the greatest country on earth, oh 'Scotland the Brave'. Here every little group claimed to be the only good Christian outfit and loudly denounced all others. The 'other side' had to be ignored, evicted, banned, imprisoned and exterminated and I was to get myself into a few predicaments even at a tender age by challenging this status quo.

I had heard that forty percent of people in hospitals were mental cases and the pubs and jails were full of people going mad with frustration but all this seemed to be totally ignored by the people in black frocks and dog-collars, the secret societies, or the 'good living' elite who apparently owned and ran the country from an English-based government many hundreds of miles away; but I was taught that it was just that 'some people were better than others and always would be'. Long live the King.

I was brought up in these beliefs and the penalty for anyone who questioned them, or even dared to think for themselves, was to be reminded that hellfire waited for all those who wandered from the straight and narrow, whatever that was.

Now that was not too bad as long as you did not believe such nonsense. The tragedy was that I, in my naiveté, tended to believe everything that the grown-ups told me; after all I came from an honest and respectable family. Somewhere in the back of my mind I knew that something was all wrong but the possible consequences of THINKING for one's self was not worth the risk of being, as the sombre figure in the black frock put it, "damned forever!" Perhaps I would be able to escape from it one day and even be able to THINK!!!!!! I would then plan a good simple life and…,"Come on, son, it's time to get off." The bus screeched to a halt. Out in the rain the gas lamps reflected on the wet pavements and somewhere in the dark night a voice sang 'I belong to Glasgow'. I would, at all costs, avoid offending the family or inviting a telling-off, but my well-guarded deep secret was that, unlike the night singer, I did not feel that I belonged to Glasgow.

As I grew up and started to sort out dogma from reality and informed opinion from bigotry, I became increasingly sensitive to the daily verbal and practical abuse and degradation, which seems to permeate all levels of cross-border intercourse with England. At the same time I have been forced to acknowledge that this would seem to be unavoidable where any small country tries to live next door to a much larger neighbour. China and Tibet, Germany and her neighbours and Russia and her satellites are just a few examples.

This may be the appropriate place in the book to say quite clearly that I have never indulged in the questionable luxury of allowing myself to feel hate for anyone. At times some of my friends have offered me their approval and support by saying things like, "I understand why you hate the English so much". Well, let me make it clear that I do not hate the English. I do, however, have a very deep, sad frustration and feeling of hopelessness regarding some of the irretrievable damage suffered by the Scottish nation at the hand of rulers and politicians ruling from London. When I contemplate the Scottish gentry who Robert Burns is referring to when he says, "We're bought and sold for English gold, what a parcel of rouges in a nation" I also feel deep hurt and sadness and must acknowledge that when I try to express such feelings it could be construed as hate; but it is not.

If you read the following verse of an emotive song called *Eternity*, written by Dougie MacLean for his grandfather who only spoke Gaelic, you may catch a glimmer of my feelings which are shared by many others, not all necessarily Scottish.

"I'll lose a son to the German wars
– we'll lose the land he was fighting for
Lose our language to greed and gain
– all washed away by a southern rain
Washed until we can't see
What our own destiny meant us to be."

I DID IT MY WAY

At Home in Patagonia

Hard Magic

My escape from life in post-war Britain in the late '40s had initially taken me shipbuilding in Uruguay; then ranching near the Brazilian frontier; cattle ranching in the province of Cordoba in Argentina; and running a quarry high in the hills overlooking the Calamuchita valley, also in Cordoba. But for now I felt at home here in Patagonia as I sat on the corral fence aware of the mules and the men, the dust, the noises and the smells, with the towering majestic Andes as a backdrop.

I felt at one with the hard magic of this land, its indigenous people, brutally subdued, yet still very much part of the atmosphere that casts its spell on the unwary and never quite leaves anyone who has ridden, and lived, in these parts in the company of what is left of these tough, secretive people. I sometimes felt a common bond between this land and the country of my birth, where wholesale genocide took place and the prohibition of our language, music and culture was for years punishable by death, but that's another story.

I would be happy to go back to Scotland one day but for the present this vast land, from the south Atlantic coast across a thousand miles of desert and scrub to the foothills rising into the indescribable Andes, and then stretching south to the Antarctic, would be more than I could explore in a lifetime. In spite of man's efforts to destroy it, the indigenous wildlife was still there to be enjoyed. The condor, one of the largest birds of flight in the world, yet on the wing so graceful and majestic, jet black against the sky with a ruff of white feathers almost surrounding its neck, and just a touch of white in the wings can be seen sitting apparently timelessly on the wind, rising on the thermals without any obvious effort, never moving a wing but always observant and keeping well away from humans. By the end of the 19th century, eating the carcasses of pumas poisoned by the cattle and sheep farmers as well as shooting had destroyed great numbers of these birds. The condors are now mostly to be found in the mountains where they are safe from man, although they do travel and could be seen at times over the pampas or out over the desert.

Patagonia was, by the accounts of some early explorers, a 'land of giants'. The large condor, which can have a wingspan of up to eight or nine feet, no doubt, helped to create this myth. The actual name Patagonia comes from the word *patagón*, a word used by Magellan in 1520 that meant 'big feet' or 'giant feet' (pata meaning foot). It described the native people that his expedition thought to be giants. It is now believed the Patagons were actually the Tehuelches who have an average height of 180cm compared to the 155cm average for Spaniards of the time.

Years later, when I was working on the ski slopes near the tourist town of Bariloche, it was my privilege to stay behind on the mountain after the many thousands of tourists and skiers had descended to their hotels and lodges. I would sit on one of the now silent and motionless ski lift chairs and the peaks, the valleys, the lakes and the trees would all be mine for just a while. As I sat there, keeping as still as possible, first one black shadow, then another would appear in the thin mountain air above me. Several pairs of condors would wheel and glide high above. They could see me but I would try to sit motionless until the cold forced me to move. Then, as I quietly put my skis on and glided slowly down the slope I would stop and look back to see them inspecting where I had been sitting, but they were always careful not to get too close.

I briefly enjoyed this wild, untouched side of Patagonia each evening, and then would go down to the lights and warmth of civilization that the ski industry had brought to the area. My temporary job allowed me to enjoy the best of both worlds and I made the most of it.

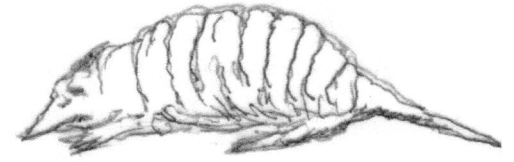

Armadillos and Funerals

One wild creature I came across during my ranching days was the armadillo, known locally as a *pichi*. These small animals were numerous and would very quickly bury a dead sheep by burrowing under it and would, with equal efficiency, disinter a human body that had been buried without a sufficient supply of stones placed on top of the body or coffin.

I discovered this the hard way.

My first Patagonian burial took place at Estancia Alicura where I, in the absence of the *mayordomo*, was expected to officiate as boss, undertaker, priest and, at times, paramedic. The death of one of the men was unexpected on one such occasion when I was standing in for the resident mayordomo and so I was suddenly expected to do something I had never even contemplated. The foreman by the name of Montenegro and whom I greatly admired had filled me in with the details and I had agreed that I would officiate at the burial.

While the grave was still being dug, the coffin containing the body was being carried across the saddle of the deceased's horse, supported on each side, and followed by some of the friends and ranch hands who had been present at the fight that had caused this poor fellow's death.

Suddenly the horse carrying the coffin broke into a trot and the whole party all desperately trying to prevent the precarious coffin from falling off the saddle started whooping and shouting as though they were at a rodeo. They arrived in a disorderly fashion in a cloud of dust where I was standing and doing my best to look the part. Eventually the grave was dug and with a few words (invented by me on the spot) the coffin was lowered and the ropes removed. I had planned to solemnly finish off my first burial by throwing a handful of earth on the grave and saying ashes to ashes, etcetera but I was beaten to it when a number of large stones were noisily dropped onto the coffin, almost smashing the lid. I was getting used to surprises but this rather noisy, uncouth way of throwing rocks on the coffin rather than handfuls of earth caught me unprepared. More rocks and earth were added as I retreated, bowing to the mourners and shaking a few hands. As I was congratulated on my performance and thanked by the deceased's relatives I secretly felt like a complete fraud.

I was to learn that this was standard practice and the stones were a necessity, being a protection against the *pichi* or armadillos, but it took several such occasions before I would get used to the way things are done at the graveside or, for that matter, at the wake during which drinking and dancing were very much the order of the day.

Mourners had arrived earlier in the day, mostly on horseback from different places and now as these dark-skinned, very rough looking individuals drank and danced, this whole scene seemed unreal and perhaps from a far-off time. I had, however, to remind myself that it was I who was the odd man out and that I had no right or justification to judge them.

Graceful Wildlife

The animal, which is always synonymous with Patagonia for me is the *guanaco*. This graceful creature could, in the 1950s, be seen in herds of twenty to fifty. It seemed more regal than its cousin the *vicuña* or the *llama* or *alpaca* of the north. This beautiful creature, sometimes known as the 'camel deer' or 'Spanish sheep', was reported by Darwin in herds of five hundred or more, and there are even reports of thousands being seen all together in one herd but, alas, this was no longer the case in the '50s. The *guanaco* had always been hunted for their meat and skins and some preferred the meat of the *guanaco* to beef or mutton. The dried *charqui* or jerked meat made an excellent stew, while the fillet was second only to the *chulengo*, or young *guanaco*. The poncho or *quillango* made from the hide, which is soft, warm and waterproof was the only clothing worn by the indigenous inhabitants before the invasion by the Europeans. By the end of the 19th century, thousands of these skins were being bought up by white settlers and sent to Buenos Aires and overseas.

The indigenous people, as well as the settlers tended to eat anything that moved and today they seem to have a tendency to kill everything, whether they want to eat it or not. There is a line in the classic Argentine poem, *Martin Fierro*: "Todo que camina va a parar al asador". Everything that walks ends up on the roasting grill, or barbeque; and this still seems to apply.

The puma, or cougar, locally known as the *leon* was very shy. It had been greatly reduced in numbers, but was still holding out in some areas. A century before, the sheep farmers called it the 'cursed lion' and Darwin reports puma tracks 'almost everywhere', while later in the twentieth century they were still regarded as a pest in Rio Negro. I have come very close to the *leon* while driving a lorry on two occasions and have had to stop as they stood apparently hypnotised by the headlights. Their size, their beauty and their graceful movements are impossible for me to describe and the fact that the old army truck which I was driving had long since lost both its doors helped to speed up the blood rushing through my veins.

When I lived in Patagonia in the 1950s the ostrich was still hunted with the *bolas* and the various 'pieces' of this large bird were used in unexpected ways. A favourite with so many was the tobacco pouch or *chuspa* made from the neck. The skin would be removed like a stocking without cutting it lengthwise and, once dried and cured, was very soft and pleasant to touch. One end would be sewn up and the skin often beautifully embroidered. An excellent meat dish could also be prepared from the wing muscle while the tendon from the long legs was very sought after for sewing raw hide and, of course, the feathers had been a great money earner or trading article ever since the first white man (or lady) discovered them.

The Ever Gentle Guanaco

The animal looked upon as the main pest when I worked there, however, was still the *guanaco*; the reason for this was quite simply that they eat grass. The whole of Patagonia had been overgrazed by sheep, cattle and horses for years by the mainly English land companies who, after shooting the *guanaco* and then poisoning them, declared them a pest in the early '50s, and decided to kill them all; although, as I say, all that the indigenous *guanaco* were ever accused of was eating grass.

Special *guanaco* hunters were taken on to do the job and were paid per skin brought back. One hunter whom I met was one of five brothers whose father had run away from the USA at the turn of the century and, so the story went, had only to kill a few Indians to take possession of a small empire on the edge of the incredibly beautiful Nahuel Huapi lake. Stories went around that this man had been an outlaw in the American wild west but, whatever the truth, those who met him or his wife were left in no doubt that they had brought a piece of the old west with them and the family still lived, even in the 1950s, the way people had lived a half a century before.

The method used to kill the *guanaco* was to get as near to a herd as possible and then, on horseback, ride full speed at them with the *bolas* and bring down one or two in this fashion. The next stage was to draw a rifle and try to shoot as many as possible as they ran away while, at the same time, doing as little damage as possible to the hide. This caught my imagination and following a *guanaco* hunt I asked this colourful American-Argentine cowboy how he had managed to shoot these swift-footed *guanaco* and avoid lowering the value of the skins by making holes all over them. It must be remembered that this was all done on horseback.

"Well, if you watch them," he said, "they always lift their heads, stop for a second, then turn tail and run off in a straight line. Well, it is when they turn tail and run that I shoot them up the arse." This was followed by lots of laughter and backslapping. It was all part of life and distasteful as I found it one had to live with it. The young *guanaco*, called *chulengo*, would not leave their mothers even after they were shot and the hunter would return to his quarry and, reversing the *rebenque*, a kind of heavy duty riding crop, would club the young to death. In spite of being hardened to some degree by different life experiences I always felt like crying when I came across the slaughter of the *guanaco* and as I write this now it still has the same effect on me.

I only visited the ranch on which this fellow had been brought up on one occasion. Their father had died and the old lady ruled the family with a rod of iron. She dressed in a dark dress down to the floor, with a shawl over her shoulders. Nothing was allowed to change and everything in that house – from the oil lamps to the spinning wheel and the old heavy irons for ironing clothes, her husband's revolvers hanging on the wall – were the kinds of things only to be seen in museums where I come from, yet here they were in everyday use. Nor was this unique, for instance Pilcaniyue, which at one time was my nearest village, looked like the old North American west and was part of the territory owned by the land company I worked for. It boasted a railway station where large herds of cattle would arrive following weeks or even months of being herded from farther south. The 'town' boasted one 'hotel'. This was a drab building containing a bar, living quarters for the owners, and a few rooms looking on to a patio. The owners were Lebanese and were known to one and all as *'los turcos'*! They also owned a petrol pump, a precarious affair with a long handle, which had to be vigorously pushed back and forth by the client wishing to buy petrol.

In addition to the hotel, there was a small hut where an old Russian practised medicine; immigrants with foreign qualifications were allowed to practise in the Argentine national territories without revalidating their qualifications. The best building in the street had been built by the *Gendarmeria Nacional*. The *'gendarmes'*, as we called them, were in charge of the national territories, (as opposed to the provinces). Their local headquarters consisted of two offices, sleeping quarters, and several cells, in which anyone unfortunate enough to end up, was guaranteed a rough time. Another bar and a few houses made up the row of buildings, each with hitching rails for horses. All of the buildings were on one side of the road. They faced the railway sidings and the station, all built by the British at the turn of the century. The roads were made of earth and the only attention they got was an occasional scraping and bevelling with a bulldozer. Horses, horse-drawn carts, sheep and cattle all did their best to plough up the surface, which would alternate between red powdered dust inches thick and heavy, clinging mud. Perhaps the best time was in winter during the snow, which made it easier to ride, or even drive, on.

Drovers

I remember seeing a very large herd of cattle, which had been on the move for months arriving here at the railway siding. The men appeared to be in a rather sorry state. Their clothes, their boots and even their hats seemed to be falling apart. The foreman or trail boss had a revolver strapped to his chest and a rifle on his saddle and they all had a hungry, almost desperate, look about them. They had clearly been riding for a very long time but I could not help feeling shocked at their appearance. I decided to find out more about them and made an effort to start a conversation with two hard-bitten looking characters, but they just eyed me up and down very suspiciously then looked the other way. These men were undoubtedly at the end of their tether and could perhaps easily turn nasty. I decided to leave them alone but just watch them for a while, so I leaned against my horse and observed them over the saddle. They were a tired, sullen lot and did not appear to talk much even to each other.

Then I noticed that one man was leading a very thin horse away from the others, I watched him until he was well clear of everyone; he then stopped, casually drew his knife and after sticking it right through the horse's neck just below the jaw, he sawed outwards. As the blood gushed out he and some others got their tin cups and caught the warm blood and drank it. The horse showed no sign of alarm or pain but slowly got down onto its knees and then toppled over.

These were the people I lived and worked with, but as I mounted and slowly rode away it became unmistakably clear that my world and theirs were miles apart.

I was later to learn that in spite of my revulsion, this practice was not uncommon amongst some groups who believed that one could acquire the strength of a horse this way. I have always taken a great deal of interest in meeting unusual people and customs and I felt that this was an invitation for me to consider that we really are all equally vulnerable and perhaps each one of us is just the end product of our particular upbringing and mind conditioning.

There is a dinner held each year in London, or at least there used to be, which is attended mainly by people connected with the beef industry. It is known as the Drover's dinner, but few of the guests, if any at all, seem to me to even know the stories and the history of the drovers. This is a formal affair where evening dress, speeches and small talk are the norm. On the one occasion I attended, I had very little success in getting a conversation going about the original Scottish drovers who brought the herds of cattle all the way from the Western Isles down to Smithfield market to supply the ever-growing carnivorous market in London and the south of England. Although there were a number of Scots present at the dinner, no one seemed to be interested in the original drovers, who later went to America and conducted the great cattle drives to the Chicago stockyards that did so much to enhance the image of the American cowboy and the Wild West. In the end I had to admit to being an old romantic and that the kind of conversation, which I had been looking forward to was all in my head.

Keery

One of a number of Irishmen I met at the time I worked on the Estancia Alicura was Pat Keery. He had the job of looking after the store and the office on this ranch on the Rio Limay where I was still a young assistant ranch manager, while he was probably in his early fifties. I should point out that these isolated *estancias* usually had

ESTANCIA KITCHEN   SIDE VIEW

a large stock of just about everything that was required to live in such areas and this included clothes, food, tobacco, knives, belts and boots, all of which were sold through the company store. This, together with the office jobs, was Keery's responsibility.

This large *estancia* or ranch was a long way from anywhere and I found that his active mind, his knowledge on any subject from classical music to history or mathematics and his willingness to have a go at almost any mental task made him good company.

On occasions a lorry on its way from the wine-growing Rio Negro valley to the railhead at Bariloche would roll up, its driver looking for a bed for the night. Some of these lorries carried enormous wooden barrels filled with wine and weighed about five tons each. In exchange for our hospitality we would be invited to take an enamel milking bucket out to a barrel and, after drilling a small hole in the wood, fill our pail with new wine before banging in a small wooden bung. The result was usually about twenty litres of excellent wine. When one of these welcome visitors arrived some six weeks after Keery's own arrival at Alicura he was instructed on how to acquire the wine and duly supplied with brace and bit, wooden bung and pail. The weather was bad and Keery put on a poncho and hat and went off into the rain.

A good hour later he was found lying in the rain, soaked with wine and quite drunk. How much wine had been lost nobody knew but his body was totally doused in wine, inside and out. We were soon to learn that he was, in spite of a brilliant mind (or because of it), an alcoholic. He stayed with the company for almost a year during which time he began to act very strangely, telling stories of how "that wee man in the bowler hat" used to come through the keyhole in his bedroom and talk to him, keeping him awake. Eventually he was asked to move on and I reckoned that although I missed his wide knowledge and interesting conversation I would not be seeing him again.

Some years later I was being kept in overnight in the British Hospital in Buenos Aires following a rugby injury when, on walking out onto the balcony, who should I meet but Keery, who was beginning to show the signs of alcohol abuse. We chatted for a while and I enquired as to what he had been doing with himself. "Oh!" said Keery, "I've been travelling. The Salvation Army paid my passage for me to see my folks back in the old country". I politely commented on how nice a sea voyage was and how nice it is to see the old country after being abroad. "Oh, yes!" he agreed, "and a fine upstanding family I have too. Do you know they put the hat round and got enough money together to send me all the way back out here again? So here I am in this wonderful city enjoying life."

Mora

There was, and probably still is, a law in Patagonia saying that anyone arriving at a ranch in the area must be fed and given shelter, at least for one night. This law was not necessary in my experience, as Patagonian hospitality was as good as any to be found anywhere. Mora was one regular visitor at the Estancia Pilcaniyue who took full advantage of this hospitality at a number of *estancias* as he journeyed from one to the other all year round. He dressed in boots covered in cowhide, several pairs of trousers, coats and jackets. He appeared to be fat, had jet black long hair and always wore a smile, showing white teeth against a dark brown face. My first experience with this colourful tramp was when he arrived on his quarterly visit. The cook informed me he was outside asking for any old papers we did not want so I sent him a pile of newspapers, only to have them rejected and to receive a request for *Country Life, Fox and Hound* and *The Illustrated London News*. My curiosity was aroused and I decided to make the acquaintance of this nomad with a refined taste in reading material. He was standing in the yard with his back to me and as I approached I called out his name, "Mora!" He turned slowly and after eyeing me up and down asked me what I wanted, as if I were the visitor and he would somehow have to deal with me. "They tell me that you rejected the newspapers I offered you and that you asked for these quality magazines." I gestured with a copy of Fox and Hound I had brought with me. He confirmed that he liked the shiny posh magazines, then went on to inform this rather slow and obviously thick foreigner that the paper was used to insulate him from the cold and that it was meticulously spread out in layers in between the pairs of trousers and jackets he wore and that the thick shiny paper was much warmer than the newspapers he had rejected. So much for my high hopes of discovering an indigenous (English-speaking) intellectual in the middle of Patagonia. This fellow apparently never entered a building of any description and would sleep on the wood pile even in the most severe weather so his taste in paper made a lot of sense when seen from his point of view, while my romantic ideas and high hopes were brought a little closer to earth.

Marcachifles – Los 'Turcos'

In the 1950s roving merchants known as *marcachifles* roamed the southern Argentine territories. These men, usually of Syrian or Lebanese origin, would appear at the *estancias* in the most improbable, overloaded vehicles. They would buy almost anything form horsehair to wool, hides, meat and even old papers. They sold knives, mirrors, tobacco, drink, boots, belts, hats, soap, bullets, guns, shop-made reins and tack, long johns and leather coats, in fact almost anything you could ask for.

While I was still trying to learn so many new things and trying to fit in I found myself suddenly having to temporarily move from Alicura to an *estancia* called San José. This was to be my first job as an *estancia* manager all on my own. The reason for the move was simply that the manager had taken ill and I was detailed, at short notice, to get myself out to this very isolated place on the Rio Colorado and keep things going until his return. This was a particularly far-out and isolated place where I found myself in charge of an unusually introverted sullen bunch whom, for the first week or so, refused to cooperate one little bit more than was absolutely necessary. Following a few days of feeling my way around I told the horse boy to put the horses for the following day's work in a paddock near the bunkhouse, which was on the outside perimeter of the ranch. Nobody made any comment on my orders and the horses were duly put into the paddock. The following morning I saddled up and went round to the paddock, where the men were catching their mounts. There was a lot of laughing and noise but nobody looked in my direction.

Every horse had had its tail and mane hacked off, giving an overall effect of a very motley moth-eaten bunch indeed, which seemed to amuse my contentious cutthroat crew.

I had to look confident and not allow anarchy to take root. Shears were produced and I lost no time trying to make things a bit tidier, but still no comment.

It later transpired that a couple of lads who lived a few miles away on a small holding and were always on the lookout for something to sell to the *marcachifles*, had been busy during the night but there was no way of proving this and nothing I could do about it.

It was this kind of situation that could win or lose the cooperation of these simple people so I tried my hardest not to show any annoyance or weakness. A chance to make a joke of it came when the foreman suggested that some ewes that had collected an excessive number of burrs might be hand shorn. My reply was not to waste time but just to leave them overnight in the infamous paddock. This 'joke' was quite well appreciated and was my first small success in trying to thaw the tense atmosphere, which I seemed to have inherited; an apparently insignificant point perhaps but life in these isolated and simple communities often tended to centre around trivialities. The *marcachifles* were, as I said, Syrian or Lebanese, but were known as *los turcos*, or the Turks. This may have been due to the fact that they could be seen sitting by their trucks smoking the hubble-bubble.

What's in a Name?

Giving misleading names to peoples is however an unusual habit in Argentina, where Jews are called *rusos* or Russians; anyone from the Indian subcontinent is a Hindu; their own indigenous Indians are *cabezitas negras* or 'little black heads' or sometimes *chinitas* or 'little Chinese'. All Arabs are *turcos* or Turks; and Scots, Irish and even Americans and Scandinavians become 'Johnnys' and *ingleses*, or English, while at the same time you must never call a local Indian an Indian. On one occasion I narrowly missed having a knife stuck into me when we were sitting around the campfire and I indicated to the fellow who was teaching me their native Mapuche tongue, known as Mapudungun that they were Indians, and should be proud of the fact. This was seen quite plainly as a direct insult by these people, which led one surly fellow to draw his knife and to make a lunge at me. My teacher, Yanquehuen, saved the situation by intervening on my behalf, as I unceremoniously rolled backwards and away from the threatening blade. To understand why this was so offensive to these 'Indians' I had to learn that when Christianity was forced on them, they were taught that there were only two species of beings that walked this earth. These were either *'cristianos'* or *'animales'*. Anyone refusing to join the Christian brotherhood was therefore an animal and could be treated as such. Since Indians were not *cristianos* they were obviously some type of animal so calling an Indian *'indio'* was the same as calling him an animal.

I did not sleep in my sleeping bag for a couple of nights following this incident and I never called an Indian, *indio* again.

Saints and Virgins

An amusing incident occurred to me in San José shortly after losing the horses' tails and manes to the *marcachifles*.

Things had improved slightly as I worked day to day with this sullen bunch, and I had settled into the job quite well. The housemaid who looked after my house was young, very attractive and would come into he house without bowing or looking subservient, as so many of these people would. These indigenous people who had been taught to call themselves *'cristianos'* were easy targets for the missionaries and often had no idea what they were talking about when it came to religion. They saw being Christian as being submissive to the 'Holy Virgin', the 'Holy Saints' and the Holy Cross, but their confusion around holiness, virginity, saints and religion was to be amusingly illustrated.

I was in my bathroom shaving one evening when I heard a repeated scratching behind me. On turning around I was startled to see the largest spider I had ever seen leap high in the air in an effort to get out of my bathtub. My automatic reaction was to exit the bathroom, covering myself with a towel. I came face to face with the housemaid to whom I tried to explain my behaviour. Her reaction was to show some frustration at me then to break into a broad smile as she pushed past. She then took a towel off the rail, dropped it over this large hairy fellow and, gathering the four corners of the towel together, proceeded to wallop the whole thing against the wall. Following this she shook the towel out of the window and then returned to the bedroom where the new 'boss' was standing, looking quite impressed, if somewhat inadequate.

My thoughts had strayed on more than one occasion to wondering if it would be wise to make a pass in her direction, and in my wisdom I had decided that I would definitely be careful not to offer offence in any way.

Suddenly this seemed the perfect moment to broach the subject quite openly and in a way that I hoped would sound casual. As I drew on my dressing gown I asked, "Are you a virgin?" There was an awkward pause as she tried to absorb what I had just said. Her easy smile slowly evaporated then she looked at me in a very odd way, as if perhaps the sun had got to me and asked in reply, "Why do you ask? Are you a saint or something?" I still laugh when I remember this incident and every time that girl looked at me after this I could see her perception of me as definitely not being right in the head.

Horsing Around

On these large Argentine ranches, lamb marking took place about October or November, followed by shearing and culling. The object was to mark the newborn lamb with the earmark of the ranch, castrate the ram lambs, dock the tails and to count the number in each category.

The ram lambs, or young wethers as they were after castration, had their tails left a little longer than the female lambs, which would grow into hoggets and ewes. This was partly for easy identification when they were later separated but the docking was done largely in the interest of hygiene. On this particular ranch I had been christened Don Diego and as was the custom I was given a string of six horses. Although most of the men knew these horses and their peculiarities, it was part of being accepted not to ask too many questions, but merely to saddle up and get on with it. Some of these partly broken-in animals might kick the stirrup, others would bite, buck or even lie down and if they had a novice in their midst all this would be enhanced by whoops of laughter from the men who, I have to say, were very tolerant of anyone who had less experience of horsemanship than they did. They would get a laugh out of these situations as long as you were willing to laugh with them, and laugh at yourself. It was far more important that a novice should be willing to have a go than that he should be a capable horseman. One thing, which always surprised me, no matter how often it happened, was the way they would land on their feet if they were thrown or if the horse went down.

One day we had been working cattle since early morning when about midday I changed my mount for a large grey, which I had not yet ridden. I was sure that as I mounted it there were some knowing glances between some of the men but nothing untoward took place at first, although I was still certain that something was in the air. This constant tension waiting for something to happen was quite wearing but it was well past midday when this big fellow with no warning got down on his knees and tried to roll over with me still on his back. This, although not dangerous, or requiring great dexterity, caught me unawares. It caused a great amount of hilarity, perhaps because it was such an unusual characteristic or perhaps it was the look of surprise on my face. Eventually, with some help, the saddle and tack were removed and the offending horse went off to graze with the others and I got a new mount. This was another small event to be gone over and to be enjoyed later on sitting round the fire, and when it came to talking about incidents of this kind, the laughter would be just as loud as it was when the actual incident took place. It might even be mentioned night after night, until every little bit of fun had been extracted. I personally always enjoyed the way these hard men enjoyed going over everything and making each other laugh, sometimes at my expense. The way one accepted these amusing moments, and the way one accepted being laughed at, was of utmost importance and had a great influence on how the men would accept a new overseer or *mayordomo*.

Cruel Reality

The ranch hands were mostly Mapuche Indians and half-castes and although life on the big *estancias* could be vey hard at times, the kind of hard existence these people had to endure on their own was at times beyond belief and could be quite cruel. The national territories, before becoming national provinces, were - as mentioned earlier - policed by the 'National Gendarmerie' *(gendarmería nacional)* who tended to exceed their authority when dealing with the indigenous people.

There are any number of distressing stories to be told, largely originating in character from the official approach by central government during and following the infamous Conquest of the Desert. Once an attitude has been officially sanctioned and given the blessing of the people in authority it is normally impossible to change it and it can endure for centuries. This can be seen in the attitude officially created by Christianity towards the Muslims a thousand years ago, or the current attitude towards the Kurds, which the Turks sanctioned long ago, or nearer to home we see the result of the London establishment making second class citizens of Catholics. The Conquest of the Desert was not seen as a war but was officially referred to as the slaughter *(faena)* of the Indians native to these lands. So it was that my friend Yanquhuen, who was teaching me Mapudungun, was to die in the cells of the local *gendarmería* after being arrested for owning a horse with saddle sores. I was fully aware that brutality toward the indigenous people had unofficial backing from many of those in power, and so it was that while I got the unofficial version of the way he had been murdered I was up against a brick wall when it came to getting any kind of satisfaction from the authorities. I was obliged to walk away from this distressing experience, perhaps wiser but definitely frustrated and sadder.

Nobody's Fool

But before this happened we had a visit to one of our campfires from the new Irish-Argentine office assistant called Walsh. We had been out for about ten days and had planned to stay the night not far from a small track, which meant that our visitor, who could not ride, could be brought out in a pickup truck to experience a night under the stars. When we had finished our work we found him with the cook, sitting on the largest bedroll ever seen in the middle of this wilderness. Now these Patagonian cowboys were just as touchy and wary of city folk as country folk anywhere in the world and this fellow's reputation for being a bit of a leg puller had preceded him. Eventually we had our meal and settled round the fire and the talk of the day's activities ran its course. Our guest, who looked very out of place in his brown shoes, neat clothes and pale skin, was far from being shy and obviously did not feel out of place. We drank *mate*, smoked and warmed ourselves at the fire. The conversation inevitably swung to the big city of Buenos Aires where our visitor Walsh had been born and brought up. The men asked him questions about city life and what he did in the big city. Eventually my friend and tutor asked him what he was referring to when he had said *'subte'* (pronounced soobtay). It was explained that *subte* was the abbreviation commonly used for *subterraneo*, or underground railway. We were working near the railhead that came from Buenos Aires so these men were familiar with the railway and some had even travelled short distances on it. However the word *subte* or *subterrraneo* still intrigued them and on asking for some clarification on what exactly it was, Walsh explained that it was just a train that went below the earth. This clearly challenged the group and glances were exchanged and heads shaken in disbelief, then one young man, who had decided not to be made a fool of by this city slicker, made his opinion loudly heard, "We're not daft, you know!! An armadillo runs along the surface then goes under the ground and runs along making a tunnel, but not a train, do you think we swallow everything people like you tell us?" All around the fire heads nodded in agreement, accompanied by gestures of dismissal and even anger.

I stared at Walsh and on the spur of the moment said very loudly, "It was only a joke he did not mean to offend." Walsh, who I suspect had been feeling a bit threatened, was happy to go along with my explanation and the situation was saved. This helped to illustrate the subdued aggression in some of these people, which I was always aware of but seldom witnessed. A week or two later back at the ranch I was able to explain to my friend Yanquhuen the reality of the claim that a train could run under the ground and exactly how it worked. I hoped that he spoke to some of the others about what I had said since I always felt that more sensible dialogue and exchanges were needed between 'them and us'.

This whole way of life was soon to change with the introduction of new tracks, roads and pickup trucks, so when I look back at these nightly chats around the fire, that have now gone forever, I feel privileged and grateful to have been part of something, which, in its unhurried way, had a deep human resonance for me. The isolation, the simplicity, together with the great open spaces created a sense of great timelessness and peace, which seems to have escaped me ever since.

Covered Wagons

The only time I remember getting a similar feeling was when some years before when working in Uruguay, I met a covered wagon drawn by bullocks. A family of five or six ambled along at a snail's pace and I overtook them in an old Ford I had been lent. Returning on the same road a week later I met them less than thirty miles from where I had originally seen them.

I stopped to talk to them and was immediately aware of the same unhurried and timeless tranquility. These people had time to take things in and digest them. They 'felt' the mood of the two bullocks who pulled them slowly along and it did not matter how far they went each day. They were polite but clearly not very interested in who I was or what I had to say.

Although I was privileged to experience that timelessness while in Patagonia I never came across a covered wagon, apart from in photographs. I have been aware for many years, however, that the story of covered wagons in Patagonia has yet to be told so let me try to fire your imagination and who knows, you might feel inclined to find out a bit more and even write this fantastic untold story.

After almost twenty years absence from Patagonia I went to visit my old friend, John Gough - for whom I had stood in at Estancia San José - and who was living in the town of Bolson in northern Patagonia. He was very surprised to see me and as you can imagine we did a great deal of reminiscing. Eventually he started to tell me a wonderful story of what his family had done for a living and how he had grown up. He broke off in the middle of a sentence and mumbled something about some very old albums as he left the room. I waited patiently and when he returned he had a pile of large brown, leather photograph albums in his arms.

As soon as he opened the first one I realised that this was not a collection of people smiling into the camera, these were large sepia photographs of covered wagons. Individual wagons, groups of wagons and some taken from a distance showing hundreds of covered wagons all one behind the other.

Some people walked beside the wagons while others rode on them; I was looking at hundreds of wagons and people but more astonishingly I was looking at a piece of history that few were, or are to my knowledge, aware of. I took no notes and so all that I tell here is from my memory of what he told me more than thirty-five years ago.

In the late 1800s and in the early 1900s transport consisted of horses, mules and bullocks. As the Patagonian sheep farms grew in number there was an ever-increasing need for a system for collecting the wool and transporting it to Port Madryn on the coast of Patagonia, from where it was sent to England by ship.

Now I simply do not know the details of how or even when the company was developed but I was given to understand that Mr Gough's father and grandfather would travel all around the sheep breeding farms and collect the many thousands of bales of wool and eventually end up in Port Madryn, where they were unloaded onto ships.

Having completed this marathon drive over a period of four or five months they would then load the wagons with the innumerable items that the ships had brought with them. Articles of clothing, tools, machinery, guns and ammunition, building materials, medicines, household goods and a thousand more items eagerly sought after by the Europeans who had settled in this part of the world.

As I listened to this story I suddenly interrupted my storyteller with, "What about family, did they never stay at home?"

"These wagons were our home," he explained. "The first wagon was our sitting room, the second the kitchen, then came the bedrooms and our personal storeroom."

I could not believe my ears. The children were taught on a wagon, they slept and ate and cooked on the wagons and they even had a sick bay wagon. The wool was produced in Argentina and shipped to England with no intervention on the part of the Argentine authorities at all. I believe that this continued right up until General Peron took office and decided in the early 1950's that Argentina should see some return on these exports, since it was an Argentine product.

Never Bite off more than you can Chew

But to get back to my story of when I was getting ready for my first lamb marking, the boss, Mr Dickson, had said in his beautiful Scottish way, "Well, you'll see about a million balls being bitten off during the next few weeks". This was yet another of these mysterious new things to be learned, or was this another joke at my expense? Like everything here, you were not helped or taught, you found out from experience.

My previous ranching experience had been with cattle only but it was sufficient to avoid appearing as a raw novice during my first lamb marking. This turned out to be quite fortunate since Mr Dickson's prediction, which I thought was some kind of a bad joke, turned out to be nothing less than factual.

The system was to round up several thousand ewes with their lambs at a time and to pen them into the mobile corrals made of posts driven into the ground, to which nets were attached. The lambs were separated from the ewes and were fed to the men at the workstations. There they were, a row of men docking the tails, short for the female lambs and long for the wethers. Then they would make the incision, bite, spit and wash the mouth out before grabbing the next one. This was the only way to do the job of castration on such a large scale in a hygienic way. The fact that I was not classed as a complete novice exempted me from going through the inauguration ceremony of swallowing the first doctoring, raw. Once the lambs were dealt with the corral netting would be removed very quietly to avoid any panic and several thousand lambs, with the occasional hiccup, would find their mothers. It would usually be late in the day when the lambs were freed like this but very quickly all would return to normal as though nothing had ever happened.

A Sixth Sense

The people I worked with had an awareness or perhaps a sixth sense, which always surprised me. One example of this amongst many was when, on one occasion, I was crossing a shallow river with about fifty men, all on horseback. The river bed was covered in stones, millions of pieces of flint all the same colour with the sparkling water running over them and carrying the flotsam stirred up by the horses. One man stopped, pulled up his sleeve and leaning over, literally hanging down from his horse, retrieved an arrowhead perhaps an inch and a half long from amongst the thousands of similar pieces of stone at the bottom of the river. I made a collection of these pieces of Indian folklore from the bits and pieces that the men presented to me and eventually gifted it to the museum in the town of San Carlos de Bariloche.

Tricks of the Trade

One deviation from the standard diet in these parts was the ostrich egg. The nests, made on the ground, could contain up to forty eggs.

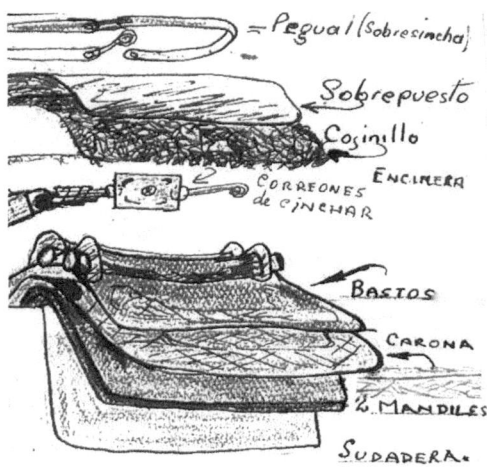

THE BITS AND PIECES WHICH MAKE UP A GAUCHO SADDLE, OR RECADO. I DREW THIS IN THE 1950s!

Rattling the eggs close to the ear, or looking at the colour, would decide if they were fresh or not. They would turn from green to blue and eventually white, as they got older. One egg was the equivalent of a dozen chicken's eggs, so no great quantities were ever taken. The top was removed and the egg placed upright in hot embers, sugar could be stirred in it if one had a sweet tooth and although I never tried this delicacy more than a couple of times, it was quite popular with some.

A month of this hard outdoor life and I learned some of the tricks of the trade. A knob of kidney fat tucked into the saddle and occasionally rubbed into the corners of the mouth and the knuckles would deter the drying out and cracking of the skin. Following cattle or any other livestock in a cloud of dust in dry weather could result in the drying of the skin to the point where a sudden movement of the mouth or hands after sitting fairly still in the saddle for a time could result in a painful splitting of the skin which, once open, took a very long time to heal. Goatskin leg chaps were also a must. I have tried other alternatives but nothing ever compared in comfort, and in keeping the legs dry and warm, than a well-made goatskin removed all in one piece and with no seams or sewing. They were worn hair outwards and, apart from being waterproof, were warm and looked quite attractive.

If one chooses not to use the *recado* or *gaucho* saddle, then the eight or ten pieces which go to make up a *recado*, and which are useful when sitting around a fire or making a bed, must be compensated for. When I rode a Mexican saddle, which consisted of a sweat sheet, one pad and the saddle, I carried a waterproof canvas bag to sleep in and in very cold weather added a couple of sheepskins.

Two small saddle bags made from old riding boots were all that one needed for a pouch of sugar, salt, a cup and matches. A spare notebook and pencils could also be accommodated in these bags and I sometimes filled one side up with a few apples or even a hip flask.

Soon after the lamb marking the shearing shed was prepared and we would work through Christmas and New Year. The suntan acquired during the previous months would soon disappear at the same time as the lanolin in the wool softened our dried skin, turning hard, rough, calloused hands into something any lady would envy.

Shearing Shed

At four-thirty in the morning I would go to the shearing shed and light the blowlamp, which was left for about ten minutes under the old diesel engine to warm it before starting it up. All was silent at this hour in the big shed and I would sit on my own drinking tea and listening to the hissing of the blowlamp. The large flywheel of the diesel engine was turned over by hand and eventually it would respond and break the silence with a spat whoosh spat whoosh spat spat spat spat, and away it would go. The exhaust pipe sticking out of the wall, which blew the most perfect smoke rings, would let everyone know that another day was about to start and, little by little, twenty-four shearers would appear. The men outdoors in the pens would start pushing the sheep up to the trapdoors and then I would move the big lever that fed power to the spindles and shears. As the men pulled the string, which started their individual shears chattering the noise and movement would rise to a certain level and a certain rhythm from which, with practice, one could sense how things were going. There was a certain cacophony of shears, sheep, sliding doors, wool grading and the wool press, all doing their jobs. As soon as the pitch changed there was something to be dealt with. A shearer had a problem with the combs or the ewes were not being fed to the shearers properly; for whatever happens, the shearers were the prima donnas of this all-important season and they called the tune. This was when most of these men made the only wages they would see until the following shearing season, as most of them were local smallholding farmers.

Wages were very poor indeed, apart from for the shearers, who were on piecework. I personally was paid each month what it would cost to rent a room in a boarding house in the city. On top of the wages, of course, I got a house, a cook, a maid, a string of horses and all the food I could eat, so perhaps it was not too bad. I compare the wage with the boarding house because I remember when I went to Buenos Aires, I had to pay for a shared room each month the same amount I had earned as a ranch manager.

Although the food and accommodation was good at the *estancias*, how one slept when out and about was up to each individual. You simply lay down as best you could. If you had had a bad night or got wet, then that was not something you mentioned. You had a job to do and nobody was interested in your problems. I remember the temperature at the *estancia* had shown minus thirty degrees centigrade on the night I slept out in my waterproof sleeping bag and it felt far too hot. This was the great danger since sweating inside the bag could result in a wet, icy bag the following night. Boots had to be tucked inside the bag to keep them from freezing to the ground or in some areas from being eaten.

I had my own ideas about healthy living in the open and the men had theirs.

Many simply slept on their spread out *recados* or saddles and used the horse blankets to keep out the cold. The whole *recado*, including the blankets, would tend to be damp from horse sweat and the truth is that as tough as these people were, TB and other ailments were not uncommon.

From time to time I suffered certain frustrations when I tried to persuade these proud, abused people to change some of their habits and attitudes. The fact is that an understandable, ingrained - but unspoken - mistrust of incomers, together with a lack of education was supported by old superstitions. So if one adds to this the damage inflicted via physical abuse and religious mumbo jumbo, it is not surprising that there remains little room for enlightened dialogue. After all, we see the fear of change as the big challenge in more enlightened societies and what I was naively trying to do was persuade these people to change in some ways, which for them were quite fundamental.

These native people seemed to have lost so much of their original culture and what had taken its place was not always in their best interests. For instance their attitudes regarding women seemed to be based on the idea that tough guys were inherently cruel and insensitive. This same approach was evident when it came to domesticated dogs and other animals. Man's dominance over all of creation as taught by the churches gave them a right to use, abuse and inflict suffering and they had learned to do these things without showing any signs of emotion, compassion or what they had come to see as weakness.

It seemed to me that having had their own innate free will strangled by the incomers it had been replaced by a very narrow, dogmatic set of rules based on politics, the law and religion with no consideration for the culture that was being replaced.

My Friend Brodie

I had been working hard for over a year at the Estancia Alicura in the province of Rio Negro. The cattle had been taken to higher grazing, the lamb marking and shearing were behind us and I had decided to take a break. I decided to ride from Alicura on the river Limay to the town of San Martin de los Andes.

After several days of rough going and becoming lost, I ended up arriving one hot, sunny morning at my destination. I must have looked quite travel-worn, deeply weather beaten very dusty and unshaven. Two rather thin horses completed the picture. As I rode through the town square I spotted a well-known acquaintance who was in charge of a large Chilean-owned ranch. This was Wing Commander Alexander Brodie-Reid, an ex Spitfire pilot. He was chatting to a group of well-dressed, prosperous-looking men and women and as I got closer to the group I became acutely aware that the whole party was looking increasingly worried. However, as I reined up and greeted my friend in English, affectionately calling him an old buzzard, the looks on their faces changed from apprehension to total disbelief. Perhaps they had been in too much of a hurry to judge me.

I managed to get the horses stabled with the local *gendarmes* and following a bath and change of clothes; I accepted an invitation to join the party that I had unintentionally startled. I was left in no doubt by this little group that my appearance had been that of a 'desperado' and it took a little persuasion to even convince one of the ladies that, after getting cleaned up, I was even the same fellow they had encountered in the main square.

The sequence to this tale is that before my intended return ride, I enjoyed several days socialising, shopping, walking and resting.

Before I had time to plan my return trip, however, my friend Brodie, as we all called him, asked me to give him a hand to pick up two of his men who, he informed me, had to be taken to the hospital in Bariloche, almost a hundred miles away. And so it was that I found myself being driven through a canyon along a mountain pass in the dark with two men lying in the back of Brodie's pickup truck. I was not clear as to the nature of our passengers' injuries but Brodie assured me that they needed urgent attention and that he would need to drive as fast as the roads would allow him. This trip was not a lot of fun and at one point we found ourselves stuck behind a slow-moving truck, which was taking up the centre of the road. My friend wound down his window, took a heavy-calibre revolver out of the glove drawer and fired three shots up in the air. The echo bounced it's way down the canyon walls exaggerating the sound and multiplying the number of shots. The truck, which had been refusing to let us pass, immediately pulled over and we shot past and on to our destination in Bariloche and I learned another lesson in driving, Patagonian style.

We eventually arrived at a small private hospital where we discovered that we were expected to carry our patients up two flights of narrow stairs by ourselves since everyone except for the doctor and one nurse who was expecting us had gone home. We struggled with the heavy stretchers between the two of us to get them up the steep stairs without these very silent patients sliding off the stretchers, but we finally made it and went back downstairs with the intention of heading for the hotel and a well-earned drink. We waited for the doctor who seemed to be taking a long time with the patients but Brodie felt happy to have got the two men to hospital.

When the doctor finally appeared he had some papers for Brodie to sign; this seemed to be a simple formality until we read them. They contained the names and details of the two men followed by the following words in large print: DEAD ON ARRIVAL.

We went to the bar in the Hotel Italia to drown our sorrows and eventually to book a room for a much-needed sleep. Before falling asleep Brodie called across the room, "Do you reckon that it's true what they say about dead bodies being heavier than live ones?"

A cheerful, talkative waiter serving me a gin and tonic for breakfast, awakened me the next morning. His explanation was that, "Mr Brodie always breakfasts like this and since you are also an *ingles* I brought you the same".

Quite apart from being a Scot I did not really fit into what the locals saw as an *'ingles'*. First of all I spoke excellent Spanish; second, I had no money; and third, I did not breakfast on gin and tonics. I have to acknowledge, however, that being classed as an *'ingles'* did give one some kind of status.

Conquest of the Desert

A very brief glimpse at the extent to which dogma has become interwoven into this culture is not an anecdote in the true sense of the word but is an essential element when trying to understand local attitudes, which to me were foreign in the true sense of the word. Many history books are available on the subject of the so-called Conquest of the Desert or *Conquista del Desierto*. My personal opinion is that anything telling the true story should carry a title something like: 'The national endeavour to rid the country of every vestige of its indigenous people' because that is what is indicated when the historians use the word *faena*, which means 'slaughter' in reference to the objectives of the army. History, of course, is usually written by the victors but in all fairness the Argentine writers seem to make no effort to hide the murderous nature of the Conquest of the Desert, which had as its official aim to eliminate all the indigenous people. Some dogma, however, tends to overwhelm some of these writings when they include opinions about their Latin affiliation coming from the "Roman Empire and producing the best political result ever known", and then for good measure they throw in a bit of Roman Christianity and end up saying that there is no other complete civilisation, or better said, civilisation is something Roman in the same way that perfect Christianity is Roman Catholic Christianity, or "the fact that it should be Spain, champion of Catholicism who should conquer these countries to incorporate them into Christianity", etc, etc.

One finds this kind of simplistic one-sided and poorly written dogma offered time and again to support hardwired points of view on subjects from dictatorship to Catholicism and from education to modern day politics and if one points out that these are mere opinions being offered as hard facts they tend to say things like, "Well that is the difference between us. We like to have rules and accepted beliefs to guide us whereas you like to pull everything to pieces; we are both right". I am of course generalising here in an attempt to convey a taste of what I understand regarding differences in culture and in attitudes and why at times I have experienced frustration when I was hoping for progressive dialogue.

The Uttermost Parts of the Earth

During the period when the native population was facing annihilation in the north of Patagonia, in the far south a family by the name of Bridges was developing farms and strengthening their relationship with the Indians there. There is a wonderful book about this family and the creation of Ushuaia, which is the most southern city in the world. The title is *The Uttermost Parts of the Earth* and was written by Lucas Bridges.

When looking into the different accounts of what took place in Patagonia, albeit in very unusual and difficult circumstances, the gift of hindsight tempts me to become more than a little judgmental, yet the more I read the clearer it is to me that the majority of the protagonists in these pioneering endeavours, whether it be the settlers or the apparently barbaric military, were in fact doing what seemed to be appropriate and totally justified to them at the time. Questions which arise may centre round the very wonderful civilising work done by some settlers - especially the dedicated Bridges family - who at the same time were Christian missionaries imposing ideas and dogmas on unsuspecting simple people. Similar questions arise around the man who led the infamous Conquista del Desierto, General Roca, who later became President Roca.

Juan Carlos Walther in his *La Conquista del Desierto* gives several accounts of attacks on the Indians and then follows his accounts with some details of the dead, the wounded and the details of the prisoners. Seldom are any soldiers wounded or killed, nor is anything said about what happened to the women and children who were captured. Here is just one typical account from this book.

"The attack was carried out by three hundred and twenty soldiers and eighty friendly Indians. On the eleventh of November we made a surprise dawn attack on the tolderías (Indian camp) and following a bloody fight the Indians dispersed into the surrounding area while some headed up the Colorado river. The panic which was caused amongst the savage masses was complete just as we had hoped by the valiant squadrons of our cavalry who with their shining breastplates and well sharpened swords caused terror amongst the 'Children of the Pampas'."

The result of this day's work was seven Indian chiefs dead, one hundred and fifty fighting Indians dead, sixty five lance Indians captured, some three hundred women and children captured, as well as six hundred horses.

"The national troops suffered no casualties."

Lucas Bridges in his book talks of the Europeans arriving in Patagonia and I quote a passage, which I think helps to illustrate the complexities and difficulties in dealing with incomers from other cultures.

"They had not been born in the country. They had not been brought up to look upon the Indian as an intelligent comrade with whom to work side by side. To them the Feugians [natives of Tierra del Fuego] were not individuals, each to be treated not only on his merits but also as a fellow human being, but as a horde of dangerous untamed natives, to be wiped out as speedily as possible. Was it any wonder that the Ona, slowly retreating from the north should look southward for help."

Having lived and worked with the Araucana Indian farther north and having experienced the attitudes towards the native population still existing when I lived in the area I was initially surprised at Lucas Bridges' unbridled praise for General Roca, both as the General who led the slaughter of the Indians and later as President of the Republic. Once again, however, I have to acknowledge that I was not present at the time these things were happening and I will not be tempted to judge from a distance and with hindsight.

There is no doubt in my mind that the Falklands (Malvinas) and all of Patagonia was in effect unclaimed by anyone until around 1884 when a sub-prefectura was established in Ushuaia and for the first time raised the Argentine flag. Even some seventy years later in the early '50s when I decided to go to Patagonia to work, my Argentine friends in Buenos Aires thought that I was mad to go somewhere that even Argentines knew little of. So while I have little to say in support of colonisation I have to say that the Falklands and even Patagonia might well have been taken over by some other foreign European country right up until General Peron came to power in the late '40s; when Peron started promoting Argentine Nationalism few Argentines knew much about or cared about these 'Uttermost Parts of the Earth'.

Intrigue in Uruguay

Jesus and a Cup of Tea

By the mid-1950s I had been working in industry for a while when I was sent to the town of Fray Bentos in Uruguay to help with a canning factory, more on this later.

Mr Henry Bruce, OBE, managed the upriver packing plant at Fray Bentos. He ran the plant not only as factory manager but as uncrowned monarch of the town and surrounding district. His home, the "Casa Grande" originally built by Count von Liebig, was an imposing square structure surrounded by gardens and overlooking the Uruguay River and beyond, across to Argentina. The wrought iron gates, a consular shield and Uruguayan and British flags adorned the entrance. I soon noticed that the Uruguayans, as well as the English, always acknowledged the Union (British) flag as being the 'English flag'.

Inside and alone except for the servants, Mr Bruce lived in some style surrounded by tartan carpets, curtains and other things Scottish.

Before leaving my new home in Buenos Aires for this temporary upriver job, I had managed to get a promise from our rather devious and untrustworthy personnel office in Buenos Aires that my long-awaited trip to the UK, to be vetted and employed as a UK-contracted employee, would be confirmed in writing within fifteen days. This was quite an achievement and I promised as I left that, should the letter not be forthcoming, I would consider the agreement broken; but for the present there was a new challenge waiting upriver.

On arrival it was immediately apparent that there were several colourful characters in this outpost of British industry.

The first amusing incident was when I visited the office of the canning foreman. This was a small office with a loft where tools were stored. When I sat down to talk things over, the foreman asked me if I would like a cup of tea and when I accepted he grabbed a broom handle next to his desk and, banging the ceiling, he called out, "Jesus, two teas!" His Man Friday had the common name of Jesus and he worked in the storage loft, where he was on hand for odd jobs like making tea. These details I was to learn with time but on that first encounter I found it difficult not to be rude and fall on the floor laughing. One other encounter which amused me at the time was when talking to the personnel manager about labour relations at Fray Bentos he explained that the communist trades union was creating a lot of challenges and with a straight face introduced me to the two men running the union. This, he said as I shook hands, is Stalin Contreras and his brother, Lenin Contreras. Contreras translates roughly as 'against' or 'contrary to'. Again I managed not to laugh. The office I used was near the entrance to the plant and so became the mail delivery point for the postman. A retired gentleman called Mr Link, who had worked all his life at Fray Bentos, would come to pick up his mail and get the latest gossip; with time he became a good friend. One day a letter arrived for him and I noticed that it was addressed to Mr Cuff Link. I put the letter to one side and when my friend arrived I greeted him with the news that someone was pulling his leg by addressing him as Cuff Link. There was a moment's silence, then in a small voice he announced, "That is my name, it is not a joke."

A certain Mr Day was less amusing, he wore a black hat, neckerchief, leather jerkin, flowing black *bombachas* (trousers worn by *gauchos*) and concertina boots, with a knife tucked into a broad black belt. A blue-grey cape held at the throat by a silver chain blanketed all this. This chap had a rather handsome face decorated with a thin black moustache but a knife wound, which came across one eyebrow, his nose and chin managed to create a somewhat sinister touch. This was the head stockman who looked after the arrival of livestock at the plant.

For visitors and short-term employees there was a house built in a square with a central courtyard; it was here that my wife and myself stayed and where I initially made Mr Day's acquaintance at the communal dinner table.

From the first encounter Mr Day refused to speak to me. In fact he managed to treat me as if I did not exist at all and would not even look in my direction. This, in a very small community, was quite awkward but since I was very absorbed in my new job I managed to ignore this strange, unwarranted behaviour.

Many years were to pass as I became more and more involved in the food industry, visiting and working in other factories and in other countries but I would eventually re-visit this same place in a senior capacity and solve a long-standing mystery. For the present, however, I had my work cut out in the canning factory.

The days at the factory were long and very busy, so as a distraction I tried my hand at writing. Little did I suspect that the experience I was trying to put down on paper, about my first introduction to ranch work, had something to do with the sinister Mr Day.

The following is based on these attempts at writing all those years ago. I use the word 'camp' to indicate any piece of land, farm or ranch. It is also an introduction to the 'Spanglish' spoken by many Anglo-Argentines and ex-pats. It is borrowed from the Spanish word *campo*, which the dictionary translates as field, countryside, ground, pitch, playing field, etc.

El Recbidor

The village of Carmelo lies about two hundred and fifty kilometres up the Rio Uruguay from Montevideo, and was reached by dusty roads, which run into impassable mud in wet weather.

Hugh, another Scot out from home, and I were always together; at work, at home and also in the local rowing club, where we qualified to represent the club in the Uruguay National Regattas in what the locals called *'el bote escoses'*, the Scottish boat.

Hugh and I worked for a Uruguayan shipbuilding organisation called MDF and we shared a room in a local boarding house. Hugh worked as a welder and I, being a draughtsman, worked in the moulding loft. Hugh was looking forward to the day his contract would end and he would return to Scotland, while I had accepted a temporary job on an Uruguayan ranch for the duration of the coming harvest. I was just waiting for the crops to ripen before finally abandoning my shipbuilding career for something I knew nothing about.

The day finally arrived when I left for my new job, leaving Hugh to the Spanish and Guarani (Indian language) speaking population. I arrived at Estancia San Gregorio after a two-hour journey, which certainly put the jeep springs to the test. Major Collie, a large big-hearted Aberdonian, and an English accountant by the name of Price ran this *estancia*.

We were served dinner in some style followed by a few drinks. I soon excused myself and went to bed where I immediately fell asleep to the silence of the *'campo'* interrupted only by the buzz of mosquitoes and the croaking of frogs.

My job was to be that of *'recibidor'*, which meant overseer (or harvest receiver), with the responsibility of seeing that the share-out between the landowners and the tenant farmer was done fairly. This 'camp' was called Media Agua and was some distance from the main *estancia*. To get there I was to travel the worst roads, or so-called roads, that I had ever come across. It was already getting hot when, with my haversack and saddle in the back of the jeep, I set off with the major for Media Agua. The roads were of earth or in parts just a faint track over grass. Perspiration showed on the Major's forehead as he smoked his black cigarettes and wrestled with the wheel. We kept this up for hours, passing *estancias*, cattle, the occasional house and miles and miles of waving corn and linseed, golden and brown in the blistering sun. Finally, on crossing a shallow river and climbing the bank, we came to a tenant farmer's very basic home built of adobe with a straw roof and some very dilapidated outbuildings.

As we drew up outside we were met by twelve noisy dogs that did not make us feel at all welcome. I remember wondering what it was going to be like arriving here on horseback and on my own, at night.

The farmer came out to meet us dressed in the usual *gaucho* attire. He wore a particularly large hat with a strap, which came across his forehead and acted like a chinstrap. He scowled at me disapprovingly as he invited us to sit and share some *mate* under a large *ombu* tree. It is not usual to invite people inside the house. During the time I stayed there I ate my breakfast outside under the tree or in a very shabby outhouse and had my other meals wherever we were working out in the fields.

Following the obligatory *mate* we went out to look at the vast fields that were to be harvested and I met the foreman and the labourers, who numbered twenty in all. The major said his goodbyes and left me the job of ensuring over the coming weeks that the proper percentages of the harvest went to the appropriate grain stores and that the tenant farmer got no more than his agreed share, which I suspect had been a sore point in the past.

I was given a very large horse and together with the foreman's son, El Chilo, went to see what this place really looked like. My experience with horses was almost zero since the cart horse that used to deliver our coal or the horse-drawn ice cream van that used to come round the streets in the summer could hardly be counted. It took me more than a little courage just to bluff my way, which I felt obliged to do, since it seemed that these people had no concept of someone who did not know how to ride unless perhaps they were mentally retarded.

Looking back on it I realise that nobody ever thought to enquire whether I had ever been on a horse although it has to be said that they did give me a very well behaved mount. It was only later when I had seen a lot more of what horses can be that I came to appreciate how they had looked after me and kept me out of danger. We arrived back at the *puesto* and I watched El Chilo as he unsaddled his mount and did the same. We turned the horses loose and I felt that I had managed to pass as an acceptable rider.

After a few *mates* we went into the outhouse to eat. An oil lamp was placed in the middle of a wooden table around which the head of the family and his three sons sat. The light was very poor and the black walls and roof did not help. The farmer's wife appeared from the house carrying a large plate piled high with meat and this was placed in the middle of the table and bread was scattered around the dish. I was given a fork and everyone waited until I had helped myself. Each then picked up a piece of meat in his fingers and, drawing a large knife from behind them, proceeded to bite the meat while cutting it in an upward direction. It surprised me then and still surprises me today that half the population are not missing the point off their noses.

I turned in to sleep, or perhaps turned out may be more appropriate since my bedroom consisted of four upright poles covered by a tin roof. One side was covered in with wood while the other three were open to wind and weather. A few large nails hammered into the posts served as my wardrobe and a candle stuck in a bottle on the ground was my night-light. This was to be my home for about six weeks. There were, however, still twelve undefined dogs to be dealt with and as I prepared to get into bed they all came to sniff at me and inspect my clothes, saddle, boots and my meagre possessions. I spoke to them, trying to sound authoritative and in charge of things, in the hope that they might accept me and not devour me in my sleep.

I slept soundly and was up at four and not a dog in sight. After some *mate* followed by meat and a large cup of milky coffee it was time to set off for the harvest fields and my first day in my new job. I had about three miles to travel across country and as the miles went by I began to wonder if I had been overconfident when I said that I would be able to find my way without help. This was rolling country and each time I came over a hill I expected to see the harvesters. When I finally spotted them they were, according to my calculations, in totally the wrong place and it took me sometime to understand how I had gone round in an almost complete circle. This was not how I had intended to start my new career but it gave the men something to talk about, and my poor navigational skills were periodically the subject of conversation over the next few weeks.

Inauguration

When I arrived the men were sitting under a large *ombu* tree eating breakfast and as I approached they watched me in silence. Nobody spoke and as I felt my way through the awkward silence I suddenly realised that they saw me as the new boss man and they were expecting me to make the first move. I raised my hand and called out *buenos dias*. Instantly, as if by some magic, the aggressive silence evaporated and after handshakes all round everybody had something to say, questions to ask and advice to share. The cook quickly became my friend and over the following weeks taught me how to make *mate*, catch and skin lizards and what to do, and not do, in this totally strange new culture.

I gradually became used to the work, which started at four or five each day and consisted mainly of checking the numbers of bags of grain that went to the barn for the farmer and how many ended up at the grain store belonging to the *estancia*.

This was not at all a simple task with men carrying the sacks on their backs, lorries coming and going and people asking questions. I soon realised that I would only need to be distracted for a few minutes for the distribution to go wrong and if I had to leave the field for any length of time then any pretence of control was impossible.

My friend the cook came to my rescue when he pointed out that as long as I insisted that each lorry took a full load on each trip there was no way that they could juggle the figures and once I had established that a standard number of bags compiled a full load all I needed to do was count the trucks rather than each bag. Not bad for an illiterate *campesino*.

I found that I had more free time as things became more organised and I started helping with loading the lorries as well as helping the cook and on one occasion helping with the repairs to a lorry, which had broken down. The days went quickly by but then I got my foot quite badly injured when my horse accidentally stood on it, and my mood changed. I went to the doctor in the nearest village and ended up with a bandaged foot, which meant I could not get my boot on. I spent about ten days either on horseback or sitting on a bag of linseed. Apart from the cook, nobody showed any interest in my plight as I dressed the wound sitting on my bag of linseed while trying to fend off the flies. Just what I felt towards camp life at that time and just what I called myself for getting mixed up in it is nobody's business.

The major came by plane to see how things were going from time to time, landing the small plane on the recently harvested fields. He brought mail and the latest news and it gave me a break from speaking Spanish. I managed quite well in Spanish but had never before spoken continuously day in and day out. On one such visit he asked me to acquire a few ostrich eggs for him to take back to an English couple who were visiting him at the main *estancia* for a few days.

I Learn About the Ostrich

The day came when everything had to stop because of a freak rainstorm. This meant that the crops had to be left to dry before harvesting could continue. This gave me the opportunity to go looking for a nest with about thirty eggs in it which I had discovered only days before on my way to the harvest field. When I was still a way off I could see that there was an ostrich sitting on the nest so, having been advised that most horses will try to bolt if confronted by an angry ostrich I, in my innocence, chose to approach on foot. Now these birds can stand over six feet high and, I was just about to learn, that when they puff themselves up and hiss like a steam engine while running at you they present an impressive spectacle, to put it mildly. I went slowly towards the nest and as I closed in the bird's head went lower and lower. I got to within about ten or fifteen feet of it when it suddenly shot up like a rocket and rushed me; wings and claws going like pistons. I pulled off my shirt and waved it furiously as I retreated, shouting at the top of my voice.

This panic response on my part caused it to slow down and make a half circle around me, which meant that it was now between the fence and myself. I picked up some stones and started to pelt it while working my way towards the fence. A short, sham battle then ensued, with me shouting and behaving like a mad dervish and the bird striding about hissing while making dabs and rushes at me, rather like a boxer. I lost all awareness of time but clearly remember seeing a free path to the barbed wire fence, which I took at full speed and dived through, cutting myself in the process. The agitated ostrich strode up and down on the other side of the fence as I took stock. The horse was very uneasy and skittish when I tried to mount it and I felt quite shaky as I made my way back to my accommodation. When I returned the following day there was no sign of the ostrich and I collected several eggs, which probably are now part of someone's memorabilia from their South American trip.

Getting Lost

Every day I learned something new, like when it was safe to plant corn or how a hide should be cut only when the moon was new or waxing. I had no idea what half of it meant, although regarding the cutting of a hide to make a lasso was something I not only witnessed but eventually participated in. Some of their beliefs and superstitions were obviously born of ignorance but there was also an intriguing quasi-spiritual dimension to some of their cultural understandings, which seemed to have been corrupted by religious dogma as their traditional knowledge was subjected to more 'civilised' ways.

The men, who slept out every night would play guitars after supper and a couple of them would sometimes sing, so one particular night I stayed on to listen. It was very late when I finally saddled up and headed back. I felt quite happy with life and was in no hurry and as the music faded in the distance my thoughts turned to getting into bed. I reached the river but it was not the usual place where I could cross in about two feet of water. I rode up and down the bank looking for a crossing but I was lost. I tried a couple of potential crossing places but the horse was very reluctant so, in desperation, I rode back up the bank, turned round and made a rush for it. I soon found myself holding the horse's tail as it laboriously swam in about fifteen feet of water as we drifted down with the current. I finally arrived back at my digs feeling cold and tired and got into bed and went to sleep, intending to keep my stupidity a secret. The story finally got out, due mainly to the state of my clothes but instead of laughing at my adventure my host and hostess warned me to stay well away from the upper reaches of the river at night since it was inhabited by 'lobos', which would attack anyone on their own. Now the word *lobo* translates as wolf, ofwhich there had not been any for at least fifty years and *lobo del mar'* would be a seal, but neither of these made any sense and in the end I never did find a satisfactory answer. I felt that this whole subject was something they were uncomfortable about and that I was not getting the full story. I decided not to pursue it any farther, but I made a point of not returning there at night-time.

The day arrived when the last lorries were loaded up and everyone clambered on board and we set off for town. I got a seat in the cab of the leading lorry - which meant we did not have to put up with the dust from the convoy - and off we went to unload for the last time and have a night on the town. There was a bit of hand shaking and backslapping with the townsfolk and then it was time for eating and drinking.

The Town

My only visits to the town had been to see where the harvest was destined and one visit to the doctor when I damaged my foot, so I was a total stranger. I soon found a good restaurant and enjoyed a meal that included vegetables and a sweet washed down with a good wine. For some reason this did not seem to appeal to any of the others so I was allowed to enjoy my treat all by myself. The weather was warm and I wandered along the main street and went into a bar where three of my workmates were doing some serious drinking. When they spotted me they treated me like a long lost brother, plying me with drinks and telling everyone that I was their friend from Scotland who had been working with them.

As I explored the town, which consisted of one main street that had been covered with tarmacadam, while the smaller streets running off at right angles were mainly just earth. I became aware that most of my working companions were nowhere to be seen as my progress took me towards the end of the street, which became poorer looking and less well lit. There was the sound of music and there was a busy feel to this area, with groups of men coming and going accompanied by occasional laughter and sounds of revelry.

It hit me out of the blue and explained why the invitation to join me for a meal had been rejected in favour of something more urgent and attractive. How could I have been so blind? I was in the red light district and this was where the men had been since our arrival. Just then a group of men I immediately recognised spotted me and started calling to me, enquiring if I was having a good time and recommending the best whorehouses to visit. I played my part and soon got free from their kind assistance and kept walking until the street came to an end and I was walking on grass in the stillness of the warm night air. Quite recently, while living in Carmelo, I had lost my virginity to a very beautiful English lady almost twice my age and I savoured the memory and had every intention of carrying on where I had left off when I returned. The prospect of going into one of these dingy looking brothels or having any contact with these girls was unappealing enough to fill me with revulsion. I returned to the place where I slept in the wee hours of the morning, having been driven back by El Chilo who, in spite of being very drunk, got us back all in one piece.

There was a bit of a party at the place where I had been sleeping and the farmer and his family were more than kind and complimentary to me and came to wave me goodbye as I took off in the small plane the Major had sent to pick me up and deliver me back to the main *estancia*.

A New Job

Upon my return to the main *estancia* I was complimented on the success of the operation and received my not inconsiderable wages. I felt sure that there was more to this whole job than was being said and this was reinforced when the accountant shook my hand and said, "Well good for you, you managed to see it though then?"

I assured him that I had enjoyed the experience, to which he replied, raising his eyebrows, "Well, rather you than me". The major changed the subject and invited me to rest for a few days and then to accompany him to another smaller ranch called Santa Anita, of which he was also in charge. I enjoyed the luxury of a private room, a proper bed and a shower, to say nothing of the food.

I spent time riding around with the major and seeing how he ran things and Mr Pierce, the accountant, showed me how he kept the books and records and the all-important diary in which everything that went on, including the weather, was recorded daily. I kept my counsel but I was aware that I was being treated better than normal and that this was probably leading up to something.

We left early one morning for Santa Anita and as suggested by the major I took everything with me, including my saddle. As we drove along in the jeep the major explained that he had nobody actually running Santa Ana and that the foreman was all right but needed someone to keep an eye on him and do the office work. So this was it, I was to become a - very young - ranch manager. WOW!

We talked as we drove along but my head was full of questions, doubts and a feeling of apprehension, so that when we arrived I had no recollection of what we had talked about. When we finally drove up to a large square house overlooking what seemed to be an orderly well-built farmyard complete with stables, drinking trough and hitching rail, I really did not know what to expect.

A woman who turned out to be the housekeeper came out to meet us and what I took to be the houseboy helped us with our luggage. There was a meal ready for us and our rooms were ready with towels laid out and the beds even had mosquito nets over them. The major showed me around and explained that he wanted me to take over the whole place. The salary was good, the house, the servants and the cook were run by the housekeeper, leaving me free to dedicate myself to running the ranch.

I found it hard to get my thoughts together. The staff in the house had been very welcoming and the job as described by the major sounded like something I could do. The only person who had come over as a bit sullen and not very welcoming had been the foreman by the name of Segundo Sanchez and I made a mental note to start off by getting him on my side.

We spent the following day riding around while I got my bearings, and by the third day I felt quite happy with the arrangements. The major left in the afternoon and I went over things in the office and turned in early to get ready for my first day as a ranch manager.

The morning was bright and it felt as if it was going to be hot. I went to the stables and asked the horse boy about a good horse. Then after breakfast I went out to find the foreman, who I wanted to cultivate into my way of doing things. Through the front door, along the veranda, down three steps and across the yard and there was Segundo Sanchez leaning against the wall, dressed in black from his black riding boots to his wide brimmed hat and even his faded neckerchief was black. I noticed the horse boy peeping round the stable door and a couple of faces at windows, all looking in our direction. Everything seemed to be very quiet and I felt that there was trouble brewing. As I approached, Sanchez lazily pushed himself off the wall and advanced with his hands behind his back and his head down. I stopped in the middle of the yard and let Sanchez come to me. When he was a little way off he looked up and as his head slowly came up he had a very large knife in his hand. Stopping about three yards away he proceeded to draw a line across the yard with the point of the knife blade. He then straightened up and, slipping the knife back into its sheath behind his back, he shouted, "If you cross that line you'll have to fight me". I heard myself bawling back at him, "What's your problem Sanchez". There was a silence, and then in a lower voice meant only for me, "Cross that line and I'll remove your innards."

This was not part of the deal and surely the major must have known that my life would be put in danger.

I felt angry and let down and so it was in a sombre mood that I packed my things and headed south to have it out with the major, who was several hours' driving away.

Back to Fray Bentos

It was not until about eight years later that I found out that a certain young man had agreed to take my place at Santa Anita only to go through the same ritual with Segundo Sanchez. This particular youngster, however, had decided to draw his revolver and cross the prohibited line, only to receive a nasty cut across his eyebrow, his nose and down across his chin.

I must presume that at the time of my original visit to Fray Bentos, that Mr Day was aware of my connection with Santa Anita and that this induced him to behave towards me in such a strange and arrogant fashion, but I will never know.

Now let me tell you a little more that I do know to round off this particular piece of the Fray Bentos saga.

A constant friend and drinking partner of Mr Day was a fellow by the name of Bowie. A bit of a poor fish from the accounting department in Buenos Aires who, it seemed, was able to go where he wanted within the company and get away with all kinds of normally unacceptable behaviour. They shared the guesthouse with myself, my then-wife as well as a colleague by the name of Tom Avis. I had a great deal of respect for this new, five feet two inches tall colleague who also had his wife with him and I enjoyed his company mainly because I found him both knowledgeable and hard working.

Our two unsavoury neighbours would come back in the wee hours of the morning from their drinking bouts in the town and wake us up with their loud voices, banging doors and drunken laughter.

Both Avis and myself had to get up very early each morning and as the weeks went by we felt more and more unwilling to tolerate this invasive, loutish behaviour but wanted to avoid outright confrontation.

The weather was very warm and sleep did not come easily in the old-fashioned building with no air conditioning or even fans.

On one occasion I lay awake as I heard the two drunks arrive shortly after midnight. They made no effort to go about their business quietly and soon they were talking in loud voices about the two good little hard working idiots who always went to bed early. I could hear Avis and his wife talking in the bedroom next door and became concerned that things might develop into a confrontation. Just then the conversation turned to comments about our wives and Bowie was saying something very personal about Mrs Avis.

Very suddenly I was aware that Avis was outside confronting Bowie while his wife was screaming at him not to get into trouble. I must have reacted instinctively because I can remember coming face to face with 'tough guy' Day as I came out of my room. He was standing with his cape thrown over one shoulder and his hat on the back of his head and the next moment he went backwards through the double doors behind him and ended up under the table with all the appearance of someone who might be dead and for some reason my right fist was painful.

Everything stopped and there was an eerie silence. Our two wives were standing together looking shocked as Avis and I surveyed the situation. After a few minutes we decided to go up to the *casa grande* and report to the manager.

It was after one o'clock in the morning and it took some time to get Mr Bruce to grasp what we were saying. We told him that we were packing up and returning to Buenos Aires immediately and that we were fully aware of the seriousness of our decision.

The eventual outcome was that Day was severely reprimanded, but there was a complete cover up on what had really taken place and we were requested not to talk about it. Avis and I returned to Fray Bentos to finish the season, following which I travelled with my wife to London on the company-owned *Brazil Star*, the flagship of the fleet. We sat at the captain's table during the three-week voyage and, after being vetted by the big chief in London, I returned abroad to work as part of the UK contract staff.

Bowie went on to become part of the economy team, which had carte blanche to look into every aspect of the business in Buenos Aires and was, in my view, partly responsible for the eventual demise of the business. I was to hear a rumour sometime later that Day had been shot in a nightclub, but was never able to confirm this. Bowie spent his last days in an institution for the insane in Argentina.

Dukes and Partridges

Let me offer one final anecdote on a lighter note before leaving Fray Bentos. Following the foot and mouth outbreak in the UK, the Duke of

Northumberland and his team visited South America on a fact-finding visit. I happened to be present when the visitors were having a look at Fray Bentos and together with Mr Bruce, Señor Camesana - a Charles Laughton kind of character who was overall head of canning - and the Duke's entourage we were enjoying a kind of working dinner. With the dessert the conversation became less formal and the always inquisitive Duke turned to Señor Camesana and, through the several willing translators present, asked Camesana about himself, his family and his pastimes. Camesana mentioned that he liked to go shooting. The *perdiz* or partridge were plentiful in the area and the Duke listened as he was told how the birds would run along the ground rather than fly. It then transpired, much to the dismay of our visitor, that Camesana actually got his driver to drive him across the fields so that he could do his shooting from the comfort of a car. In the presence of this country squire who knew so much about such things we were all feeling a little uncomfortable when the Duke asked, "You don't mean that you shoot them when they are running along the ground, do you?" Following a pregnant silence Camesana's face lit up as he replied, "No, no, no! I wait until they stop, then I let them have it". Only through a rather embarrassed and reluctant translator was the message passed on.

I DID IT MY WAY

The Paris of the South

Those Were the Days

My reason for leaving the *estancia* life was simply that following a riding accident I had been told by the doctors that I would not be able to ride again. At this point I would like to remind the reader that half the lies you hear aren't true. Basically I had been thrown by a horse while working, and ended up with a number of compound broken ribs plus two fractured vertebrae. The doc used the word compound because there was some kind if complication, which I never really understood. It is not all that unusual in the horsey world to have accidents and it could have been much more serious, suffice to say that I was not going to be a great success as a cowboy if I couldn't ride a horse.

I travelled to Buenos Aires, the big city known as the 'Paris of the southern hemisphere'. In the '50s this was still a very affluent post-war country and there were jobs galore and as yet the scourge of the drug addiction trade in big cities had not yet become a reality. *The Standard*, an English language newspaper dedicated several pages exclusively to advertising jobs. Following a few interviews I soon found myself working as a livestock buyer for the Anglo Packing House, which employed some five thousand people all in one very large complex. This place included a children's crèche, an operating theatre, five doctors, a private armed police force, fire brigade, various laboratories, a large veterinary division employing over one hundred vets and vets' assistants and a large dock where five large refrigerated ships could tie up at the same time. While working as a livestock buyer I also managed to do some business selling farm machinery like windmills and the like when visiting the ranches to buy livestock. Another part-time job, working for Sono Films, as an extra, paid handsomely and so I always made an effort to also fit some filming work into my schedule.

It was about this time that General Peron decided to put on "the greatest show on earth", which he called *El Dia del Deportista*, or Sportsman's Day. Thousands of people were paraded up one of the main avenues in Buenos Aires past a fancy podium where Peron in the company of Miss Argentina who, if my memory serves me well, was called June Hanson took the salute. The racing cars lead by the world famous Juan Manuel Fangio moved noisily up past the podium where they were hailed as heroes by the President. Golfers, boxers, tennis players, skaters, cyclists, mounted jockeys and footballers and many others all turned out.

I was a member of the Tigre Boat Cub and we oarsmen had been told that we had better turn up, since being a foreign club we might be particularly careful not to offend the regime by our absence. All the clubs were represented and together we numbered several hundred oarsmen and women, all smartly dressed in shorts and rowing shirts and carrying an oar, each with the club colours painted on the blade. The parade was several miles long and down near the assembly area there was great activity and some confusion as the stewards with 'Peronist' armbands barked orders and tried to organise the chaos. The plainclothed police and 'enforcers' allowed no dissension and stood for no nonsense. Three tough looking characters, complete with armbands and ill-disguised guns under their shirts, approached me and handed me an Argentine flag, wrapped round a flagpole. They explained to me that I was going to lead the Argentine oarsmen and present them to President Peron. "But I am not even an Argentine," I protested. The three stared in disbelief that anyone would be so stupid as to question their authority. I could feel the atmosphere freeze as they studied me and then looked at each other. One of them came very close to me and I wondered what was going to happen. He put his face close to mine and said in a quiet voice, "Do what you are told or you are going to have problems," then he stood back and waited for my answer. I heard myself saying, "Yes sir, that's okay."

I was instructed in how to carry the flag in its leather holder with a strap, which went over my shoulder. I was also instructed to walk about twenty paces ahead of the main body of oarsmen which was to feel very strange, being away out on my own, with literally thousands of noisy waving, cheering, onlookers lining the pavements. After marching for miles carrying this heavy pole and wearing thin rowing shoes I finally managed to ignore my discomfort and did an eyes right as we approached the podium and got a salute from on high. Later I was to see myself on TV and in the newspapers and I remember thinking how nobody would have guessed at my extreme discomfort.

An Air Raid

Buying livestock was all about getting the required quantities and quality shipped to the cattle and sheep pens on time. Although this particular packing house could handle up to twelve thousand head each day, five or six days a week, the operation worked well and once the buyer had completed his part of the business his time was his own. I found myself with spare time on my hands on one such occasion and headed for my favourite coffee shop.

Instead of ending up at the coffee shop I ran into an attempt by a group of military 'head cases' to oust President Peron from office. The way that they went about it was to use thirty-four aeroplanes, including British-built Gloucester Meteors, to bomb Government House in the middle of a beautiful sunny day, when ordinary people were going about their business. What they achieved was to kill almost four-hundred civilians, injure eight-hundred more and to make many others like myself sick to the core and traumatised by this savage military mentality. The raid lasted for more than four hours and, amongst other things, managed to hit a trolley bus full of people killing most of them, including the daughter of an employee of the company. Back in Scotland my mother, who read what had happened in the news, wrote me saying that she had never expected me to have to go through another air raid after the war had ended and I had gone abroad. I find it difficult to explain the total difference between the two experiences. One, when there is a war going on and air raids are part of life and the other, when out of a beautiful blue summer sky there arrives unexpected, unannounced genocide.

Before settling in at Mrs Roberts' boarding house in the suburbs I had tried other alternatives but there were ten other lodgers in this house and that offered a kind of ready-made small community. The boarding house was on the south side of the capital in a suburb called Lomas de Zamora. I joined the local sports club, Club Atletico Lomas, and was to play rugby for them for several years while in the summer I rowed for the Tigre Boat Club, where I eventually became club president.

When I think back about those magical bygone days a song comes to mind, sung by Mary Hopkin which, I feel, says it all,

> "Those were the days my friend
> We thought they'd never end
> We'd sing and dance forever and a day
> We'd live the life we choose
> We'd fight and never lose
> For we were young, and sure to have our way."

But I am getting ahead of myself. My new life in the big city working for a very large company entailed visiting the cattle and sheep markets as well as the large cattle ranches and this gave me an insight into the very questionable wheeling-dealing that went on at every level of the livestock purchasing business. The overall boss of our livestock-buying department was a certain Mr Jackson. He had a large room in his house where he kept all the (non-cash) loot he acquired. This became a major operation around Christmas time when vast quantities of gifts had to be stored and eventually sorted out. These were either kept, sold, returned to the shops where they had originated for cash or used as presents for friends and family. I soon realised that the money with which all these expensive gifts were purchased came, in the final analysis, out of the pocket of our employer.

Elevated prices were being paid thanks to the livestock buyers, who knew that by overpaying the cattle dealers they were going to receive these very handsome, if somewhat tainted, rewards.

I did not seem to function on the same wavelength as these people so when the personnel department looked at my CV and, due to my engineering experience, offered me a job in the can-making factory I jumped at the chance to remove myself from a group of wheeler dealers with which I felt increasingly at odds. This was, for me, undoubtedly a major step since it meant getting up early each morning and living a more regimented life as well as having to give up my extra jobs - and the money - but it felt more comfortable on a very personal level. Some of my friends, who had observed the lifestyle that these livestock buyers lived, said I was crazy to make such a move. I found it quite difficult to explain that I did not want to make money with which I would feel less than comfortable. Some friends refused to believe that there was not some other motive for my decision so I just had to settle for being crazy and left it at that, although I have to admit to some questions and doubts which I did harbour related mainly to the money I could have made.

Upon reflection I now realise that I could have done with a friend or mentor with whom to talk things over. The truth is that I have always been a loner and probably a rather stubborn one at that, and it is only since I remarried late in life that I have found a real friend with whom to discuss things and to get advice and support from. Why, I must ask myself, did I take so long?

Working in the can-making factory was a real challenge and it took a lot of time, effort and study to learn the tricks of the trade. I enjoyed the work, which of course meant working closely with engineers and mechanics who manned this enormous canning factory, which used millions of cans each day to produce a long list of products, from corned beef to fruit, vegetables and the more exotic spreads and jams and we also supplied the Argentine army with twenty kilo cans of Pemican dog food for the huskies in the Antarctic.

About a year after moving to the factory I was asked to work as assistant to the canning superintendent, a controversial character by the name of Pedro Ragazzi. This meant helping to look after both the can-making factory and the canning operation, which employed over two thousand operators. The head of laboratories was a brilliant boffin called Peter Boyes who was popular with everyone, the exception being Pedro Ragazzi with whom there was an ongoing, mutual hate relationship. I discovered this when I laughingly pointed out that Pedro Ragazzi translated into Peter Boyes.

On top of all this I was also asked to offer a helping hand when needed to the young men who were sent out from London as students and had no Spanish and no knowledge of the country. These well-heeled young students had mostly been to English public school followed by two years as an officer in the army and then, through the old boys network, been taken on by the Vestey organisation, who owned the company, and sent out to South America. They were a mixed bunch, some very likeable, some quite badly behaved, but they all seemed to have two things in common. The first was their lack of any idea whatsoever of how to behave around the opposite sex. This could be most embarrassing and the Argentines above all could not believe the antics of some of these cack-handed, young *ingleses*. The second was that they refused to get their hands dirty and saw themselves as something above the other members of staff who had to work their way up from the bottom. The Argentines were aware of everything that was going on and, being great at nicknames, were soon to call them the *paracaidistas,* which translates as parachutists. "Why parachutists?" I asked the yard foreman, who was a great character called Flores. "Well," he explained, "they have been in the English army and they come out here and out of thin air they land in the best jobs, so we call them the *paracaidistas.*" Few, if any, of them ever stayed on, or benefited the company in any way as far as I could see, but they belonged to that impenetrable private club that it would seem had to be tolerated, rather like Monday mornings or the taxman.

Right out of the blue I was called to a meeting with the personnel manager and had it explained to me that Ragazzi was leaving the canning department - no reason given - and did I feel that I would be able to take over as provisional canning superintendent? A very bright young Anglo-Argentine chemist by the name of Gillanders would be detailed to work with me and I always had the wonderful Jimmy Laird, also a chemist, who spent years as canning superintendent, and who was now the overall factory manager, to help me if I got stuck.

I learned from the lab's chief that Ragazzi had changed a formula for a particular product without the proper procedure and this had resulted in thousands of cans having to be destroyed. The real surprise for me, however, was that this man who I never liked had been given a desk in the front office and had orders not to go into the factory. He seemed to spend his days sleeping, betting on the horses and looking bored. His Argentine co-workers called him 'the cat' because he spent a lot of time sleeping on a pile of papers.

There seemed to be a very shady side to big business of which I was still very naïve so I was shocked when I learned that Ragazzi would never be sacked from the company no matter the blunders he might make. He was apparently one of the people who had been involved in a high profile scandal some years previous, when the company had been caught running two sets of books. The fall guy who went to prison was Mr Aron and the people who had packed the real books in a corned beef box and sent them to Fray Bentos still knew of a lot of undisclosed information, which the company wanted to be kept secret. This little group had all kept quiet and as a result had jobs for life. Aron eventually left jail and became company president and was given an OBE while the others stayed invisible until something like this Ragazzi situation arose and people started to ask questions.

I have to say that I later worked closely with Aron and found him to be a very likeable character. He was, I learned, the son of a Jewish family who had escaped from the Russian pogroms and he had been born into poverty in London. Apparently, the first thing he did when he made some money was to buy his parents a house. I was later, in the company of Aron, to see some shady dealing, which entailed giving backhanders to government officials and other questionable practices and although I always distanced myself from the sleaze of which I was aware I still hesitate to judge others who have come from a background of which I know nothing.

Time went by and in 1959 I was sent to Brazil - with a very pregnant wife - to run a canning factory just outside the town of Barretos. This place had been in mothballs for about fifteen years and presented some serious challenges.

Above: *me, aged 8, on a family holiday in Millport,*
lower Firth of Clyde

Main Photo: *Centre - my favourite grandpa, Peter Crawford Kemp & my 'wee' grannie, Annie McDonald accompanied by my uncles and aunties; on the extreme right, the one with sergeant stripes, is my father.*
Bottom left: *My father, John Watson Kemp at the Somme, 1916.*
Bottom right: *My mother, Grace Clark Kemp.*

Top left: *My maternal grandfather, John Clark, in his masonry regalia.* **Top and bottom right:** *two Clark uncles, Richard & Jim, respectively.* **Bottom left**: *My uncle Willie Clark, who never returned from the 'Great' War.*

Top: *In my gaucho bombachas, Nahuel Huapi lake, Bariloche, Patagonia, 1951.* **Bottom**: *London, 1958.*

Above: *far left, aged 20, drinking mate from a gourd and bombilla, Uruguay and my friend the cook standing on far right.*
Below: *Second from right, El Tigre Boat Club, Buenos Aires 1953.*

Above: *on my first honeymoon, Cordoba, Argentina, 1956.*
Below left and right: *making friends in Ghana 1958.*

This and opposite page: Ship board life on the Blue Star Line, 1960s, my preferred way of going on leave from Buenos Aires to the UK. *Top left*: with my first wife Jenny. *Top right and below*: enjoying life on deck.

*Above left: going for the fancy dress prize! **Above right**: dancing with my friend Derek's wife, Sonia. **Centre**: spot Boris Karloff's twin brother. **Below**: at a friend's wedding, Buenos Aires, 1960s.*

This page: home leave 1970.
Top left: Aviemore, with Four Seasons Hotel in background.
Top right: talking to Sam Vestey at his country estate.
Below: my friend Derek in front of Sam's country house, Stowell Park.

Top left and right: *my way of relaxing: sailing on the River Plate, Buenos Aires, 1960s and early 1970s.* **Left**: *on holiday, Humber Snipe going onto plane in Kent, bound for Le Toque, France, 1964.* **Below**: *my first new car, ever! Buenos Aires, early 1960s.*

Above: *rowing from Argentina to Uruguay.*

Bottom left: *My friends and colleagues, Lopez (L) & Tommy Boeche on my ill-fated skiing holiday to Bariloche.* **Bottom right:** *my chauffeur Ignacio.*

124

Top and centre: Argentine gauchos, Patagonia, 1970s.

Right: Hydroscheme on Rio Limay, home of'el vientos de los locos'.

This page: the freedom of Patagonia, the second time around: Chacra Caledonia, Mallín Ahogado. The house was built without any electric tools.

Below: trying to get the roof on before the bad Andes weather set in.

Main photo: *Half the Lies You Hear Aren't True!*
Other photos: *Chacra Caledonia*

Top left: *Chacra Caledonia, Mallín Ahogado.*
Centre left: *oxen pulling cart.*
Centre right: *weather station at El Tronador glacier.*
Bottom left and right: *interior of the cabin.*

Above: ski lodge at the top of the world.
Centre: lower restaurant on the Bariloche ski slopes, known then as 'Mil doscientos'.

Below left: *talking to a water boy, Brazil, 1970s;*
Below right: *working at at a weather station, El Tronador.*

This page: The Nile and the desert; working in Cairo, Egypt, 1980s.
Bottom left: the old part of Riyadh, Saudi Arabia.

Above: At Drovers Dinner, London, 1980s.
Centre and right: A hunting we will go.
Bottom: exercising horses in Sussex, England, 1980s.

Above left: *with my friend Bernard at Windsor Great Park, 1980s.*

Above: *at the office in East Sussex, 1980s.*

Above: *polo match, Windsor Great Park,* **Below**: *stamping the divot at Windsor Park, who is that guy in white?*

Right: My croft
house in Shetland.
Below left:
Walking the length
of the Findhorn
River.

Above: Findhorn Foundation - how it looked when I arrived in the late 1980s,
now parked cars would block that view. **Centre right**: A Findhorn village pub.

133

This page: Holism and Art of Living in Peace lecture tour of Spain and (top left) Holland, with my workshop charts in background. *Bottom right*: Radio Valencia.

Above left: *Holosapience, a symbol of Oneness I developed to explain holism.*

This page: *Back in Scotland.* **Top right**: *Still rowing after 60 years;* **Centre Left**: *admiring a curragh at Portsoy Boat Festival.* **Centre right**: *rowing coxswain on Atlantic Challenge Moray Gig.* **Right**: *selling my watercolours at a local craft fair.*

135

Top Left: Susan 'doing her thing'.
Bottom left: 'Crowfoot' symbol on floor of Rosslyn chapel crypt.

Top Right: my wife Susan and I at the Portsoy Boat Festival.
Bottom right: cycling near home in Scotland, 2011.

Top Left: walking with Susan into Vilcabamba, Ecuador, 2006.
Top right: on holiday with Susan in her native South Africa, 2001.
Centre left: Susan with our friend Vicky, the gifted healer in Italy, 2005.
Centre right: horse riding in the Andes, Ecuador, 2006; and finally,
Bottom left: tea and scones in the garden of my wee council house, 2010.

137

I DID IT MY WAY

Magical Brazil

Problemas? Let's Samba!

The difference between the working conditions in Brazil and Argentina caught me quite by surprise. The overall difference in the way of life between the two factories was like chalk and cheese. The informality, the smiling faces and the relaxed atmosphere was all a tonic for me. These up-country seasonal plants allowed the employees time to play golf, swim and socialise in a way quite unknown to the people who worked in the South Dock plant in Buenos Aires, which I had left behind. The Brazilians were more than helpful and the company house and garden were very good but the people who had convinced me to uproot myself and small family and travel to this remote place now expected me and my family to sleep on what I called a donkey's breakfast. This was a rough bag stuffed with straw that I was told I could cover with a sheet. I demanded that the personnel manager from São Paolo come to see the conditions since I was returning to Buenos Aires or the UK if things were not changed immediately. I was told that things could be arranged but I must keep it secret from the rest of the staff. I told him that I had stopped work and demanded return tickets for family and myself. Three days later a whole houseful of furniture arrived, even including beds and tables for the servant's quarters.

There was a fifty percent chance of my wife producing what is known as a 'blue baby' and it was imperative that the baby should be born in a properly equipped hospital where the blood could be changed if necessary. I was under pressure from all sides and felt unsupported by the very people I had agreed to help. Uprooting my self and family and moving with one small child and a pregnant wife to the middle of Brazil needed some support from the personnel department but they only seemed to respond to threats and angry disagreements. Before starting the difficult job of running the factory I was already feeling stressed and frustrated.

Before we could get the house furnished, and several weeks early, my wife went into labour at three o'clock one morning. José, the chief chemist, had offered to help if an emergency occurred and I had hardly knocked his door when he was up and dressed and we hurriedly set off on what had been a road but had largely disappeared during the heavy rains. We ended up at the local convent and were ushered in by three black-clad nuns. To cut the story short, a boy was born without complications twenty minutes before the doctor arrived. The stress over and everyone safe, I slept for eighteen hours.

Apart from the way the company treated its staff I found Brazil a magical land in every sense of he word. The sensual language, its music, the Portuguese-African mix where pagan rites and Christianity become entangled and indistinguishable, all enhanced by the lavish plant life, the smells and nature displaying its bright colours everywhere. This was a land where one of my foremen, a very capable, hardworking fellow would spend a large part of his time and salary on macumba or magic (black or white), a land where one of my workers seeing me in a worried mood over a broken machine came up to me and asked, "Do you have a problem? Let's sing a bit of samba!"

Getting the factory to work was not an easy job and these lovable people had to be taught the importance of complying with the new hygiene regulations imposed by the importing countries. Also the need for teamwork and, above all, that the danger of getting foreign bodies into the products meant that rings and jewellery were not allowed. This was quite a problem for some of these Brazilian women who always tried to look their best and favoured large earrings, bright necklaces and lots of rings.

The job turned out to be a challenge, but gradually it all settled down and eventually I no longer came home at night to fall asleep before dinner.

Corned Beef and Brothels

The day arrived when I agreed to accompany a group of ex-pats for a drink in town. Going out for a drink usually meant visiting the town of Barretos, three or four miles away and sitting in a large square patio complete with chairs and tables where one could order anything from a beer to a meal. There were lots of waitresses and hostesses in attendance and yes for a fee you could take the one of your choice into one of the rooms that surrounded the patio. This was how the ever so astute and 'respectable' Brazilian brothel functioned in most towns. It was about three months into my new life when I had agreed to go to town with a few of the lads. Since I had been totally occupied with my little family as well as getting the factory functioning, and since I had never experienced Barretos nightlife there was a lot of leg pulling and jokes at my expense. We went to what was claimed to be the best house in town. Soft music was playing and I was immediately taken aback by the beautiful decor, the cleanliness and oh! what an overwhelming display of charm, beauty and seductive behaviour. Some of the girls were blondes, some quite dark and each one was dressed in beautiful, if flimsy, clothing. All this was in such stark contrast to the women I dealt with daily at the factory who wore overalls, plastic aprons and 'hygiene' hats pulled down to hide their hair.

We ordered our drinks and as the olive-skinned waitress dressed in a white semi-transparent dress bent over me to put my drink on the table she said in my ear, "How are you Senhor Kemp, nice to see you again". A volley of unprintable observations from around the table followed the momentary silence. My friend Tom looked at me and said, "We thought you were working nights when all the time you've been sneaking up to town, you dirty old bastard." No amount of persuasion would convince them that I was as surprised as they were. Eventually, as a last resort, I asked the young waitress who I had never seen before in my life to explain how she knew who I was. Much to the delight of my accusers she looked at me in disbelief and asked, "You really don't remember me?" My silence only made an already poignant moment all the more intriguing. I was uncomfortably aware that everyone was staring at me, some in a bemused way, others quite openly with disapproval.

She looked around the table in silence then very slowly looked at me and turning the palms of her hands up to heaven in a gesture of disbelief, said in a small voice, "I work on the number two, twelve ounce corned beef canning line, surely you recognise me."

One long-standing personal trend of mine is that regarding the other sex I have always tended to be more interested in their IQ rather than their eye shadow, and when it comes to the sleazy side of things I am happy to be intrigued and entertained, but at a safe distance.

Magic and Macumba

I made friends with some interesting people in Barretos, including a local doctor called Luis Barrientos, whom I would occasionally accompany when he visited the sick. The poor, badly lit shacks where the poorer black population lived were the most intriguing of these visits, and on several occasions I witnessed healing by what today I would call a psychic surgeon.

The scene was usually a homemade shack, which would be full to capacity with relations, neighbours and the curious. Candles placed on boxes or in wall fittings were the only light and drums, music and singing would accompany the procedure. I remember one early experience,

143

before I got used to this mysterious land, when I was invited to be present at one of these psychic operations. My first impression upon entering the dimly lit shack was one of lots of white eyes and white teeth all peering through thick swirling smoke, which I think came from incense and whatever was being smoked. We were made very welcome and they found two proper chairs for us to sit on, close to a mattress in the centre of the floor. A young woman lay on the mattress surrounded by other women who were rocking back and forth and making noises that sounded like a cross between singing and wailing. Two men played drums and a third danced around the room wafting smoke from what appeared to be a bunch of twigs and grass he held in his hand.

Everyone wanted to shake my hand and say thank you; the doctor explained that a visit from a white foreigner to their humble dwelling was very unusual and was seen as a good omen. This helped to clarify, to some degree, why they were saying 'thank you' when I thought 'welcome' might have been more appropriate.

Suddenly everyone was talking and pointing as a tall, light-skinned man dressed in white shirt and trousers came into the room. He slowly walked over to the woman on the mattress and stood for a full minute with his arms stretched out over the patient, palms down. This was the surgeon who was about to carry out an abdominal operation. The room quietened down although the drumming continued in the background. All eyes were on this fellow who seemed to be apart and distant from the crowd around him. He bent over the woman and seemed totally focused on a point just above her body then, as far as I could see, he knelt down and his hand disappeared under the hem of the woman's blouse. He appeared to be pressing down on the woman's abdomen with some force then he seemed to be struggling with something while the patient moaned and rolled her head from side to side. The tension rose in the room and people started talking and letting out strange noises as if they too wanted to participate in what was going on. The atmosphere was surreal; I realised that the drums were accompanied by gentle music, but all these people, the noises and smoke seemed to blend and transport me to another level of awareness where nothing seemed real. I turned in my chair and looked out through the door, just to ground myself and confirm that things were still normal out there. As I turned back the woman on the mattress took a long deep breath then expelled the air with a drawn-out sigh. For a moment everything went very quiet.

Our surgeon, who seemed to be totally absorbed in what he was doing, slowly stood up and, stretching out his arm to the crowd, displayed something in the palm of a bloody hand. The drumming became a frenzy and people danced, congratulated each other and as many as could shook my hand. My mental and emotional faculties had been challenged and I needed fresh air.

Out in the night air I discussed what I had just seen with my doctor friend. He took a neutral position and told me that these people could do things that he could not explain as a doctor and that some things were better just left alone without explanation.

Psychic Surgeon, UK Style

Many years later when I ran a holistic health practice in Brighton I was invited by Jane, the nurse who worked with me, to visit a famous psychic surgeon. He lived near the Blackwall tunnel in London, and I think we called him John but unfortunately his full name now escapes me. I was interested to see this man at work for several reasons, not least of all to compare his approach to what I had witnessed back in my Brazilian days. The day arrived and we drove down to what was a fairly poor area. We were ushered into a clean and tidy working class home and then into the 'operation' room where, after a while, John came in and introduced himself. He talked rather slowly and looked the part of the bricklayer that we had been told was his original job. He then left the room and returned with a lady who appeared to be in her early forties. He asked her to lie on a bed that was against the wall opposite to where we were sitting. John then asked for total silence and sat down on a chair at the foot of the bed.

I decided to watch him carefully in every detail but I was not prepared for what followed. As he closed his eyes and sat very still his features went through a visible transformation and we found ourselves looking at a man with a more refined, slimmer appearance. This was no optical illusion; we were looking at a different person. My nurse Jane and I exchanged looks but kept silent. After a while he stood up and announced in a clear cultured voice with a foreign accent, quite different from his original voice, that his patient had a growth that needed to be removed and added some detail that I cannot now remember. His voice was definitely foreign and his whole demeanour was that of someone in authority. He put a white sheet over the patient and seemed to bare her abdomen beneath the sheet. He spoke softly as he bent over the bed then he took something in his two hands and placed it into a stainless steel bowl, bowed to the patient, wiped his hands on a towel and sat down. The whole procedure had lasted no more than a few minutes and caught us a little by surprise. He sat still again for about two or three minutes, then our original bricklayer stood up and said his local London accent, "I hope that was all right for you." We shook hands and went out to the car. "Well," said Jane, "what did you make of that?" I thought for a minute then replied, "I think I prefer the version with the heat, the smells, smoke, candles, music, dancing and macumba."

I cannot leave the subject of spiritual healing or psychic surgery without some reference to that 'illiterate Brazilian peasant' by the name of João Texeira de Faria, who I first heard of about ten years ago, long after I had left Brazil. It is not appropriate for me to tell his story here since others who know him personally, and are more qualified, have already written of this remarkable man and his story, which is still in the making. He is known as João de Deus, or John of God, and he operates from Casa de Dom Iñacio or the House of Ignacio, so called in honour of Saint Ignatius of Loyola who was born in 1491 and was the founder of the Jesuits. This house commonly referred to as the *'Casa'* is in the Brazilian interior near the capital Brasilia.

Some years ago when I was taking an active interest in the healing process I had some correspondence with the *'Casa'* and more recently have met people who have visited the *Casa*. When I decided to mention it in this book, my wife showed me an excellent article written by Doctor Míceál Ledwith, who had recently visited the *Casa* and actually stayed with John of God at his home. For those who are not conversant with this outstanding academic, his investigative gifts, his achievements in a number of fields and his capacity to pass on his knowledge to the layman is very inspiring and unique. Included in the article was a photograph of John of God with Doctor Ledwith and a lady who for some unexplained reason caught my attention. I was quite intrigued that Doctor Ledwith, who I greatly admire, should have taken the trouble to look into the *Casa* phenomena but I left it at that and moved on to address a new subject. It was then that I saw an advertisement for a film premier, which was not yet on general release. The title of the film was *Healing: Miracles, Mysteries and John of God*. There is no such thing as coincidence so I went with my wife to see the film. The sensitive photography captured that old feeling, which for me is, or was, Brazil and I shall not dilute it by trying to fit it into mere words. However the same person who had caught my attention in the above-mentioned photograph appeared prominently in the film. Upon making enquiries she turned out to be the daughter of an old friend of mine by the name of Angus Cumming, who was born in my hometown of Greenock and had become a ranch manager in Brazil where, all these years ago, we had struck up a lasting friendship. I have written to this interesting young lady who I understand was not in Brazil at the time my letter was delivered by a friend, so the story continues.

If one takes the trouble to read about John of God or has the opportunity to see one of the films of his activities, there will be no room for doubt that something most remarkable is taking place out there and since it has baffled the best contemporary thinkers, theologians and doctors I shall not attempt an explanation. I offer one last interesting anecdote, however, within this anecdote. John of God cannot read nor write but apparently can manage a rather childish signature. Doctor Ledwith, having bought a book detailing the healings at the Casa, apparently asked John of God if he would sign it for him. Once Doctor Ledwith was on his way home he took the book out, opened it and found a very stylish and mature signature in the book. It was that of the 400-year-old Saint Ignacio; but of course anyone who knows anything about Doctor Ledwith will not find this very surprising.

No Natives Allowed

In my Brazil, life was full of contradictions where we played golf wearing riding boots in case we ran into snakes in the rough. In this complex society brothels, priests, macumba and happy looking people all conspired to create a magical way of life that felt good to me, but I still could not swallow that 'superior English abroad' stuff that raised its pathetic head from time to time. One example was when I invited my very good friend José to play tennis. José was the young man who had run us to the hospital over washed-out roads at three in the morning when my son was born. His kindness had helped me in several areas that were new to me and our friendship had grown. Above all, he had a good head on him and was interested in everything. I had agreed to help him learn English and he would do the same for my Portuguese. We met at the club on a Saturday after lunch and played a bit of tennis, had a drink and talked endlessly about everything imaginable. When I returned to work on the Monday there was a message saying that the plant manager wished to see me as soon as I arrived. I grabbed my production sheets and diary and headed for the manager's office. Now this particular fellow was a bit of a rough diamond from the north of England who was good at his job and he had done well to reach managerial level but he still had a bit of a working class chip on his shoulder. "Good morning Mr Braithwait," I said as I walked into his office. He did not reply immediately but stared at me as if I had just run over his pet hamster. Something was wrong and I could not imagine what it could be. Eventually he said in a north country, measured voice, "Now I am going to tell you something and I expect you to remember it." Pause! "We… do…not…allow…natives…in… our…club! Got that?"

I did not get the point at all. "What are you getting at?" I asked.

"You brought that Brazilian, José, into the club last Saturday so don't try to deny it."

"Yes but he's an educated man with a PhD in chemistry," I replied.

"You will do yourself no favours mixing with the natives and you have to think of your future. That is all I have to say to you. Good morning."

I had travelled enough to be aware of this English affliction, so I just accepted it as another lesson and opportunity to control my own feelings of superiority if and when they arose.

This new enjoyable lifestyle was to end sooner than expected. Early in 1960 there was an urgent request for me to return to Buenos Aires to join the management team. In hindsight I should have turned the offer down but I think that my ego got in the way and the lure of top management won over a life in colourful, sunny, happy Brazil.

Back to Buenos Aires

República de San Telmo

Por cuanto el ciudadano

Crawford Kemp

ha sido designado

Ciudadano Ilustre

en atención a sus valores espirituales
y a sus deseos
de contribuir al bien de la comunidad,
ordenamos
se le reconozca en tal carácter
en todo el ámbito
en que se ejerce nuestra soberanía

Dado en el Palacio de Gobierno
31 de Mayo de 1968

The South Dock Plant

Returning by request of the company to Buenos Aires, I was offered the job as assistant to Mr Jimmy Laird, the manager of this massive plant in the capital city of Argentina.

A chemist by profession, he was fair, honest and very knowledgeable and I felt privileged to work under him, but to my great disappointment I discovered that he was preparing to move on. At the time I was not aware of the animosity that existed between Laird and the new General Manager and I was totally unaware of the fundamental changes taking place under this new management, who looked after all the company's interests in Argentina. The truth is that I had never been involved in politics nor am I a natural wheeler-dealer, so I was ill prepared for what this man was to bring with him. He was called Ronald Bent and he eventually ran the organisation through a network of cronies, wheeler-dealers, informers and 'yes men'. Part of his plan was to put a certain Mr Davis in the post of plant manager when Laird left. Davis had been demoted in the past for gross incompetence and in recent years had created a name for being dim-witted to put it politely. By having a weak manager at the head of the factory Bent hoped to bypass the management and run things his own way and, as I was to uncover, for some very questionable personal interests.

The first signs of a very worrying change were when rumours about Mr Laird started to spread. I was in a position to check these attempts to dirty Mr Laird's name, and I soon realised that this was all originating from Bent's office. Once Mr Davis replaced Mr Laird, a few of Bent's selected collaborators were then given free access to visit the factory and go into any department without the permission, or the knowledge, of the management. Although this was unheard of and was an invitation for confrontation and division within the plant, Davis did not protest and I, who by this time was virtually running the plant under - and in spite of - Davis, would not go over his head.

To be honest I still did not have the self-confidence to challenge what I saw as 'authority', partly because I was twenty years younger than anyone else in a senior position and perhaps at the time I still felt, mistakenly, inhibited by my working class background. I had not yet learned that most successful people had a support team, an exclusive club, or perhaps a 'mafia' to back them. I naively believed that honesty and hard work would see me through, and in spite of the eventual disastrous financial consequences of this approach I am really quite happy to say that - like Frank Sinatra - I did it my way.

Bent's influence gradually changed the whole atmosphere at the factory. People started looking over their shoulders and the feeling of being a family or all working together slowly evaporated. Jimmy Laird had been a father figure and this had greatly enhanced the image of the company and working cohesion within the factory. Now Davis was seen as bumbling and incompetent and this had a detrimental effect on the coherence and quality of the 'factory family'. To be specific about what changed is not straight forward, but isolated remarks by visitors and by the staff working under this new Bent-Davis set up affected discipline and authority, rather like water dripping on a stone, and gradually it became a little more difficult to get things done as focus on one's job gave way to mistrust, suspicion and, at least in my mind, some doubts that the organisation could survive Bent's new way of doing things.

New people appeared at odd times and nobody could define what their job was and a less desirable element began to grow amongst the work force.

Workers' Strikes

But before I get to the consequences of that particular management team, let me return to 1958 when Mr Laird was still manager. All the factories in the country went on strike and our supervisory staff members were asked to stay at the plant to look after things.

This meant keeping the engine room running, which supplied all the refrigeration, electricity, water, sewage, etc. In addition to this there were millions of cans to be processed, hundreds of tons of meat in various stages of preparation as well as cheese, eggs, canned and fresh food to be dealt with, as well as the reorganisation of the security arrangements. Most of the forty or so security guards stayed on, as well as our ten police officers, including a sergeant. Between the management, supervisors, and some foremen we organised shifts to cover each twenty four-hour period. We worked long hours and the closeness of working in this unusual way did a lot to create bonds between people who, in spite of working under the same roof, had never really got to know each other. Unsuspected qualities surfaced and we discovered that we had some good cooks amongst our number while others who had always been seen in suits and ties rolled up their sleeves and did heavy manual work. We lived in what was a siege situation, carrying guns and sleeping anywhere including, in the early days, on cement floors.

This way of life lasted for over three months during which time we saw nobody from outside. Several attempts were made to sneak through the picket lines but three men returned very badly beaten and one was actually shot. After this shooting incident Mr Laird, the manager, prohibited any more attempts to get out.

When we eventually returned to normal and went home it actually took some readjustment. I remember looking back at the sacrifice and hard work that the loyal staff had put into averting a disaster and wondering if the owners back in London had any idea at all of what was being done for them and their interests by the ordinary folk, who always seem to end up doing the decent thing.

Challenging Work

The political situation in the country was deteriorating, and there was a great deal of in-fighting within the CGT (*Confederacion General Del Trabajo*).

This national trades union centre or General Confederation of Labour was founded in 1930 and had become the centre of power for many politicians, including General Peron. General unrest permeated all aspects of life in Argentina. People in prominent positions were being taken hostage by the rival gangs and held for ransom. There was actually a list of executives who were considered vulnerable and in danger of being taken by these gangs.

Only later, when I took over the running of the plant, did I realise that the police and the army were fully aware of this list, as well as the insurance companies and the individual companies. My name, together with several others from the company, figured on this list and alongside was my alias *El Escoses*, The Scot.

Eventually, once I had the police organised, we took measures to counter these plans and avoid capture. But all this was later on so I'll go back to the Bent-Davis set up.

Death And Destruction

Sometime about 1962 we changed our supplier of ammonia gas. This was used to run the refrigeration plant where we could hold some seventeen thousand tons of refrigerated produce prior to shipping. I was later to learn that if one has a tank of ammonia containing a small but specific mixture of hydrogen and one suddenly changes the pressure in the tank, an explosion could result. Now we had ninety tons of this 'new' ammonia in the storage tank, as had been the normal procedure for thirty years.

One day I was asked by Davis to accompany him and Señor Ranea, who ran the factory personnel office, to the dock where there was a report of a fire on board one of the ships. As the three of us left the office together, Mr Wallace, who worked as a bacteriologist for our sister company next door, stopped me to enquire about some laboratory reports that I had asked for. Davis and Ranea walked on slowly then stopped about forty paces away to wait for me. I had finished talking to Wallace and had turned to catch up with them when, without any warning, the world exploded around us. Ranea was on his back, and I remember wondering why the inside of his mouth was all black. Davis looked like a rag doll lying on his side with one leg twisted so that his foot was touching his lower back. A workman who had been on a ladder was in the air flying towards me. There was a cloud of dust and bits and pieces were falling out of the sky. Something was triggered in me and I felt as though all my senses had become super-alert. My head was clear and I knew that I was going to take charge of this situation to the exclusion of all else. People were running about; injured people were everywhere, some lying on the ground, some crawling on hands and knees. People screamed and some seemed to be in a total daze. When I spotted Señor Lanceloti, head of civilian security, I grabbed him and told him to relax gate security since we would have to allow ambulances and emergency people free access to the area. Meanwhile I returned to my desk and phoned Bent's office and since nobody seemed to know where to find him I left a message explaining what had happened and that I would be too busy to answer my phone.

For the next twenty-four hours everyone worked non-stop to get things cleared up. The two engineers, Newhouse and Wood, who were in charge of that side of the plant did a heroic job of getting things into some kind of order. Nobody questioned orders and the wounded and the traumatised were attended with a minimum of fuss. The challenging job of collecting body parts of friends and co-workers and putting them into black bags was handled with little obvious emotion, although I have to say that the delayed reaction to the whole experience was to show up later in different ways in different people.

Ignored by Everyone

About four or five hours into this unreal nightmare I was outdoors in front of the main building trying to get some idea of progress and what the current situation was, when I was grabbed by the arm and a voice was demanding, "Who are these people there?" It was Bent and, standing there with all this death and horror surrounding me, I could only stare at him in disbelief. Here was a wonderful team of labourers, managers, doctors and volunteers all desperately involved in a very unpleasant humanitarian exercise and Bent, arriving five hours late, was acting like a spoiled child trying to get some attention. Everyone, including myself, ignored him. He then turned to the security guard who was with me and, pointing to a group of men, told him to throw these people out of the factory. The guard looked at me for guidance and when I shook my head ever so slightly he turned away and left Bent looking very inadequate, and frustrated. The people he was at pains to avoid confronting personally, but wanted someone else to evict, were part of the communist trades union who were an extremely nasty outfit and had sneaked into the factory in the back of an ambulance. Once Bent had taken himself off somewhere else I walked over to these characters and politely told them that we were having a hard time and I wanted them to leave. Two of them were obviously bodyguards and moved towards me only to be stopped by the leader raising his hand. "Who are you?" he asked, to which I answered, "I'm the guy who runs this place since Mr Davis was taken away in an ambulance with his leg somewhere up the middle of his back". We stared at each other for a tense moment then, much to my surprise and relief, they agreed to leave and were soon in another ambulance leaving the property.

Lasting Effects

Somewhere in the following twenty-four or thirty-six hours Doctor Pagola, who was head of the medical team, ordered me in a no-nonsense tone of voice into his surgery. He examined me and talked to me about getting some rest. My vocal chords were in a mess and my hearing was a bit strange but this was, in his opinion, a temporary problem which only time would help. Apart from this I seemed to be tired and hungry and, as must be expected, affected by the stress and the shock of events but otherwise fit. Today, fifty years later, I have still not fully recovered my voice and I have to use two hearing aids. Just for the record I have never received any recognition or compensation and was even denied the company pension originally promised by Gower, the personnel manager at the time I took the job. This is an observation on my part and not a complaint.

The major job of getting production back to normal took time and slowly we returned to full capacity.

Davis was given a company pension and never returned to work. Ranea, who was a heavy smoker, never touched another cigarette. The death toll was six; a large number of people needed hospital treatment mainly due to breathing in the escaped ammonia. Broken bones and cuts from flying glass meant that many people were absent for periods of time and some were able to claim compensation, but eventually things got back to normal and I was eventually - still in my early thirties - named factory manager and so I moved into the hallowed office of my hero Mr Jimmy Laird.

I Take Over

The following ten years were very busy, at times great fun, at times dangerous, but always inspiring because of the challenges. The job gave me a great deal of power and authority, which I enjoyed. I met some incredible individuals, mixed with the great and the good as well as some of the less savoury and, when on UK leave, I always opted to travel by ship where again one tended to meet interesting people.

There are a number of little anecdotes worth recording concerning these years between 1962 and 1971 and I will tell them as separate stories, although they are all part of the bigger picture.

In spite of Bent giving me a hard time whenever he could I was blessed with excellent collaboration and respect from those working under me and I felt confident with regard to the running this varied and complex organisation, with only one exception. I needed help with reorganising and running the police force that I had inherited. Although things were not to my liking I found it difficult to put my finger on what had to be done in this one department.

Lopez

My circle of friends outside of work were almost all Argentines with a few Latvians, a Russian and some Europeans who had escaped the various 'isms' imposed on them by religion or State. They all knew me as *El Escoses* and most of my English-speaking friends called me Scotty. One good friend, Hans Schoen, who was originally from Czechoslovakia, introduced me to one very bright, retired police commissar who went by the name of Comissário Mayor Carlos José Maria Lopez. Hans was the manager at the Parker Pen factory and married to Lucy Lopez, sister of the police commissar. I talked to my new policeman friend and mentioned my inherited police force and the challenge it offered me. The eventual outcome was that he offered to come and have a look at the set-up and offer me any advice he could.

Now I was aware that the police were quite paramilitary and even used the same ranks system as the army, but I was not quite ready for what developed when Lopez paid us a visit.

We went into the factory police station, known as the *comissária*, and sat at the desk. I had one of the security guards tell the police sergeant that the manager and a commissar wanted to see him in the office. Our unsuspecting sergeant walked into the office all smiles and said, "Good afternoon". Lopez simply exploded, "Get the hell out of here then come back in and present yourself correctly!" The poor sergeant who had been doing things his own way for a very long time, eventually reappeared in the office, made a brave attempt at clicking his heels, saluted and said, "Sargento Gonzalez at your service, sir!" There was a brief silence as a look of exasperation came over Lopez's face. Then he shouted, "Where in the name of God were you trained?" I sat tight lipped and observed.

The sergeant was forced to repeat this exercise until Lopez dismissed him with the promise that he would be back to see if things were improving.

Birome

Before leaving my good friend Hans, who introduced me to Lopez, let me tell you a wee yarn concerning a certain Miss Parker. This lady inherited the multimillion-dollar Parker Pen empire and eventually appointed one of her relations as general manager to run the Argentine side of the business. He in turn appointed my friend Hans as factory manager and so it was that one day while visiting Hans I ran into a little bit of history. Hans introduced me to yet another two Central Europeans who were living in Argentina and explained that they were the people with whom his company had been negotiating with for some considerable time. I only vaguely remembered having had this mentioned to me but my interest was awakened when he pointed out that these were the two inventors he had talked about in the past. Well, to cut the story short, I was apparently sitting between the two fellows who had worked in a garden shed for years until they produced a pen that, instead of a nib, had a little round ball like a ball bearing. They had named this first ever ball point pen the 'Birome' pen, but had eventually sold the patent to the Parker Pen company because they could not find the finance to experiment with and improve the special ink required to perfect the ballpoint concept.

"So," I asked, "what does Birome mean?"

"Well said Hans, this man on your left is Mr Biro (pronounced beero) and on your right is Mr Maine (pronounced my-nay), so they called their invention the Birome Pen."

I wonder how many zillions of Biromes, or ballpoint pens, have been manufactured since that day I sat between Biro and Maine and observed a little piece of history.

As things turned out I eventually employed Lopez who, through his contacts in the police and in army intelligence, helped us to keep ahead of the kidnapping, beatings and the blowing up of private residences that took place during the 'dirty wars'; but more on this later.

My Friend Spam

I felt just slightly embarrassed over the whole police discipline episode and it took me some time to get used to the sergeant throwing out his chest and saluting whenever our paths crossed. On one occasion, following the foot and mouth outbreak in the UK, I was showing the Duke of Northumberland and his entourage round the plant when we came across the sergeant, who duly did his number. The group exchanged glances following the unexpected military type salute and the Duke said something complimentary about us still having some of the old qualities, which had been lost back home.

Lord Vestey, the head of a vast empire, made periodical visits to Argentina to keep an eye on the business and also to play polo with his Argentine friends. During these visits he seemed to enjoy having a break from his obligations in England. On a few occasions he came home with me after work and took potluck with what we were going to eat, and several times the two of us went out for a drink or to visit a club. These unplanned little outings were always incognito and I introduced him to my friends as Sam, a friend out on a visit from England. Some of his polo playing friends affectionately called him 'Spam' but I never did.

We came from vastly different backgrounds and had our different views on life. While I was trying to bring up a small family and pay the bills he was one of the richest men on earth, yet we got along very well together and built an easygoing friendship. He would turn up at home unannounced and on two occasions telephoned Bent to cancel a dinner appointment saying that he had been called by the British ambassador or that something unforeseen had cropped up. The whole joy of being away from the UK for him seemed to be getting away from the social climbers like Bent who wanted to be seen with him or to have him for dinner as often as possible. I support few of the institutions that are Sam's whole life, be it rightwing politics, English public school, the English military, or Royalty, yet I genuinely liked this guy and enjoyed his company. I must also admit that I got some satisfaction from the fact that he seemed to feel the same about Bent as I did. We enjoyed a real, personal friendship, which had nothing to do with work and he would eventually invite me and my family to stay with him at his country seat, Stowell Park in Gloucestershire. He talked to me in some detail of his private family life and while at Stowell Park I was invited into his private 'secure quarters' where, locked away, he kept his valuable private collections, including coins and stamps. These gestures on his part were seen by me as confirmation that we were good friends and enjoyed a mutual respect. I mention these facts because of the way that things were eventually to turn out.

A New Regime

Getting back to the situation at the South Dock Plant, there had been a gradual change in the way people were treated, it was a move from seeing the employees as people to treating them as statistics. This new way of doing things was introduced by accountants and efficiency clerks who appeared more and more in the factory and I suspected had filtered all the way down from a change in policy back in London. All the old hands saw this as the death knell for the business and of course, as it happened, things did go from bad to worse and eventually the whole place closed down, leaving thousands without work. Contrary to other opinions, I am convinced that this could have been avoided had the top management in London not been so distant from the reality on the ground in Argentina.

Threats and a Girlfriend

We were at one time in almost in daily communication with the Argentine intelligence services and on one occasion Lopez was advised by military intelligence that Señor Ranea's house was to be bombed. I was at home in the evening when I got word and we immediately put an agreed procedure into action. Lopez requested the cooperation of the local police in the area where Ranea lived and we put a police cordon round the block. I personally went to Ranea's house and tried to get him, his wife and daughter to go to a hotel for the night but he would not move so we organised what was termed an 'intensive guard' until daylight. Two suspicious cars were spotted going round the block but, presumably because of the police presence, did not stop. We were satisfied that we had averted a nasty incident but still left a police presence at the house for a few days.

Ranea and myself, a plainclothes officer called Cruz, together with Lopez - who unexpectedly had a tall blonde girl with him - all went to a local bar to prepare the official document that is required by law following any incident involving the police. This bureaucracy tends to raise its head in Argentina all the time and must be dealt with seriously. It is also quite normal to do such things in bars where a large proportion of business is normally transacted. We were halfway through these papers when, out of the blue, into the bar comes Lopez's girlfriend and his sister. Now, quite unknown to me, this girlfriend who had just walked in was of an extremely jealous nature, so Lopez was at pains to have no apparent connection to the tall blonde who had come with him. What he did was to casually point out that, "Writing all this legal police language was going to take time, so if I were to accompany the blonde girl to the bar and buy her a drink we could both be spared the monotony of preparing the documents."

I was aware of his ulterior motives but was happy to play along. What was revealed much later was, that to further his case, he had said to Cruz that this lady, whom I had never seen before, was my wife. We eventually finished in the wee hours of the morning and went home satisfied that we had done 'a good night's work'.

A Challenge

It was about this time that two friends with whom I played rugby, and who worked under me, decided to become qualified public speakers and signed up for a Dale Carnegie public speaking course.

After the first few evening sessions they decided to ask to be allowed to come to work later than normal. Now these two fellows were good workers and deserved anything I could do to help them but firstly, they were rugby friends and secondly, although they were born in Argentina, they were seen as '*ingleses*' and I could not be seen to be favouring them over the other Argentines. I refused their request only to have them say behind my back that I would not let them do something that I was not capable of doing myself.

This challenge stayed with me until the following year when I decided to do the same course just to prove to myself that I could. When it finally ended I was top of the class and was duly named President of Dale Carnegie Argentina 1965. As if I was not busy enough!

Paraguay and London

On one occasion I flew up to Paraguay with our chief chemist, Peter Boyes and George Newhouse, our chief engineer. We landed at the General Stroisner Airport in Asunción where the Manager of the Liebig's organisation met us. We were there to look at a new evaporator system and eventually we were shown round and looked after and wined and dined in true South American fashion. In the evening their engineer invited me to go out on the town with him and I gladly accepted, the other two in my party opting to spend the evening at the hotel. The Hotel Guarani, where we were staying, was impressively fronted by a long flight of stone steps leading up to the entrance. As we descended the steps we were surrounded by a mob of street urchins with trays full of cigarettes held up by neck straps. Neither of us being smokers, we were not interested in their wares. We were amused, however, to observe the lengths that some of these kids had gone to in order to emphasize that their brand of cigarettes were CONTRABANDO LEJITIMO! Legitimate contraband!

We ended up in a cosy little nightclub where the Trio Paraguayo was playing and eventually we invited them to join us at our table. They were keen to talk to visitors like us who, in those days, were not all that common. We learned that the British Ambassador had 'discovered' the talent these young men displayed and had organised the group, buying them guitars and harps and starting them on their way to fame and fortune. These impromptu encounters are usually interesting and sometimes have a habit of invoking the unexpected. We learned that the Ambassador's name was Millington-Drake and that he was a larger than life character but that the numerous invoices arriving at the embassy did not always keep up with his philanthropic tendencies, which were nevertheless greatly appreciated by his benefactors.

We arrived back in Buenos Aires and filed our report only a few weeks before I was due to sail to London and my home leave.

I was in need of a break and thoroughly enjoyed the first class three-week sea voyage to the UK.

A few days after arriving at Tilbury docks in London, I invited some Brazilian fellow passengers to join me at the Edmundo Ross nightclub in Upper Regent Street for a drink and a chat. We settled down at a front table and ordered drinks just as the highlight of the evening was being announced, "Please welcome to our wonderful club here in London, THE TRIO PARAGUAYO!!" On to the stage walked the friends I had made about two months earlier in their hometown of Asuncion in Paraguay. When their act came to an end they, having spotted me at a front table, came over to handshakes and hugs all round. My Brazilian friends asked, "How the hell do you manage to have friends here in London when we only arrived two days ago?"

"Charm," I answered, "just charm."

Threats and a Girlfriend, Continued

As what was to become known as 'the dirty war' got more vicious it became necessary to put guards on certain people's houses, and I was allocated this plainclothes officer called Cruz, who had been part of the team protecting Ranea's house.

What transpired was that Cruz arrived at my house to introduce himself to my wife - who was tall and blonde - and children who were going to see a lot of him in the future. When, in a friendly gesture, he offered his hand to my wife she made it plain that she did not know him and had never seen him before.

To this Cruz replied, "Oh yes Señora, do you remember that night in the bar when you and your husband had a drink while we finished the legal stuff with Commissar Lopez?"

My then-wife never accepted the true story, which I explained to her, and she always held it against me until we eventually parted and went our own ways.

My job was to run a large factory and so these police encounters took up only a small portion of my time, but thanks to the professionalism of my friendly Commissar Lopez, not one of the people we protected were ever taken hostage or hurt in any way. There was a list of people who were vulnerable and since Bent was one of them I offered him our protection. He treated the offer as a joke and almost paid for it with his life when he was taken hostage and eventually cost his employer something like one million dollars to buy his freedom; and that was a lot of money in the '60s.

Trujillo

Before leaving my good friend Carlos Lopez there is a little story to tell regarding an excellent employee by the name of Trujillo, who worked for over twenty years in our chemical laboratory and was the butt of many jokes regarding his nine-year engagement to a very attractive - and patient - lady. The time eventually came when he announced that he was getting married and following the great day the happy couple boarded their first ever aeroplane flight, bound for the ski resort of Bariloche in the south of Argentina.

The plane and all of the honeymoon couples on board disappeared in the Andes Mountains and, in spite of extensive searching, were not found until about three months later when a local police patrol found them about twelve thousand feet up, covered in snow and ice.

It was several years later when Lopez had been working for me at the factory that the conversation came up about 'good old Trujillo'. The chief chemist Peter Boyes mentioned his name and how he could do with more people like him in the laboratory. Lopez, who happened to be present, asked why he had left and on being told of the tragic accident and the disappearance of the plane, Lopez asked if it was a small passenger plane and asked if it had disappeared on a certain date. Of course it all fitted in and it turned out that Lopez had been in charge of the patrol that had eventually found the plane.

Everyone in the lab wanted to know more but, apart from the comment that all the passengers were still in their seats and that there was little visible damage to the plane, Lopez had little to say. I had the feeling that there was more to this story but I never got Lopez to talk about it again and his silence only added to the mystery.

Threats at Home

My attitude to all the nasty stuff and personal threats that was going on, was to see these 'bad' guys as basically a bunch of bullies who would try to avoid serious personal conflict at any cost. With this in mind I purposely created a name for myself as being a bit of a head case capable of personally attacking anyone who threatened my family or me. On one memorable occasion I managed to reinforce this image when I became aware of a man standing at the bus stop opposite our house. I observed that the buses came and went yet he did not get on any of them but seemed to be more interested in my house. What I did was to walk out to my front gate and start filming him with my 8mm camera, which actually had no film in it. When he realised what was happening he took off at a smart pace. I got into my car and caught up with him just as we came to an empty building site. I drove up over the pavement and trapped him against the wall. I took my revolver and pressed it hard against his nose until he gasped in pain and I asked to see his identity papers. He produced a stevedore's employment book and said his name, which I cannot now remember. He left with a promise that I would shoot him if he ever came near my house or my family again. Lopez actually heard about this incident before I had the opportunity to tell him about it and it transpired that this poor fellow, who had a criminal record, had been sent to watch my house and report on the comings and goings with a view to taking me hostage. What it actually did was to convince these nasty people that I was probably too much trouble and better left alone. As it happens I am simply not capable of shooting anyone but my strategy was built round that old adage 'give a dog a name' and my friend Lopez helped to promote this image by spreading some outrageous tales about my imaginary exploits from imaginary police records. The evidence that it worked was in some of the intelligence details we got from the military who quoted - who they termed - 'the subversives' as saying, "it would be safer to leave *El Escoses* alone, he is too unpredictable and could cause us problems".

Playing the Godfather

Another similar incident that was to come back to haunt me years later was when we got confirmation that the head of the trades union or CGT, which supported the 'Peronism without Peron' faction, and which we found best to deal with, was to have his house blown up. This fellow went by the name of Papio and, although he had a bit of a bloody reputation, he fought his corner when it came to disputes and he always seemed to me to be fair and straightforward.

The trades unions were run by a very rough and tough bunch of people who used everything at their disposal to hold on to power, including assassinations. While I could not be seen to be taking sides in an inter-union war it was in the company's interests to keep this fellow alive and in power. I got Lopez to contact the local Commissar and fill him in on the details while offering the cooperation of our own police, but making it clear that this was strictly a police affair and not coming from the company or myself. To cut a long story short, this turned out to be an operation lasting several long nights and daily meetings involving difficult decision-making but in the end Papio and his family, who were scheduled to be killed, escaped unhurt and another report was filed with the various authorities and - I believed - had passed into history.

The years went by and as fate would have it I found myself lying for six months in hospital with hepatitis. I was in a general ward in the British hospital in Buenos Aires and due to the exhausting nature of the disease was only allowed a limited number of visitors for a limited time. I was surprised, therefore, when the nurse informed me that I had three visitors waiting outside who had promised to be brief and not to tax my energy.

When my visitors walked into the ward everyone stopped and stared. These men were so out of place in this pristine hospital ward that I could only lie there and stare at them myself. Papio and his two bodyguards walked up to my bedside. The bodyguards turned their backs to me and looked the place over, while Papio gave me a hearty handshake. I started to say thank you for the visit but I was cut short when Papio asked, "What can we do for you?" I lamely said, "Well nothing really." But he would have none of it.

"We can fix a couple of your enemies for you while you lie here."

I shook my head. Papio bent closer and drawing his hand across his throat he whispered, "Bent?" Then standing up, he laughed and said, "Just say the word".

What took me time to understand was that these men were much more aware of what had been going on within the company than I had ever suspected. They had their own opinion of Bent and they were aware that he had been running a campaign to discredit me before I was made aware of it. Papio saw this as an opportunity to say thanks for saving his life and that of his family and went about it the only way he knew how.

The other patients and their visitors must have got the impression that I was some kind of mafia godfather or underworld character and I had great enjoyment playing this role as I lay in bed and thought back over the good fortune I had had to live such a full and interesting life.

Foreign Travel and the Film Stars

While I was still running the factory I was periodically called to travel abroad for a variety of reasons. One of the first trips was to show a fairly new product called 'cooked frozen beef' to the Campbell's Soup people in New York State and then to travel out west visiting one company in particular, which had the whole operation from livestock procurement through to delivery of final products all computerised. I do not recall the name of this company but I am not likely to forget the man who ran it. Everybody called him Joe. He was about six-feet-four in his high-heeled cowboy boots and when I met him he was sitting at his desk in the middle of a sea of desks. There were no walls or divisions and my host asked me to take a seat. He watched me as I looked around and quickly explained, "We have no secrets here, we are all here to make a dollar and we all help each other". He then called a young woman over who just happened to be walking by. I had noticed that above his desk there was a piece of string hanging from the ceiling with a dollar bill tied to it. As the young woman approached he called out to her, "What are we here for?" Pointing to the hanging dollar bill she replied. "To make a dollar", and she walked by and sat at her desk. He pointed up at the dollar bill and said, "Yes sir, that's what we're here for. Let me show you around". We drove out to see thousands of geese take to the sky as the pick-up approached. We had lunch at a diner where I met a bunch of cowboys who all seemed to know who Joe was. One of them asked me what I thought the chances were of the Yellow Socks winning on Saturday. The looks of disbelief that someone did not know about the pending game were all too evident. "Oh Scotty here is a visitor," said Joe, helping me out, "he's just flown in from Buenos Aires."

"Really?" came the reply, "what state is that in?"

Joe was a great host and never stopped talking. Some of his stories about John and him having holidays in Mexico together were from funny to far-fetched but always entertaining. Eventually I felt obliged to ask him who this buddy called John was who seemed to figure in all his stories. "Oh I thought you knew," came the reply, "my drinking partner and best friend is John Wayne. You know, he is an actor from Hollywood".

I had actually met a couple of film stars in the hotel in Chicago, one was Jack Palance and the other I can't remember, all this kind of thing gave me a kick which is understandable when you look at my dreary, humble beginnings.

In an era when computers were almost unknown, Joe's computerised system covered the ordering of packing materials, the preparation of invoices, the arrival of new stock, the shipping of goods and provided just about anything you wanted to know, it seemed. The control room looked like a scene from Star Wars with a semi-circular console, easy chairs and what looked like TV screens. I wrote a report on all this but whoever had asked for me to be sent on this job kept his own counsel and I heard no more on the subject.

Job Offer

I was asked to return to the Campbell's Soup Company by the head of the company and after discussing our products and how we made them, he informed me that they had decided to buy from us rather than the competition. I explained that I was not a salesman but actually ran the plant at South Dock and was just promoting the product because I knew how it was made. The CEO took me into an office and without sitting down he said, "I don't know what they pay you in Buenos Aires but I'll double it if you come to work for us."

I returned to Buenos Aires, to a job that was beginning to take its toll on my health, and for some reason I, perhaps foolishly, felt that I was not going to let Bent beat me.

The job at Campbell's Soup was not the only one I was offered and at one time a very good offer came from Johnson and Johnson in Chile. There was something in me, which felt that I had to finish what I had started while at the back of my mind I felt that Lord Vestey, or perhaps somebody else in the organisation who was on the side of common sense and decency, would wake up and put things to rights. Although I was to be bitterly disappointed and still feel totally let down, I know that I did what was right, and I am aware that these painfully hard lessons helped to temper my character and make me the entity that I am today. I have to acknowledge that my current poverty is largely due to my refusal to join or support 'The Establishment' who can be viciously unforgiving of those who, like myself, steadfastly believe in sovereignty and freedom for my country (or for any country) and refuse to be bought or bribed into bowing to the status quo. As I grow older and find it hard to earn

174

money I have to admit to some hardship, but I am proud that I followed my instinct and stuck by my beliefs and did it my way.

I was not aware of it at the time but some of my Argentine friends who were aware of these injustices took the unusual step of inviting me to a dinner in the original, old part of Buenos Aires called San Telmo. To my surprise I was invited up onto the podium and presented with the title of 'Illustrious Citizen'. That little bit of recognition came entirely voluntarily from people who had nothing to gain and I treasure it more than anything the *"ingleses"* or the Establishment could ever offer.

Home Leave

In 1970 I took my home leave, which turned out to be full of problems. My son broke his leg skiing in Aviemore, my wife and I were not hitting it off but, worst of all, my mother had an accident while I was staying with her and my Dad and after ten difficult days at home she died.

After the funeral I was invited together with my family to spend a few days at Stowell Park, Lord Vestey's country seat. This was a wonderful break as well as a great experience and helped me through the various difficulties that I was experiencing.

Staying at Stowell Park, meeting the people who my friend Sam - as I used to address him - mixed with, experiencing the great house with it's butler and twenty-eight of a staff, and all that goes with this lifestyle was a privilege that I could write about at great length; but it is sufficient for me to give thanks for the wonderful hospitality, the authentic friendship, the insights and the experience, all of which I enjoyed.

An old friend called Derek Birchall, who I had originally met when we were both livestock buyers years before, was also a house guest during our stay at Stowell Park. We had travelled together from Buenos Aires with our families and while enjoying three weeks on the high seas had re-established our old friendship. Derek had been born in South America of an English father and a German mother. As well as being very good-looking, very athletic and a thoroughly likeable individual, he had lived what I saw as a comfortable sheltered life as enjoyed by many Anglo-Argentines. I mention this because years later we were to meet again and he had an extraordinary story to tell me about what happened during a voyage to the UK from South America.

On these ships you were expected to dress for dinner and so, before dinner, the public areas would be very quiet as the ladies put on the dresses especially bought for the trip, while the men got into their dinner jackets. The story Derek told me was about what happened when he, having got dressed one evening, had wandered out onto the now-abandoned afterdeck, where he was able to see an able seaman securing a canvas wind breaker on the lower deck. As the seaman leaned back and pulled at the rope it unexpectedly broke, catapulting the unfortunate fellow backwards into the sea. This happened in mid-Atlantic, where the view in all directions was of limitless sea. Derek ran forward toward the bridge yelling, "Man overboard! Man overboard!" as he tossed lifebelts, deck chairs and anything else that came to hand over the side into the sea.

The story had a happy ending; the seaman, against all odds, was rescued thanks mainly to the large amount of flotsam thrown overboard by Derek to mark the area where he was last seen. What transpired was that the grateful survivor insisted that Derek should visit him at home in Glasgow and meet his family, who wanted to thank him. As Derek told me this story it became apparent that the most memorable and disturbing feature of the whole incident and the subsequent visit to Glasgow, had been the revelation of how his Glaswegian friend lived. He put great emphasis into describing what these tenements were like and, when I tried to tell him that I actually knew all that anyone could know about tenements, he didn't even hear me. As I stood back and listened, I realised that my old friend with whom I had shared the good life in South America and on board ship had no idea who I was, or where I was coming from. I reckoned that some things are best left unspoken, and this seemed to be one of them.

When we were returning to Argentina by ship after the 1970 visit, a shore-to-ship wireless message from Bent instructed me to leave the ship at the earliest opportunity and to fly to Buenos Aires urgently.

My working trips had taken me to places like Japan, Hong Kong, Hawaii and, on one trip, to the Philippines, during which I probably saved the company all the money that I would ever be paid by the Vesteys and much more, in a few days work, but I had never before been called back in the middle of a trip or told to cancel my schedule; so I was curious to find out what was going on.

I got off the ship in Rio and flew down to Buenos Aires only to find that there was no emergency and that Bent merely wished to spoil my well-earned, if difficult, holiday. In the interim, however, between being recalled and arriving back, London had requested that I should go to Australia to compare certain systems and report on why one of their products was so inferior to the same product coming out of Argentina. If this Australian trip had not come up I suspect that Bent and I would have had a head-to-head and things would have worked out very differently.

So, feeling unhappy, tired and not keeping well, I travelled the thirty-six hours to Sydney and spent a couple of weeks flying and driving around Australia and then thirty-six hours back again. The Australians could have produced a far better product if they had been able to follow my instructions but, as usual, after these jobs there seemed to be no follow-up. It was years later that I was told that Bent had got me off the ship in a fit of rage when he learned that I had been a house guest at Stowell Park.

Corruption

In early January of the following year I got an unexpected visit from the head of a stevedoring company who asked to see me on a confidential matter. The Vestey organisation owned a number of companies in Argentina and one of these was called Warskett and Edgar. This was a stevedoring company that worked at the South Dock, which adjoined the factory. The requested interview was from the owner of another large stevedoring company whose name escapes me right now. I must explain that in Argentina there was a bonus system, introduced by Peron, which obliged all employers to pay a thirteenth month's salary. This was known as the *'aguinaldo'*. Now in order to collect this *aguinaldo* all the stevedores had to have their stevedore's registration book stamped by the company that was paying the *aguinaldo*, and this of course would not take place unless the individual had indeed worked all year for the company that was paying the *aguinaldo* or thirteenth month's wage. What my visitor wanted to show me was that twelve of his stevedores had their books stamped by Warskett and Edgar and had been given a month's salary, in spite of having worked all year for his own company.

This meant that somebody was figuring these men as working all year for Warskett and Edgar and putting twelve men's wages in their pocket. Now this was a considerable amount of money that was the equivalent to the price of a good quality house. So someone was pocketing what today would be two to three hundred thousand pounds a year. After digesting this latest scam I felt that I should report it to my immediate boss, Bent, who was also the boss of Warskett and Edgar. I took all the details to

Bent, who studied them then said that I must leave it with him and that I should not put anything in writing or tell anyone. I did as instructed and waited to see what happened. The only obvious result was that the port captain who ran the Warskett and Edgar operation never spoke to me again and things went on as before.

More of the Same

I was aware that the livestock-purchasing department, in which I had started out, was deeply corrupt but it did not end there. All materials and machinery bought through the purchasing department had a percentage added on, which ended up in the employee's pocket. I had proved this to my satisfaction on several occasions. Then there was a very charming chap who earned a meagre salary and lived like a millionaire. He ran the commercial side of the hides department, and so on and so on, throughout Bent's entire domain. I only came to understand the extent of these rackets and thefts towards the end of my time with the company and so I gratefully put it all down to that thing called experience, which I am informed is the main ingredient in the recipe for producing wisdom.

Revolvers

The time was coming when I was going to go over Bent's head whether I liked it or not. One incident almost triggered a full-scale row but was averted at the last minute. It happened when Bent walked straight into my office while I was on the phone. He sat down across the desk from me and started to pull at the drawer handle. When I put the phone down he bellowed, "I do not want you to lock the drawers in your office."

I just stared at him afraid that I might do something I would later regret.

"There is nothing secret in here and you have no reason to lock these drawers," he went on. I opened the drawer on my side, removed a key and handed it across the desk to him. He took the key and opened the offending drawer at his side, to be confronted with fourteen revolvers that I had been slowly collecting from our civil security people, and which I felt were not necessary. Without an apology or an explanation he marched out of my office and into the factory, where I have to say he always felt uncomfortable and out of his depth. The security guards later advised me that soon after storming out of my office, his car left the premises. I know now that I should have flown to London with all the evidence against him before it was too late but I missed the opportunity and I have paid dearly for it ever since. Having said that, the truth is, since it has been an extremely tough experience for me it has also made me more resilient, and I am thankful for that.

Salay and Salay

Meantime two sisters, by the name of Salay - also known as the Mata Hari twins - who hailed from Hungary, were working for the company. They were both highly trained secretaries and had won prizes and awards for their outstanding capabilities in this field. One was Bent's private secretary and the other, after spending some time at the head office, was offered to me as my private secretary. I suspected at the time that this was a plant within my organisation that could be used by Bent to keep an eye on or even to undermine me. Having nothing to hide and being aware of what might be behind the move I gladly accepted the offer, and Miss Salay moved into the office next to mine. This woman was dynamite. She organised everything with such efficiency and seemed to read my mind and do things even before I asked her.

I was well pleased with this arrangement, especially since she had arrived at a particularly busy period, which meant that it was quite some time before we managed to have an informal conversation. Her first informal observation was that the impression that Bent's head office staff had of the factory and its people was quite opposite to the reality she had experienced. When I asked her to explain she mentioned that she, and the other head office staff, were not accustomed to the good-humoured politeness so evident at the factory from the supervisors and management, the engineers and even the laboratory helpers and cleaners.

I was left in no doubt that there was a conscious effort within the head office to deliberately denigrate our very professional, hard-working team at the plant. This attitude had grown up since Bent took over, and I puzzled to understand why he would deliberately foster such a false impression and disharmony. I might point out that our team included a number of professional engineers and chemists, a doctor of bacteriology, five medical doctors and a great number of highly skilled specialists in a host of disciplines and crafts. Miss Salay was able to reveal all kinds of hitherto unheard of activities and gossip about the office under Bent's influence and I was getting close to taking some kind of action to expose what was going on.

These conversations eventually lead to (my) Miss Salay confessing that she was indeed expected to inform on my activities and on me. My Miss Salay then went on to tell me about a number of very confidential false reports that Bent had sent to London about how he personally was running things and how worried he was about Mr Kemp's inability to run things at the plant; how aggressive Kemp was with his staff and even the irresponsible way he drove his car. She had her own proof that these were false allegations and I was actually alarmed at one point just how angry she became at what was going on. Her suggestion was that she should put together a file with all these false reports in it - which her sister would supply - and I should go to London and spill the beans on Bent who, it was evident, these two sisters wanted to see brought down. I confessed to Miss Salay that I was at a loss to understand why Bent was doing these things and trying to ruin me. She stared in disbelief then slowly said, "Everyone knows that Bent is sick with jealousy," but I did not get this at all. She kept staring at me and then said, "You really don't know do you?"

"What do you mean?" I asked.

"The way people respond to you, the way you get things done. The immense power you have and the way you handle responsibility."

"So, that is my job," I replied.

"Yes but Bent would give his right arm to be able to do things the way you do and have people look up to him the way your staff and even the union bosses look up to you. On top of this he does not like Scots, you saw how he treated Mr Laird because he was Scottish and now you."

I really had no awareness that this could be true. I may have a blind spot or be a bit slow but I did not believe that this could be true.

I sweated over these extremely unpleasant goings-on. I was unable to sleep for thinking about it. This was not the kind of thing that I handled well and I did not want to earn my living by playing dirty games. I convinced myself that Lord Sam would get wind of what his old enemy was up to and I felt that as long as I kept working to the best of my ability, the truth would come out in the long run and at least I would have a clear conscience, whatever transpired.

The stress was affecting my health so, much to the displeasure of the personnel manager, I took time off and went on holiday with the family.

182

Seventy-two people contracted hepatitis from contaminated drinking water at the ski resort and I was one of them. I spent six months in hospital and upon discharge was told not to work for at least a year.

Gateway to Freedom

When I got out of hospital the personnel manager came to my house and gave me a year's wages, would not allow me to keep the car, informed me that I would not get the promised company pension and asked me to clear my desk as soon as I could get out and about. I did not have the energy to defend myself or to argue. Bent had finally got what he wanted and nobody lifted a finger to help me, and so I retired into myself and quietly accepted my fate.

Twenty years of hard work had come to an abrupt end. Anyone who has had hepatitis will understand how weak and vulnerable one becomes following this disease. My vulnerability had been Bent's opportunity to move in and, true to his predatory character, finish me off, yet I could only feel sorry for him. For some reason my very presence disturbed and haunted this deeply unhappy man and he seemed to be prepared to go to any length to make my life a misery.

I slowly, and impatiently, recuperated and eventually saw this as my gateway to freedom and a real opportunity to find my true self. So I mean it when I say, thank you Ronald Bent, you gave me an insight into a side of life I never dreamed of, thank you for exposing me to such an important, if unjust, learning.

I must mention at this point that I was blessed with a driver called Ignacio. He had driven me many thousands of miles while putting up with my impatience, my moods and demands. Just after I got out hospital he casually gave me an envelope, which he said I should open when I got home. To cut a long story short the envelope contained his meagre life's savings, which he thought I could use to get myself going again once things collapsed. I had been slow to understand the quality and sincerity of some of these friends and it was much later on looking back that I began to realise that many people had been aware of the nasty and underhand aspects of Bent's activities. I confess that I was naïve and very slow to believe that he was really as twisted and devious as others would have me believe. That deep smouldering hate that led him to harm me behind my back in every way he possibly could is still beyond my understanding. I can only say that it did me no harm but that kind of attitude may have contributed to his fatal heart attack. I send him my blessings.

It was not long until I got divorced and lost my home and my money, finally let go of the worries and unhappiness that I had managed to create for myself and so I walked through this magical gateway to freedom and started yet another phase in this unpredictable lifetime full of unexpected experiences.

Exploring the New Freedom

The Royal Navy

Once I had left hospital, followed by an unpleasant divorce, I found myself in a foreign country with no home, no job and no prospects. This was not an enviable state to be in yet, following almost thirty years of working, I was filled with a great feeling of liberation. My large American Ford Fairlane car became the only territory I could claim as my own and at times I would lock myself away in this tin capsule where I could go inwards and feel safe.

This was 1972, the year the British Navy decided to "show the flag" in Argentina and so it was that a number of British warships, with much fuss, flag waving and the Royal Marines Band arrived in the port of Buenos Aires.

Soon the streets of the city hosted considerable numbers of British sailors who, in the time-honoured way of sailors abroad, went from bar to bar. They looked lost as they wandered the streets with their hats on the back of their heads taking in another foreign land.

It struck me that in spite of their large numbers, few of them were officers or petty officers and that almost all of these boys who wandered about looking lost wore bell-bottoms and were sometimes known as 'matelots' or 'lower rates'.

After having lived a very active life I found having no job and few obligations a bit disconcerting so I decided that, since the one thing I had plenty of was time, I would organise some kind of entertainment for these rather lost fellow countrymen.

When I suggested to some friends at the rowing club that we could organise something, almost immediately things started to take shape. A large German brewery offered us three barrels of beer, two hundred beer glasses and an 'expert' to draw and serve the beer. With this under our belts we organised a dance at the club to which - partly due to my protracted stay at the British hospital - all the nurses there were invited. I then got in touch with a Captain Forbes who was in charge of the fleet's entertainment and invited all petty officers to come to our Tigre Boat Club dance. There were all kinds of logistics to be worked out, including transport for both the nurses and the naval officers but the big night eventually arrived and we had a hall full of sailors and nurses, music and beer. After a slow start it turned out to be a highlight for the sailors and a great success all round.

How to entertain the very large numbers of these bell-bottomed matelots was, however, a different challenge and needed a different approach.

Following a long conversation with Señor Duggan, who was the president of the Argentine Jockey Club, I was able to offer free entrance to any British sailor who turned up at the San Isidro races. This not only got us over the matelots problem but also meant that all ranks could spend the day at this very beautiful racecourse free of charge. Our little team felt that we had done a good job, although we were eventually a bit disappointed to see so few matelots had accepted our invitation to spend a day at the races.

When the time came for the navy to depart, the British Embassy laid on a gala event for all officers, those who had cooperated during the visit plus a colourful gathering of diplomatic and military personnel from other embassies.

This was old style pomp and ceremony as only the British can do it and in my civilian attire with no decorations or medals to adorn my chest, I felt very much in the minority.

There were men who wore breeches and brown jackboots. Uniforms covered in clinking medals were all around me and I scrutinised one

American whose whole left side was a sea of ribbons, medals and badges. This whole situation felt very unreal to me and perhaps even bordered on the ridiculous.

Braided ropes complete with tassels hung from uniformed shoulders and swords of varying sizes got in the way as the wearers mingled with the guests. Swallow-tailed coats mixed with well fitting, button-covered jackets, while civilian decorations were hopelessly outnumbered by the military variety. It was the ladies in all their finery who quite unintentionally managed to bring some sense of balance and dignity amongst all these mind-numbing excesses.

With a large single malt in my hand I soon struck up a conversation with a British naval officer who, like myself, did not feel at ease in this heady atmosphere. It was his suggestion that we might escape this torture by visiting his ship, where we might enjoy a more relaxed drink. I accepted this invitation and suggested that we might then proceed to the suburbs where a Latvian friend with whom I rowed called Siegfried Rubilis, was hosting a party. Russians Lithuanians, Poles and Czechs amongst others were all invited, as well as a few Italians and Spanish. Their common bond was that they were all 'escapees' from post-war Europe.

We went to the cloakroom where the shelves were overflowing with a most impressive array of fancy gold-braided hats; some even had feathers on them. My new friend produced a cloakroom ticket and duly received his cap while I, on the spur of the moment and without thinking, picked up an old ticket, pointed the attendant to a very fancy white hat festooned with gold that caught my eye. The poor girl was quite flustered and handed me the hat without question and so, tucking my new acquisition under my left arm, I proceeded to march down the very long hallway to the embassy entrance. This grand hallway entrance was made up of stretches of carpeted floor with four stairs at ten or fifteen foot intervals. At each of these small flights of stairs there were two Royal Marines who came to attention as we passed. As we proceeded through this gauntlet I was aware of the knowing glances exchanged by the Marines, who could plainly see a civilian with a naval cap tucked under his arm leaving the embassy.

When we arrived at the port in my car I put the collar of my jacket up and put the gold-braided hat on my head and instead of being stopped we received a salute as the gates were thrown open to let us in.

My naval companion seeing the hat on my head raised his hands to his face while declaring, "Jesus you've nicked a bloody admiral's cap!"

Following a quick tour of the ship and a drink we headed for my friend's party in the suburb of Olivos. It was attended by a mixed bunch of Argentines, central Europeans and one ex German U-boat commander, who I later remembered had left the party early. When the tale of how I acquired the admiral's hat got out everyone wanted to try it on and, it was not until much later, when we were leaving that I discovered the hat could not be found.

Several months went by before my friend Ziggy as we called Siegfried, confessed that the ex U-boat commander who had been at the party had taken the hat.

The temptation to own an admiral's hat belonging to the old enemy was perhaps too much for him to resist and since it was not my hat in any case he was welcome to it and I hope he got some pleasure from owning it.

Forty years on and I still have the letter dated 30 January 1972 from captain Forbes thanking me for my efforts at entertaining his senior rates – with no mention of the lower ranks at whom my efforts were mainly aimed.

I have to add one parting observation, which only helps to confirm that I am perhaps somehow different and think along non-conventional lines. When all the fuss and hard work was over I visited Captain Forbes on board his ship, and during our conversation commented that I had been surprised and somewhat disappointed that so few bellbottoms had taken advantage of the invitation to the races. After a pause he looked at me as if I had broken some sacred rule and indicated rather tersely that the Navy did not expect people to entertain these lower rates.

I might have pointed out to him that I had gone to a great deal of trouble to persuade the president of the Jockey Club himself to extend the invitation, which was especially for these lower ranks or what the Navy term 'junior rates', who seemed destined to wander aimlessly from bar to bar and had nothing laid on for them.

I knew that any honest comment from me, however, would have sounded to his ears more like an invitation to start a mutiny.

I wished him 'bon voyage', walked down the gangway and got into my four-wheeled tin capsule, where I felt safe from this crazy world with which I sadly seemed to be at odds.

From Captain J M Forbes Royal Navy

HMS TRIUMPH
at Buenos Aires

The President
Tigre Boat Club
Victoria 158
Tigre
Buenos Aires   30 Jan 72

        Before our departure from Buenos Aires,
I must thank you for the hospitality which
you extended to my senior rates on Saturday.
We all welcome an opportunity to get away
from the ship for a few hours and spend them
in the communial atmosphere which you offered.
Your gesture has been much appreciated.

        Thank you again.

Casas

"You may not be aware of it but I was the one who introduced the two greatest people in this country to each other."

"Really?"

"How do you think I made so much money if it was not by knowing the man himself? You see when the earthquake demolished San Juan killing ten-thousand people in 1944 there was an effort to raise money to help the victims and rebuild the city. At that time I played the guitar in a group that, after some success at home in Mendoza, travelled to Buenos Aires and I became involved with the fundraising efforts. We put the money we collected in barrels, and twice a week there was a colonel who would come in a lorry to collect the barrels. Well, one night we invited the colonel to have a glass of wine and I suggested to a young actress friend who lived in Vicente Lopez that she should come and meet the colonel. I introduced them and they were immediately attracted to each other. The colonel eventually became President Peron and the actress Eva Duarte de Peron and between them they made this the best country in the world."

As I listened I caught the passing remark that Eva had lived in Vicente Lopez so I asked, "Do you remember the street she lived in?"

"Oh yes, very well," came the answer, "it was La Prida 822". This house that Eva Peron had spent some years living in was the house that I had bought twelve years earlier and then lost thanks to my divorce. What an interesting life I lived.

The storyteller was a man in his forties, five-feet-seven with jet black hair combed straight back, long black sideboards and a thin black moustache. Silk shirt, handmade shoes and a tailor-made suit of grey shiny material were all part of this fellow's make up. The end result was appalling, but this man just knew that he was God's gift to women and nothing could change that. He went through life with great zest and enthusiasm and told me his story with this same flair and energy, which made it impossible not to be attracted to him. His many stories were at least based on fact although one could never be sure where the fact ended and the enthusiasm took over.

His name was Raul Casas and we had met when I decided to stay for a while in Buenos Aires to recuperate from my hepatitis and to start working for myself. The projects Casas and I put together included importing cattle from Uruguay, renting a large passenger ship and creating a floating exhibition in New York and other imaginative schemes but we actually made very little money and eventually parted company. The reason I mention him is simply because he was a colourful rouge who taught me about a way of living that I had never experienced and although the partnership did not last I took with me some interesting memories.

Using the influence he had created through his friendship with General Peron and his wife Eva, Casas had made a fortune through the beef industry while becoming unpopular in certain quarters by denouncing the monumental swindle being supported by the Argentine national meat companies, who he felt should be setting an example to the foreign beef exporters. The foreign companies had, according to him, been making vast profits for many years by buying off the Argentine meat board inspectors in London, who were there to oversee and confirm the tonnages and prices of chilled beef being pitched on the Smithfield market. As it happened I had heard firsthand about this illegal practice from one of our employees called Burns, who had worked in the head office in London and later in Buenos Aires before moving on to greater things. Burns' story was that while he had been in London, chilled beef was being sold for £300 per ton, but thanks to the Argentine inspectors turning a blind eye only £100 was being declared for Argentine tax purposes by our organisation; presumably the same applied to the other beef importers.

The amounts of money being stolen in this swindle were, according to both Casas and Burns, in the billions. I had never thought very much about this super fraud until Casas mentioned it as he went into detail about these billions being stolen from the Argentine economy through these practices and his intention to do something about it, but I don't believe he ever changed things.

I found it interesting that he greatly admired the '*ingleses*' who, according to him, were stealing from 'his' Argentine nation. When I challenged him on this he was adamant that he had the greatest admiration for any country or any individual that could steal from others as well as the *ingleses* did. He scoffed at the Argentine crooks, who dressed badly and used force to extract money.

"Just look at the *ingleses*, how well they dress, how cool they are and how they only send in a gun boat as a last resort. The *ingleses* have got style. The *ingleses* have been milking the world dry for years, even before Queen Elizabeth appointed the bloodiest pirate in history as Governor of the whole Caribbean. You know it was after Morgan was appointed that we started using the term '*piratas ingleses*' and we still use that phrase today. The *ingleses* are the most professional confidence tricksters in all history and I take my hat off to them. The Americans have stolen a lot of money too but they have not got the class or the style that the *ingleses* have."

He also told of his incredible journeys across the Andes with thousands of cattle. He too always liked to do everything in style and he told me of how, when he went on these cattle drives over the Andes mountains, from Chile, that he was accompanied by a Chinese cook and a butler, complete with white gloves, and that he always had a white table cloth for the evening meal. He also claimed to be on first name terms with the Chilean President Allende and that before leaving Chile he had had dinner at the Presidential residence eating from gold plates, which had been a present from the Kremlin.

When eventually I told him that I was swapping my city clothes and habits for blue jeans, boots and a log cabin, he was horrified and warned me that I would not be able to make good money in the mountains and that I could even die of starvation.

Tiny

During this period when I found myself without employment and before moving south, back to Patagonia, I took a room at the rowing club of which I was still president. This was seen as the British rowing club and was known as the TBC, the Tigre Boat Club. I tended to spend all my weekends on the water, either rowing or sailing a small two-berth yacht that I had bought and renovated some years earlier. It was called *Malabar*, apparently because the hard wood from which it was made came from the Malabar Coast of India.

Most weekends I slept at the club and often went out in the middle of the week just to celebrate my new freedom from timetables, labour unions, danger, stress and the twenty very busy years for which I had nothing to show.

There was only one small fly in the ointment in the form of my neighbour, who rented the room at the club through the wall from mine. He was a strange, rather eccentric Englishman called Charles, who kept very much to himself. The problem arose when one night at about two in the morning I heard what sounded like a shot from a small-calibre gun. I lay awake and listened for a long time but eventually dismissed it as my imagination and went to sleep. About a week later again in the wee hours of the night, there was a shot, which alerted all my senses; this was followed by another shot. I was quite sure this time that it was not my imagination and that the shots were coming from my neighbour's room.

In view of the fact that the wall separating our rooms was made of adobe and no deterrent for a bullet fired at close range, I decided to take action. Two friends cooperated with me, engaging Charles in a long conversation at the bar while I searched his room. I eventually found a loaded .38 Smith and Wesson revolver, of which I took possession. Being club president I carried a little bit of clout so I removed the bullets and took the offending weapon to the manager's office and had him lock it away in the safe. I left instructions that, should anyone make enquiries, the truth should be told and the reason for my action explained. The manager was a large Charles Laughton-like character who addressed everyone as "me old" and had many yarns to tell about the ten years he had spent in the French Foreign Legion. His name was Holsworth and we all called him Tiny. The weeks went by and to my surprise nobody mentioned the incident, not even my neighbour Charles.

Some time later, probably a couple of months, I arrived at the club to be met by an old rowing friend who ushered me into a corner and said in a hushed voice, "Have you heard the terrible news?"

"What news?" I asked.

"Jackie went to visit Tiny last night and found him slouched in a chair with a hole in his head and that revolver you gave him lying on the table."

My mind immediately went to the revolver with my fingerprints all over it.

"So what has happened?" I asked. What transpired was that there had been no enquiries made by the police and the body had been removed

196

with a minimum of fuss. The whole thing went very quiet although there were a lot of rumours and speculation about Tiny's past life and why the suicide.

The years went by and I returned to the UK and a new life. One day, in the early 1980s, I had just acquired a new book from the library in Haywards Heath in Sussex and was leafing through the pages as I walked slowly along, when my eye caught a familiar face looking through a car windscreen at me.

I stopped and pretended to be absorbed in the book as I tried to decide to whom the face belonged. In the end I walked the few paces to the car and stooping down I enquired, "Do we know each other?"

There was a pause and the lady who owned the face said, "You are Scotty Kemp and I am Joyce Williams and the last time we met must have been over twenty years ago in Argentina."

She had married a very successful English businessman who worked in Argentina and they now lived in a beautiful house with their three children not far from where I lived. What a small world. We became friends and I would visit them and occasionally do something together. It was after an enjoyable day watching the polo at Windsor Great Park that I was enjoying a drink at their house when Bernard asked, "Were you not president of the TBC at one time?" "Yes," I replied, "many years ago."

"How well did you know the office manager, Tiny Holsworth?" he enquired. "Well, I replied, "the big hail-fellow well-met Tiny Holsworth was a bit of an enigma and nobody really knew very much about him. Then, following his rather mysterious and untimely death, the mystery only deepened but I cannot say much more than that, although the riddle as to why he decided to end his life has always intrigued me."

"Well," went on Bernard, "I cannot say too much about this but you will be interested to know that Tiny was in the RAF during the war and he was sent to Yugoslavia on some special hush-hush job. However, he apparently became a double agent and caused havoc back at headquarters in the UK before his double-dealing was eventually uncovered and he evaporated into thin air." After taking a sip of his drink, Bernard continued, "Now, as you know, I was in the navy during the war and when I decided to work in South America I was approached by the security people who told me about Holsworth and asked me to keep an eye open for them. Well it took a long time but we finally caught up with him and he must have realised that the game was up."

I sat in Bernard's comfortable house in a beautiful part of England and thought back over the time I had spent at the rowing club. I thought of the private, almost secretive lifestyle that Tiny lived, then of course there were these ten years in the Foreign Legion. Things began to fall into place and make sense and I felt that I would at last be able to close this little mystery and put this story to bed. When I was leaving I said, "Thanks Bernard for the story about Tiny Holsworth." He looked straight at me and said, "No idea what you are on about, never heard of the fellow."

Back to the Land of the Giants

Mallín Ahogado

I had decided, after twenty years absence, to return to Patagonia and live in the foothills of the Andes. My intention was to never go back into so-called civilisation ever again but to live close to the land in a simple unpretentious way.

I acquired a piece of so-called 'frontier land' in an isolated place called Mallín Ahogado and decided to develop it as a far-out adventure base where riding, rafting, fishing and other outdoor activities were all potential ways of making a living. This meant digging a well, cutting trees to build a house, learning how to build a house, etcetera all without electricity or things like running water or a shower. This piece of land was blessed with some very old fruit trees, planted by Jesuit priests who were, in 1768, expelled from all of the Spanish Empire. After my six months in hospital with hepatitis, divorce and escape from the big city this felt like paradise.

My nearest neighbours, indigenous Patagonians with whom I had become friends, had come to help me pick the fruit and it was due to this that I discovered that one of the boys, who was about seven years old, had what appeared to me to be several broken ribs. On learning that the mother had already been to the little hospital in the town of Bolson, only to be sent home, I reluctantly felt obliged to take a hand in affairs. I was actually trying to keep a low profile, and not get further involved in this kind of thing, since I was becoming at times a bit of a judge and jury when it came to disputes or selling land in the area. They owned the only form of transport for miles around in the shape of an old sulky or buckboard so I got the father to catch their horse and prepare to go to town.

The little fellow was eventually bumped and jolted on the back of the sulky for the hour it took to get to the village while I followed on foot. When we arrived at the hospital we were virtually sidelined and ignored by the staff until I confronted one of the doctors who had been carefully avoiding us. I eventually had to raise my voice and insist that the boy be attended to until eventually the doctor shrugged his shoulders and said that if I insisted he would get the boy attended to but that, "These Indians were not worth bothering about".

It turned out that the wee fellow had several broken ribs and his lung had been damaged. He appeared to be well looked after in spite of the initial experience and within weeks the patient was back to his energetic smiling self.

Still disturbed by the original lack of treatment I found the opportunity some weeks later to talk to the head doctor about my dissatisfaction at the initial reluctance to attend to the boy, only to get the brush-off with, "Well these things sometimes happen, I think you worry too much". Being just another very insignificant smallholding farmer with no power or authority took some getting used to. I had no money, no friends and only my own two hands to build this new project. It is undeniable that a large slice of humble pie, while not always easy to swallow, nevertheless can at times be revitalising and inspiring.

When I lived on this piece of land in the Andean foothills, riders would occasionally appear from the other side of the mountains, having ridden for many days over the cordillera from Chile, coming into Argentina illegally or legally. These men, without exception, rode thin, hungry horses, were hard looking, dirty and often hungry but in spite of their often desperate look they would always be polite and grateful for any food or drink they were offered. It is all too easy to get a completely erroneous impression of someone who has been outdoors on horseback for some time, and I can vouch for this personally as I described earlier in the anecdote I call *My friend Brodie*.

Perito Moreno

In addition to these travelling horsemen, one tended to run into the most unexpected and interesting characters in all kinds of circumstances throughout Patagonia.

Back in Victorian times there was a famous Argentine explorer who, amongst other things, worked on the establishment of a frontier between Argentine and Chile and actually called Queen Victoria in as arbiter in the ensuing dispute. This fellow is seen as a bit of a hero by many Argentines and is known as Perito Moreno (*perito* meaning expert or connoisseur). He is credited with having opened up new areas in southern Chile and Argentina, where there is a famous glacier named after him. As well as discovering fossils and skeletons of prehistoric animals thus farther promoting the myth that giants at one time populated Patagonia, he had the final word on the shape of the frontier between Chile and Argentina.

But to get back to my attempt to develop my piece of frontier land in Mallín Ahogado I had grand ideas of establishing an American style "Dude Ranch" which would be a very far-out and original place to ride, explore and live off the land. It soon became quite obvious that if I was going to get even a temporary road built into my property before the snows came, I was going to need some help. I sent a message to a neighbour who lived further down the valley and who, I was told, owned a ten-ton lorry and would, for a price, deliver road-building material for my project. This message was apparently delivered to an Indian lady on whose property I had seen a lorry parked. About three days later I was having breakfast when I heard an engine coming up the road that led to my place. In what was a quiet backwater the sound of a vehicle was not all that common so I stoked the fire and put the kettle on in anticipation of a visitor. I did not have long to wait to see a large red lorry slowly swaying and rocking its way through the trees. It came about half way down the projected road towards my cabin, which was further than any lorry had ever managed, and then the driver apparently considered that he had come far enough and switched the engine off. As I went out to meet the lorry I was surprised to see an Indian lady get out of the passenger side. When I got closer I was again surprised to see a fair-haired florid faced fellow approach me with his hand extended. We shook hands and the new arrival said in beautiful cultured English, "How do you do, my name is Moreno, I'm a great nephew of Perito Moreno, you know, the explorer."

It turned out that this was indeed the great nephew of the great man himself who, following an English public school education and a few years travelling in Europe, had opted for an Indian wife, a small piece of land in Patagonia and tranquility. We enjoyed several interesting conversations and although we always started off in English he inevitably had to fall back on Spanish due to a lack of vocabulary. He was yet another example of the great affinity and cultural ties that exist between Argentina and Britain, not only through well-known individuals like Perito Moreno, Luis Borges, Guillermo Hudson, General Rosas - who was nicknamed *El Ingles* - and many, many not so well-known Anglophiles. Of course, ties were also strengthened between the two countries through intermarriage, business, sport and mutual admiration.

I dwell on this because, as I see it, these are the truly important human values that seem to be totally bypassed by the military or political consciousness when an opportunity to go to war arises, as in the case of the invasion of the Malvinas, which I expand on, in the appendix under the title *The Falklands War.*

Without wishing to support one approach over another it is apparent that the way the Bridges family - that I mentioned in context of the Conquest of the Desert - handled their situation in the far south was highly successful, compared with the never-ending conflict in other regions and this has led different people to speculate what might have been had the influx of so-called *ingleses* been more substantial. I say so-called because by far the largest number of these *ingleses* were Welsh-speaking people from Wales who, when I was in the area, could still be found speaking Spanish and Welsh but no English. The numerous Scots, Irish and English who followed were, and still are broadly known as *ingleses*.

In spite of the English having invaded Argentina in 1806 and again in 1807 and having been forced to retreat there has always been a large and influential presence in Argentina of these so-called *ingleses*.

Some of them, like Mr Halliburton who, we are told, became a highly respected resident of San Telmo (the original Buenos Aires) actually arrived on one of the invading frigates. There are names like Temperley, Banfield, Coghlan, Henderson and others who gave their names to Argentine railway stations while Mr Thompson became port captain for the port of Buenos Aires.

The nearest town to where I live in Scotland is called Forres and we find a Forres railway station in northern Argentina, the railways having been built and named by these '*ingleses*'.

It is interesting to note that while there are books, including school books, in Argentina telling of the attempts by the English to invade Argentina there is little or no acknowledgement in English history books regarding these events. These historical conflicts can be confirmed by visiting the Cabildo, the old municipal council building, in Buenos Aires, where large numbers of English flags, documents and memorabilia can be viewed, all captured during the '*invasiones ingleses*'. I personally had never heard of these invasions in my schoolboy history lessons but one might ponder what may have become another little piece of English history had General Beresford or General Whitelock won their wars against Argentina.

Right up until the twentieth century in parts of Patagonia, and further north in Uruguay, the gold sovereign was the accepted currency. When visiting an English family in the small town of Conchillas in Uruguay I was told that the port of Buenos Aires was built from stone quarried at Conchillas and ferried across the river Plate in barges. This English family was extremely welcoming and, I suspect, longed for English conversation. They told me of quarry foremen being brought out from England who regarded the Uruguayan labourers as 'bloody dagos' and, although unable to learn Spanish, would yell at them with phrases like "put the hooky on the wagonoo and vamoose bloody pronto!" This family had many stories that they were eager to tell, and I was happy to listen. They told me of a strike when the English quarry company decided to pay the workers with paper pound notes. They had always been paid in gold sovereigns and would hear none of it. There may have been more to their preference for gold sovereigns, however, since I later learned that the gold sovereigns were usually kept in small, smooth leather bags, which the men would continually shake, thus producing gold dust, which could be sold, while the sovereigns maintained their value.

Michael Mainwaring in his *From the Falklands to Patagonia* quotes a German engineer who visited Punta Arenas in 1894 as saying,

"One hears almost exclusively English voices; you get the impression that you have arrived in old England or at least the Falklands. Apart from the port officials everything is British. Money, sheep, language, drink, and the ladies and gentleman."

When I first went to Argentina I was amazed at the number of English or semi-English words in use like *futbol*, *el toorf* (turf), folklore, *bif tec* (beef steak) *lincons* (referring to Lincoln sheep), shorthorns and of course *negros* (referring to the very popular black Aberdeen angus cattle).

And so I come back to the point I made earlier when I referred to human values and long standing, slowly developed relationships being pushed to one side and destroyed when there is a chance to create yet another stupid destructive war, of which the arms dealers and undertakers are the beneficiaries, while unsuspecting civilians pay taxes to support them.

Doc on Rio Limay

At this time, when I was living in my cabin at Mallín Ahogado, there was a very large hydroelectric scheme under way on the Rio Limay in the province of Rio Negro.

Following an operation to remove a kidney stone, I decided to try for a non-physical job while I recuperated. This hydroelectric project was an English-Italian consortium and I managed to get myself a very unpretentious job checking all incoming materials. This was a new, very rough site in the desert where the wind blew for three months each year non-stop and was called *el viento de los locos* (the mad man's wind). The river Limay flowed through what is called the Valle Encantado or the Enchanted Valley. The name comes from the monumental red, green and grey rock formations and outcroppings that straddle the river for mile after mile, turning the landscape into an uncompromising, rugged Disneyland. This was the Wild West where everyone seemed to carry a gun and where, in the windy season, nobody went outdoors without goggles and a face covering.

206

Due to the poor living conditions and the cold wind I managed to get an infection in the stitches along my side. This proved to be a bit of good fortune since it put me in contact with the site doctor by the name of Doctor Patola. He was a very hale and hearty sixty-four year-old Ukrainian who had been through some of the most harrowing experiences in war torn Europe, including forced marches and sixteen concentration camps. He could have filled several books with his stories but his favourite pastime was fishing for the beautiful and plentiful wild salmon to be found in the unpolluted wilds of Patagonia. Unpolluted, that was, until the project to dam the river started up. Dressed in a cap, rather tattered jacket and old flannel trousers complete with rod and bag he looked more like an English squire than the site doctor. The fishing season had not yet started, and hare being the kind of pest that the rabbit is in Australia, Doc would wander off with his shotgun looking for something for the pot. Our common language was Spanish and Doc had his own amusing version. Because of his own unique way of speaking Spanish I recognised the voice that called through the letterbox of my miniature pre-fab one evening, inviting me to come hunting. I went to the door and he explained that the water wagon was going down to the river and we could ride on top of it and shoot any hare that might get caught in the headlights.

He stopped halfway through his explanation of how things worked and said, "I suppose you do have a rifle?"

I replied that the rifle, which I had brought with me, although only a . 22 calibre, was very powerful and since the water wagon was planning to pass fairly close to the shacks where some Indians lived I did not want to accidentally shoot one of them by mistake.

"No is problem," beamed my new friend. "I Doctor in Rio Negro with revalidated doctorate. I sign all death certificates, no worry."

I am still not sure how serious he was but I had no desire to find out. There were few interesting people to talk to on the site so his friendship was a blessing. His wife was no less charming and her Spanish even more amusing. She had been on the forced marches with her husband and had seen thousands of fellow marchers die along the way before escaping to South America and she was now not going to let anything get her down. She treated Doc rather like a difficult child while she spoiled and scolded him alternately. This plump sixty-something-year old survivor always made a point of telling everyone, in her own brand of Spanish, that if she had to do it all again, it would be numerous lovers for her and definitely no husband. Doc would look on lovingly and agree with all she had to say.

The Maddening Wind (Viento de los Locos)

One little incident shook the place up when the two warring workers' syndicates locked horns and after months of arguing finally had a shoot out.

The labourers living quarters consisted of long huts with eight rooms per hut. Each room had two single beds and two wardrobes. I was walking past one of these huts when simultaneously a young labourer burst through the door at the end of the hut and gunfire erupted. I had no idea what was going on but I dived for cover under an adjacent hut and observed several men coming and going, accompanied by shouting and a couple of more shots. When it quietened down I made myself scarce and later learned that a very large pleasant fellow, who I often talked to, had been shot fourteen times by one of the rival union members. What a place!

There were several cases of men going mad, and I accompanied Doc Patola on one visit to a lad who was sitting in his wardrobe talking to his mother on an imaginary telephone and who told us, as we approached, not to disturb his conversation.

A rather tragic-comic incident took place down by the river where a group of labourers were digging a trench using picks and spades. This was not a popular job and, although I am not certain, I suspect that being sent to do this work was a kind of punishment. What was apparent was that this was a rather disgruntled group who did things as individuals, rather than as a team. All the labourers seemed to carry knives and many were armed with a variety of handguns. Carrying firearms without a permit was illegal, but there seemed to be an unwritten agreement to turn a blind eye to the practice.

Loss of Manhood

So this group were digging away, when one of them brought his pickaxe down with a thump while simultaneously his gun, which was tucked into his waistband, went off with a bang. Following a moment's silence while everyone took stock of things, the one with the pickaxe rolled over on his back and let out a list of expletives, punctuated by groans, sobs and incomprehensible language that seemed to be directed at Mary, the Mother of God. My friend Doc Patola later filled me in on the details but basically the bullet, after passing through this poor guy's penis, had passed right through his leg and out the other side. A painful experience but not life threatening.

The whole camp talked about it for days, jokes and rumours abounded plus some questionable theories and unfounded gossip about what had 'really' happened. Before I left this harsh, inhospitable, windswept camp, which I was soon to swap for my little piece of land back at Mallín Ahogado one more ludicrous event took place, which may be hard to believe, but actually did happen.

The Hold Up

There was very good looking young man who was employed as a driver and would go to pick up the visiting dignitaries and the engineers who came and went continually. He was tall and blonde so tended to stand out amongst the predominately dark-haired people on the site. His name was Eduardo Velez.

The chief engineer from Italy had been at the site for several days and was having a casual conversation with the night watchman when he suggested that it was perhaps a boring job sitting in the middle of the desert with nothing to do all night. The unexpected reply was that he did not mind being out there on his own and he did get an occasional unexpected visit. What the watchman told him was that only a few nights earlier the site wages had arrived and had been locked away in the safe. Then, at about one o'clock in the morning, he had heard a noise and when he opened the door to see what was going on he was confronted by a man wearing a stocking over his face and a .45 calibre automatic pistol in his hand pointed at him.

"Good God!" exclaimed the engineer, "what on earth did you do?"

"Well," came the reply, "I asked him to come in and sit down, then I said to him, "what are you doing Velez with that silly stocking over your face?""

"Wait a minute," said the engineer, "how did you recognise him?"

"Well, he is the only tall, blonde man on site and I could see through the stocking anyway."

Following this unreported attempt to steal the wages it was discovered that the charming Velez had a string of convictions to his name and he was eventually charged with firearm possession and intent to carry out a robbery. The watchman was replaced and swore to get even with Velez for making him lose his job. Such was the character of this place and I won't go into the skulduggery that went on both officially and unofficially; but I was glad to put it all down to experience and to move back to my piece of land in the foothills at Mallín Ahogado.

Making Films

It was hard work developing the land, planting trees, building and enlarging the cabin and the never-ending job of cutting wood. Money was needed, although I paid no rent or rates and I mostly bartered for meat, eggs and milk. One unexpected and welcome source of income came my way when, on a visit to the town of Bolson a few miles down the valley, I found myself offering a helping hand to an Englishman who was struggling to communicate with the local hotel owner. It turned out that he was working with a film company making advertisements for some kind of skin cream. Their story, especially for someone like me who had run away from the modern busy mentality, seemed mad, or at least bizarre.

In total there were some eight or ten in their group. This included a director, two 'stars', three extras, a camera crew and eventually myself. The man I had initially contacted was the scriptwriter and general organiser. They had originally flown out from London to the north of Argentina, to make a short film with peaches as the main theme, the product they were out to promote being a cream which contained peach products and produced a peach-like complexion.

On arriving at their destination they apparently discovered that they were at the wrong end of the country for peach growing. They were then told to fly to the town of Bolson, many hundreds of miles to the south, where they were guaranteed that peaches were grown in vast quantities. This latest information was quite correct but when they arrived the peaches were not due on the trees for several months.

I was invited to work with this group, initially as a translator and progressively as an organiser, special effects creator and odd job man. One job I did for them was to find out where peaches might be found. Then I had a dozen boxes flown in from Uruguay, about a thousand miles away. Next I bought a large roll of thin wire and proceeded to tie several hundred peaches on to the bare peach trees.

The weeks I spent working for them was like a holiday for me, speaking English, being inventive, working with people who seemed to have no end of money to spend on their poorly organised endeavour and, above all, being paid for it. The 'extras' seemed to have no idea of what was expected of them and seemed to me to be more of a liability than asset, standing around most of the time with nothing to do yet unwilling to give a helping hand when asked. I enjoyed creating rain by dipping a large branch full of leaves in the river, then shaking it over the heads of the young lovers who both used the peach-based skin cream and as a result had peach-like complexions. When a misty romantic scene was needed I borrowed a chain saw and stirred up a cloud of dust from the exhaust. The dust was caught in the shafts of sunlight coming through the trees and created a wonderful, surreal effect.

They eventually returned home and left me in a reflective mood, financially solvent but wondering if these people really came from the same planet as I did.

One of them actually returned to purchase a piece of land near the town. He then turned up in a bus with a wife, several children and several friends. This was a most unusual bunch of weirdos, drug users and drug dealers from London and I most sincerely regret to this day ever having had any part of introducing them to the area. My only defence is that I had no idea that they were going to turn out to be to be such an undesirable lot. One of them was a rather loud individual called Hamish, who soon got into trouble and chose to blow his brains out; he is buried in Bolson's boot hill.

Visitors

Some of my friends in Buenos Aires decided to pay me a visit in my second or third year in Patagonia. Once the snow had disappeared it was not unusual to hear the sound of a vehicle going up the valley, and one got used to listening as they changed gear, stopped or turned off the road to come down into this beautiful little haven. Unexpectedly one warm, sunny day, two cars arrived bringing a welcome group of faces I had not seen for a long time. I really enjoyed their company as they enjoyed my homemade bread, barbecued meat and local wine, accompanied by news of people I had almost forgotten and references to what was going on in the world I used to belong to.

This visit left me unsettled and I had to accept that the novelty of simple basic living had worn off, and the limited contact with the locals was no substitute for stimulating conversation.

On a few occasions people would turn up who were travelling through South America; one couple came all the way from Alaska and was headed for Tierra del Fuego.

Hippies, adventurers and professional travellers would appear, hoping for a bath or looking for a safe place to empty their truck and reorganise things. They were almost without exception great people to have around. The only exception was a couple of German girls who spent a week resting and organising themselves, only to steal a large part of my emergency stores and a felt hat when they left. I had bought the hat in Vienna a few years earlier and it was warm and waterproof and was one of my treasures. The canned goods and chocolate they took were eventually replaced but my favourite hat had gone for ever.

Another factor, which hastened my eventual departure, was the corruption in official circles. I had cut down some trees to build my cabin but I needed to cut more to finance my vision of creating a 'Dude Ranch'. With this in mind I planted some eight-thousand trees, mostly cypress pine, before applying for permission to cut down more trees. Convinced that the office dealing with woodland and forestry would be impressed with my attempts at reforestation, I made my application.

From the outset it was obvious that these people were out to feather their own nests and saw me as nothing more than a potential source of backhanders.

Everything I had done was problematic and what I wanted to do would require all kinds of legal work. It was made clear that there might be a solution but it would depend. Depend on what exactly was not made clear. This was transparently some kind of racket and I went away to think about it.

Here was my old enemy back to haunt me again, dishonesty and wheeling dealing by little men with a little bit of authority. I had looked after the forest that I owned and had planted many more trees than I would ever cut down, yet I could only see distasteful expectations being created in my future by these greedy little bureaucrats.

My attempts to become self sufficient by growing vegetables became a serious battle. The rabbits, the deer and the hares were eventually wired off and I began to have hopes of success when, in one night, the wild boar came in and totally trashed the whole garden, including the fence posts, wire netting and the produce.

I started having thoughts about returning home to that distant land called Scotland.

Skiing

Once I had decided to return home I got the offer of a job on the ski slopes near the tourist town of Bariloche. The slopes were attracting thousands of skiers from all over the world, especially enthusiasts and professional skiers from countries in the northern hemisphere who, once their ski season was over, could move south and carry on skiing. This ski resort, situated on the *Cerro Catedral* or Cathedral Mountain, almost seven thousand feet high, is simply spectacular. It gets its name from the pillars of rock stretching heavenwards like medieval cathedral spires.

The man made architecture of the whole region, perhaps in an effort to compete with, or complement, this natural spectacle, has a unique quality. The solid magnificence of some of the modern buildings reflects the essence of old Patagonia so well and the overall effect of natural and man made beauty never fails to catch the first-time visitor by surprise.

The first requirement for this job was to be able to speak English and also to have some kind of qualification in the food industry. The main job was to do something about the catering, which was unable to cope with the ever-increasing demands. There was a restaurant, known as the *"mil doscientos"* at one-thousand-two-hundred meters, and a smaller one at about two-thousand meters and then, at the very top - something over two thousand meters - there was an alpine hotel, which was not always accessible and was known locally as the 'hotel on top of the world'.

I had a good look at what was going on and came up with a simple plan, which not only got over the problem of feeding more people but eventually, once the system got under way, also gave me lots of free time to polish up my poor skiing skills.

I had twelve set meals photographed and displayed high on the walls of the entrance areas. They were written in Spanish and English and the prices were clearly displayed below each dish. In order to acquire the meal of your choice, you simply had to get in the queue, pick up the dish you wanted and pay on the way to the tables. The new challenge then became to keep the hot counter supplied, but that soon fell into place and we quickly went from selling two thousand meals a day to seven thousand a day. Since the cooks and staff were paid according to the meals sold, I was able to count on their collaboration. The one person who challenged my authority was the union boss, so after watching him for a while I named him overall foreman and increased his wages. You never saw such a transformation in a human being. From that day on he defended me whenever the cooks and waiters had a problem and I was able to leave him to keep order and discipline while I mixed with the tourists and improved my skiing skills or sat on the raised deck and got a suntan. Being part of the administration, I wore a badge that allowed me to ignore the queues for the ski lifts and always go straight to the front. I got used to this privilege and only when I later became a 'normal' skier back in Scotland and had to get in line once again, did I notice the difference.

The Stranger

I had noticed a smart looking chap in the lower restaurant several times, mainly because he did not ski and so was dressed differently to the majority of our visitors. One day he invited me to have a coffee with him and we chatted for a while, then arranged to have lunch at the mountain top hotel the following day, weather permitting.

Over lunch he asked me if I would be willing to go to Chile with him to advise the Association of Agriculture and Livestock on how to handle the cattle situation in Chile. I was quietly alarmed that this fellow had picked me out and quickly explained that I was just a poor farmer with a smallholding doing a job to make some cash. He looked at me for what seemed a long time then he told me who I was, where I came from, and even mentioned the rotten deal I had had from the Vesteys; he also hinted at my precarious financial situation.

I felt numb, exposed, my anonymity had been blown and somebody had tabs on me!!!

I felt a bit scared.

Eventually I told him to cut out the small talk and asked, "Just who are you and what is going on?" His reply went something like this, "Well I was told that you would not beat about the bush, so I'll talk to you frankly and clearly".

I was all ears; my senses were working overtime.

It turned out that he was a very rich hotel owner and tourist operator and had interests in several South American countries. He was very well connected and helped the national security agencies to keep an eye on anyone living near the frontier. I had a piece of land near the Chilean border, I was a foreigner, I was worth investigating. The authorities in Buenos Aires were able to tell my whole story, and there you have it. When he got the whole picture of who I was, he realised that I may be of help with the situation in the Chilean cattle industry, with which he was also connected. He was very persuasive that I should inspect the situation in Chile and then address the Association of Agriculture and Livestock in the south of Chile before talking to the government in the capital.

Across the Cordillera

When this new situation presented itself my focus had been on winding things up in Argentina and returning home to Scotland. This unexpected development threw me completely off course, not only because it had been so unexpected but it was a shock for me to discover that, far from having disappeared into the mountains and having been forgotten, somebody was actually keeping tabs on me.

I eventually agreed to go to Chile and meet the cattle breeders and give them my view of things, but I made it clear that I had no intention of becoming any more involved than necessary. As it turned out the job was fairly uncomplicated and after two weeks of visiting the ranches, talking and inspecting the processing plants I gave a talk to the Association. The situation was roughly that just at the time when the health gurus were persuading us that fat beef was no longer good for us the Chilean beef industry was producing some good quality, lean cattle, which seemed to fit in with the new requirements. The processing plants were in a mess due to over-staffing, which was an inheritance from the communist 'jobs for everyone' policy and they just needed a strong management and to be slimmed down in order to become efficient. The challenge was how to get the beef from the Pacific coast to the world markets, and this was a job for the Chilean government together with the big international beef importers with whom I had no desire to become involved. Everyone seemed pleased with my visit and, for me, after having lived in a very simple log cabin with no electricity nor running water for almost four years, the luxury of chauffeured cars and exquisite food in five-star hotels was quite a pleasant, and a totally unexpected, luxury.

It had taken me four years to get the desire to hide away from it all out of my system, so now it was time to move on. I sold the piece of land, which I had only partially developed and, after a month in Buenos Aires, took passage on a Dutch cargo-passenger ship back to Europe.

The new phase in my life would be a little less about travelling the world and a little more about a personal journey homeward and inward.

I DID IT MY WAY

.

Goodbye to Big Business

Out of Work in the UK

I returned to Scotland and received a letter confirming that my UK pension contributions had been paid during my time in Argentina. A few weeks later the company wrote saying that actually during the years I had worked for them, they had not paid my national insurance contributions as promised, also that they were unable to assist me with the pension I had paid into in Argentina. This meant that my UK pension had not been paid, my Argentine pension was not forthcoming and of course my promised company pension had never materialised.

I found extreme difficulty in obtaining employment but this was eventually explained when I was confidently and secretively informed that I had been blacklisted by the Vesteys. Someone must have accepted all the nasty stuff written by Bent, and so the personnel people had put out the word that I should not be employed. My belief in humankind has been seriously challenged, especially when it comes to those individuals blessed with so much wealth and privilege but unwilling or unable to acknowledge their responsibilities. This blacklisting was quite apparent when, as soon as I took the Vestey name out of my CV, I had no problem finding employment. It was quite ironic and amusing that when I spent some of my unemployed time at Queens College, Cambridge, in the company of several hundred fellow Mensa members from across the world, it transpired that about fifty percent of these top international IQ people were, like myself, unemployed.

In spite of all these setbacks I still like to believe that Lord Sam Vestey was unaware of what transpired because I still believe that he is, or certainly was, a decent human being at heart and had the truth concerning these developments ever got through to him, he would certainly not have believed Bent, nor would he have accepted that after twenty years of totally honest hard work that I should be treated so savagely. I also understand that my assistant in Buenos Aires received a company pension as well as a UK and Argentine pension, all of which were denied me, although I spent about four times as many years with the company as he did and I did a much, much better job for the company on all levels. He is just one of my staff but there are literally hundreds who have retired with a decent pension and this includes those who stole from and embezzled the company. I just feel that it is appropriate that these things be put on record although I hold no anger or bad feeling in this regard.

My life experiences have made me who I am and I have no regrets or hard feelings, so I give thanks for the adventures, past present and future and get on with finishing this wee book. It is partly these wonderful, if incredible, anecdotes that fill my rich life and hold me in anticipation of the next new adventure.

Odd Jobs

After returning to the UK I worked as a consultant, designing and building refrigeration plants as well as being appointed chief executive of a small organisation in Shetland, where I had the privilege of meeting some of the nicest people in the world. I spent a year in Glasgow working in the beef industry followed by another stint abroad working in Saudi Arabia and Egypt as a project manager for a German company. This experience finally convinced me that the business world had taught me all that I wanted to know and that I wanted nothing more to do with clever or sharp business practices and money grabbing. This was not me claiming the moral high ground; I was just truly sick of the attitude that if it put money in your pocket, then it was acceptable.

My great wealth, for which I give my deepest heart-felt thanks, lies in my independence from any man-made club, society or institution. I have given my power away to nobody and I am free to manifest my own destiny, which I do together with Susan, my mate. (When I give this to my friend Carol to read she will tell me to get off of my soap box and return to the anecdotes.)

The Laughterhouse

In Saudi my job had been that of project manager for the German company that had built nine large factories around the kingdom. These were, according to the German company, all finished and ready to operate. The Saudis, however, who had been learning how to do business the hard way, said that they would not pay the outstanding monies until they had seen the factories in operation. This was to be my job as project manager and it was not long before the enormity of the job became obvious. One outstanding feature, apparent from the beginning, was the large number of forms, sheets of rules and detailed paperwork to be filled in before and after even the smallest job could be carried out. The big halal slaughter house built as a show piece in Jeddah was to be the first to be commissioned, so when two large trucks arrived full of tea chests containing the paperwork for the factory we started unpacking the hundreds of thousands of bits of paper, which would be required for the place to function. Now I was working with a group of men from the UK, and for several weeks we had little to do as we waited for things to arrive. One result of being confined to a boring house with no music allowed, no social life, no alcohol, and so on we had become like a bunch of naughty schoolboys looking for a diversion. It was in this frame of mind that we unpacked the chests full of these millions of papers, only to discover that someone back in Dusseldorf had misspelt the word

Slaughterhouse. The first S was missing. We had literally millions of LAUGHTERHOUSE requisition forms, job description forms, receipts etc, etc, etc. In our frame of mind we found this to be hilarious and we spent days inventing things we might be able do with all of these laughter papers.

When the chief engineer came out from Germany I was invited together with Major Donald Cameron Caruthers, one of the team, to dinner at a local restaurant. All was going well, when in an effort to entertain our rather loud, overpowering and intense boss, I told him the hilarious story of the Laughterhouse. When I had finished telling my funny story his face went bright red and the veins in his neck swelled up as he thumped the table and screamed that there was nothing funny about such a disaster. I was afraid that he might even hit me at one point, which would have been interesting since my good friend Carruthers had spent all his time in the army with the SAS and was very protective of me. Needless to say the dinner was not a success, which did not bother me very much but my heart really went out to the poor unfortunate who had made the initial spelling mistake back in the fatherland.

The real truth is that my heart was no longer inspired by the business world; especially this multi-billion dollar melee that dominated life in Saudi Arabia. As dozens of international corporations, attracted by the sea of oil dollars, vied for contracts and very large money deals, this money-fever seemed to permeate down through the ranks to affect the ex-pats from all over the world who would, at times, do anything and put up with uncomfortable situations as long as they made money. I did not finish my contract for a number of reasons, so following a short time working in Egypt for the same company I returned home to look for an occupation that would be meaningful and also give me a sense of fulfilment.

Alternative Practice

I had not felt particularly comfortable with so-called successful businessmen ever since my days in Argentina but having worked in the food industry and taken a BSc. equivalent in food technology I had become interested in nutrition, microbiology and things like supplements and vitamins and general health.

I also had a dramatic introduction to self-healing when, following a parachuting accident in the '80s, I was told by the doctors - for the second time in my life - that I would never walk again. Yet, after renouncing conventional medicine, I was able to walk again within a few months. This, I must emphasise, is not to say that I would want to promote any negative approach to conventional medicine. I merely wish to say that my experience did teach me that other options and attitudes are at times very effective; and of course I went through this experience just when I was contemplating natural healing and complementary health care in general.

I also had a long-standing interest in the effect of personal attitudes and habits on health, which include an invisible dimension. When I say 'invisible dimension' I am referring principally to thoughts and attitudes, and the multitude of ramifications that affect our health. These include things like homeopathy, acupuncture, placebos, absent healing and other aspects of our being, which do not sit comfortably with Newtonian thinking. So, as I looked around for a new career I eventually gravitated towards the world of natural, complementary health care.

With a few certificates in disciplines like Spagyric medicine, kinesiology, reflexology and others, I set up a practice in the English south coast town of Brighton.

Holism

This was the early '80s and I could not avoid this new buzzword, HOLISTIC, that was being increasingly used in connection with alternative or complementary health care.

The more I looked at what was being claimed to be holistic practice, the more I became aware of the abuse and unfounded use of the word by many who chose to use it without taking the trouble to ask what it meant. I started looking into this subject and eventually ended up writing and lecturing on it, so what had started out as a question in my mind became an almost fulltime occupation for a while.

What developed for me was a basic approach to all who came for help, where what I was doing, and why I did it the way I did, was explained before any commitment was made by either party. I developed what I named my HOLOROSE; a kind of matrix symbol to guide one through the fundamental areas in which we exist, mentally and physically as well as emotionally and spiritually and this symbol was to eventually develop into something more fundamental and far-reaching.

When transferring ideas or feelings into mere words it is inevitably disappointing to observe how the intended message becomes less than the original, creating a watered down version.

The HOLOROSE eventually developed into the HOLOSAPIENCE and was always an attempt to express my feelings and knowingness through symbolism, in the hope that it may do a better job than a verbal approach.

What is printed on page 135 is an attempt to symbolise the oneness acknowledging itself, as well as symbolising some of the invisible components that are all part of who we are.

Many years after creating these symbols I was to learn how 'The Creation' took place when the Oneness went inwards and contemplated itself, so an alternative title might be 'The Creation' or 'In The Beginning', but the title is of little importance alongside the message and that 'knowingness', when words alone are not up to the job.

Over a period of several years I was to have some interesting and even spectacular results with my new occupation. I experienced inexplicable changes in some of the people who came to see me and I found that at times I could touch someone suffering pain and the pain would go away. Due to my initial lack of understanding what this was all about I tended to be secretive, while at the same time I gave it a lot of thought. Again my instinct told me to accept that something was working through me from time to time and that I should not make too much of it. In spite of keeping a low profile I was eventually interviewed and photographed by the Brighton Argos, which I must admit promoted my practice and helped to increase my badly needed income.

It should be remembered that in the 1980s alternative or complementary health care was still seen as something akin to witchcraft, mumbo jumbo or worse by most people; while I saw the positive results of my work, I was also constantly reminded that this was a pioneering venture and, as such, I would not be allowed to make any mistakes or to be seen as less than totally authentic. Two little anecdotes from this period may help to illustrate what went on in my self-invented and, I believe, unique, practice and what the results could be. Let me add that I was always aware that, while I was obliged to learn these new disciplines, I knew that whatever healing took place was always through me rather than from me.

There appeared one day a lady who was well into her seventies. She did not have an appointment but was willing to wait in the waiting room until we had a spare moment. I say we, because I had a nurse who helped me part time. When I asked this lady why she had come to see me, she said that she felt that she was going mad. She went on to explain that she had been attending a psychoanalyst for eight years and a friend had suggested that since she wanted to see someone else who would listen to her I might fit the bill. My nurse and I exchanged glances and we sat very quietly and listened. She repeated her suspicion that she might be going mad and we learned that her husband had died eight years previously and had left her a large sum of money, in spite of which she had been getting progressively more unhappy and worried over the years.

I went through the normal procedure, explaining how the blue area in my holorose represented the mind while the red and yellow indicated body and emotions respectively. In view of the intensive eight-year psychoanalysis that this lady had been subjected to, it was decided to give the mind a rest and start off by paying more attention to the physical body and, eventually, the emotions.

This approach was largely exploratory and guided by intuition and a little common sense. We started off with reflexology, which is always a gentle, non-invasive way to touch people without frightening them. She relaxed immediately and responded so well that we asked if she would be interested in a full body massage on the following visit. She thought this was an excellent idea but once she was dressed and ready to go home we could not get her to make an appointment. Three days later she appeared in the waiting room once more, and again waited until we had time to attend to her. She was very quiet as she went through the process of being wrapped in warm towels then being invited to relax as her body was gently worked on. There was very little conversation during the session and I got the feeling that something quite significant might be going on in her head. She left once again without an appointment. After about ten days we thought that we might have lost her and I was actually going over her notes to see if there might be something I had overlooked when, unannounced and quiet as a mouse, there she was in the waiting room. On enquiring she said that she was feeling fine, although to me she seemed to be a little uptight.

I suggested more of the same and left the nurse to attend to her. Again she was very quiet but seemed to relax and enjoy having her body worked on. I think that we had accepted that she was never going to make an appointment and, sure enough, she left without any commitment to return. Two days later she appeared and asked if I would please work on her or at least be present when she was being treated. I complied with her wishes and about twenty minutes into the session she suddenly started crying. More than crying, this was a deep wailing and sobbing from some place deep within. We supported her all we could, and allowed the emotions to surface. Over the following weeks we learned during numerous sessions that she had had no physical contact since her husband had died eight years previously. She had also been treated for depression, insomnia and all manner of suspected mental problems. She confessed that the only treatment that made her feel well was the physical massage, and it was during one of these sessions that I showed her the holorose again and pointed out that the blue area, representing the mind, had perhaps had all the attention in the eight years of psychoanalysis while the other areas had been ignored. I also explained that when we worked on the red area representing the body, she had eventually allowed the yellow - emotional - area to come to the fore and balance things. This was what gave her what she called a 'cosy, safe feeling'. Once she had accepted this, I made a point of going over the holorose chart once again, this time pointing to the centre where there was a large 'S'.

"There is a fourth area," I explained, "which is different for all of us, so I call it 'S' for 'something'. What is this missing 'something' in your view?" I asked.

"Oh," she instantly replied, "that is my spiritual self, and I know that that is what ties everything together for all of us". Towards the end of her treatment the nurse asked how she was and did she feel all right mentally. Our elderly patient turned to face the nurse and replied in no uncertain terms, "Now don't you dare insinuate that I'm mad, THERE IS NOTHING WRONG WITH ME!"

Holosapience

As I mentioned earlier, this word developed as a result of my work with the holistic concept and it is an evolution of the holorose symbol. Holosapience takes the concept further and attempts to explain the concept of oneness and of the oneness sometimes acknowledging itself, hence the experience of Holosapience, the human being aware of itself as the Oneness on a journey. I found that this concept was a powerful part of the healing process for many who came for help.

When I started this kind of work most people were very sceptical but some grateful patients who understood the uphill battle I had with this widespread scepticism sent me thank you letters and testimonials and I take the liberty to print one such communication. By the way, the nicest name this man called me was a fraud, he ridiculed all non-allopathic health care until his wife, out of desperation, read him the riot act and I was allowed to see him.

He sat in a chair and refused to do anything when I first met him. This letter, which he wrote to me following his treatment, tells the rest.

Crawford Kemp
140 Valley Drive
West Dene
Brighton, East Sussex

Dear Mr Kemp,

I am writing to thank you, most sincerely, for all your help recently, which has now resulted in a complete recovery after some six years of misery. I cannot emphasise enough the difference now to when I first came to you. I am now able to resume a full life, both at home and at work. I sincerely hope your practice will continue to prosper and have already recommended your expertise to family, friends and business colleagues.

Let us hope that those who are initially sceptical, as I certainly was, will open their minds to what is possible and not necessarily, understandable. Likewise let us hope that the medical profession comes to acknowledge the obvious necessity of considering alternatives when they are unable to find the solutions by conventional methods. I shall recommend your certain talents to others, but in the meantime please feel free to show this letter to both your clients and others, as evidence.

For convenience, I have detailed my history, as far as I am able, to give some idea of the condition I was in prior to your assistance. I shall be pleased to confirm any of the details to those who may be interested.

In March 1983, having suffered nothing more serious than an occasional bout of hay fever, I found myself totally incapable of doing any kind of work at the age of 30! The reason being that I was suffering from such excruciating headaches I had to be continually sedated.

The apparent cause was diagnosed by two senior Consultants at Addenbrooke Hospital, Cambridge; namely a trapped nerve in the neck area of the spine. Addenbrooke being a foremost research hospital, I had no reason to doubt this diagnosis until horrified by the proposed treatment: operate to remove one or two 'discs' and weld the vertebrae together! After being told that this would probably result in 30% loss of movement to my neck, I began looking for another solution! I found an Osteopath who did alleviate the pain after some 6 weeks but it returned 10 months later and subsequent treatment did not help.

As a result of my doctor constantly being called to help, he had me admitted to the Royal Sussex Hospital following a particularly severe attack, when injections of heavy sedative failed. The hospital specialists referred me to Hurstwood Park, the foremost neurological centre in the U.K. Their investigations, including a mylogram, resulted in contradictions of previous ones insofar that they proved no trapped nerve had existed or did then exist. This caused a further investigation and I eventually found out that I have migraine; or at least that was the diagnosis by the senior Neurologist at Guys Hospital in London. His treatment, however, was to keep me on more sedatives and anti-depressants since he found that they worked for migraines!

Needless to say, this did not really help as I still found it difficult to do my job and I still suffered ever-more frequent attacks, which were beginning to gain intensity. To such an extent were these headaches being painful and unbearable, that I could not drive and I could not do my work. At the time I last saw you I had already been off work for nearly two weeks. When I first came to your 'surgery' I did not really believe you could help where so many specialists had failed. Your treatment then and subsequently has not only stopped my headaches altogether but I am now fit and healthy as I was 6 years ago! My doctor has no answer.

I can only emphasise my admiration for your treatment and offer my profound and sincere thanks for changing my life from the problem it had become. I now look forward to resuming my successful career and enjoying my family life. Please keep up the good work and if you ever need to reassure a sceptical patient, just show them this, which I certify to be entirely factual. Indeed I have not, if anything, emphasised enough the sheer agony of those attacks. However, with your continued presence I am assured of continued good health. May yours be as good!

Very best wishes and grateful thanks.

Yours sincerely Ian R. Cleaver

30th June 1989, East Sussex

Going Home

New Age Or New Edge?

For some time I had been feeling homesick, and as I moved into my sixties I started to look for a way to move back to my native Scotland.

Another new period of my life was looming over the horizon but, perhaps, was about something more than just physically moving to Scotland. The accent, quite unintentionally, seemed to be on me just being more than doing, which I found a bit scary, since it invited me to stop, and to take a good frank look at myself.

When I eventually came home to Scotland, more than twenty years ago now, it felt like arriving in a completely new place, since that person who had moved away all these years before no longer existed and a different me was here to take his place.

I had no desire to return to the Clyde, to my place of birth or to my childhood memories, but I definitely wanted to live in Scotland once again.

I had been told to expect the unexpected when I was recommended an alternative lifestyle at a New Age community in Moray on the east coast of Scotland, an area I had briefly visited in the 1930's as a child but remembered nothing of.

After a very brief look at the place I decided that this might be as good a way as any to get established in an area where I did not know anyone. I have to confess to some unrealistic illusions about living in an anti-establishment, non-conformist, free-thinking and futuristic community. However, In spite of encountering some really sincere people and many well-intentioned individuals, the old saying 'you cannot be disillusioned unless you start out with illusions' became my reality. This place, although it gave me a foothold to start off with, turned out to include mainly pro-establishment, conservative individuals who were often incomers from places which tend to be over-disciplined, conformist and establishment-oriented. In spite of being disappointed at what I found, and partly because I had no better alternative, I decided to stay in the area.

This New Age community does attract some interesting visiting lecturers and musicians from time to time; as well as, I'm sorry to say, unscrupulous opportunists. I enjoyed the woods and the beach and soon had my own boat on the bay. In spite of this very non-Scottish, foreign community not being what I was looking for, I was back in my native Scotland and so I decided to enjoy what was available; after all I had never had a new experience that had not taught me something.

It took me some time to understand that most of these new age people were incomers who had no interest in Scotland but saw themselves as living in a kind of bubble where the Germans and the English very much ruled the roost and being Scottish actually made me a bit of an outsider. Another interesting observation was that many of these people in spite of their tendency toward arrogance, seemed to be misfits who had found a place where not fitting in did not seem to be a drawback, and I could not fault that. The level of religious belief and so-called spiritual practice was, as one visitor from Switzerland put it, 'at kindergarten level' and when one of the longtime residents asked her what was wrong with that, she replied, "Nothing at all, but this is the first time I have come across a kindergarten where the pupils do the teaching", which seemed to sum it up very well. One old - religious - misconception that seemed to be rife was that of confusing the symbol with the reality. A profundity of symbols, Angel cards, lucky charms and things to dangle round the neck or wrist or stick on the bumper of your auto machine are witness to this tendency, and is big business at the community shop. Giving one's power away to stars, crystals, workshop leaders, and gurus is popular amongst some members and visitors. I have taken the trouble to look into the workings of this rather undefined organisation and come up with some of their commonly shared concepts, which seem to take the place of any fixed credo or dogma. For instance it would seem that the New Age heaven which is referred to, is for many a destination somewhere out yonder, and more a physical place than a personal practice, or an experience; in other words for most it is a noun and not a verb. My observations only served to make me feel at odds with the place, which in all fairness, never claimed to be more than what it is. If, however, we take into account the fact that modern quantum physics has shown beyond doubt that our consciousness and energy create our reality, then I would respectfully question exactly what reality it is that they are hoping to create.

Amit Goswami in his book *The Visionary Window* states that:

"the social effect of this new-age brand of spirituality has been to enable opportunists to co-opt spirituality for selfish material pursuits."

Whilst he was not referring to the Findhorn Foundation specifically and without going into detail there is ample evidence of this opportunism in practice within this community, and to their credit I have on several occasions heard some members voicing their concern around this issue. I consider some of the people who come here to make money at the expense of the gullible to be nothing short of fraudulent, while at the same time I acknowledge and appreciate the presence from time to time of intelligent, inspiring people and interesting lecturers.

In this community, much is made of workshops and, having participated in workshops, and indeed having run a number of workshops in the UK and abroad as well as talking about workshops, self-development, holism and Oneness both on radio and TV, I have some personal observations on the subject.

The enormous workshop industry has made money for a lot of people but when compared to the useful impact that it has had, I would suggest that there is much to be questioned here.

I have seen these charming workshop leaders - and I have been one myself - as they invite you to make a breakthrough. They are sincere and hard working and they make you feel so good. While you are attending the workshop you look up to them and you enjoy their company.

It is not only you, the participant, however who is being affected as the workshop plays itself out on its mythical stage. The workshop leader is also being invited to accept the energy that you are offering her, or him, and to use it to become your temporary guru. This is a subtle but very common situation, which can sometimes result in workshop leaders being unable to resist the temptation of adulation, compliments and requests for help, inflating even the most cautious of egos. I observe that some workshop leaders actually start to see themselves as gurus and display varying degrees of arrogance.

You, who have paid good money to have this experience, may find on returning home that it is difficult to tell your friends just why you felt so inspired or exactly what happened at the workshop. After a week or two when the magic has worn off, you want to repeat the experience and so you sign up for another workshop and so for some people this becomes the start an unfulfilling career as a workshop 'junkie'.

Sooner or later you may look back on all the wonderful workshops that you have enjoyed and ask yourself why you have not changed after all these inspiring, if expensive, experiences and why you still have the same challenges or issues in your life. I would suggest that the message might be that since more than 90% of all the things we do are directed from the subconscious mind, it is therefore the subconscious that needs to be addressed. That of course, will not happen by listening to lectures, or reading books nor, as it happens, attending workshops.

I see this as being a parallel journey to those community members who have been going through all the New Age rituals and practices for twenty, thirty or forty years without much evidence of moving on, getting rid of their old challenges or the issues in their lives.

New Edge science recognises the need to address the subconscious and to this end effective belief-change modalities are available for those who are willing to swap the workshop habit for these simple disciplines like Psych-K, EFT, or any one of a long list of well-proven modalities.

This is beginning to sound less like an anecdote and more like a sales pitch, which it isn't. So I'll leave it by suggesting that you reconsider spending your money on workshops, and instead that you address your subconscious.

Even though I have stayed geographically in the same area as the New Age centre I initially visited, my interests have centred on New Edge Science, and it is here in the quantum world, where "science and spirit meet", that I have been able to enjoy more adventures, while I seem to generate even more questions.

So, having come to the end of my wee book of anecdotes, I have to recognise that there are many aspects of my life that I have not shared with you. Of course a few more interesting anecdotes come to my mind, like the time I rowed from Buenos Aires in Argentina to Carmelo in Uruguay with my good friend Peter Lewis, or the exploits of Johnny G. who won the cropdusting rights for all of Peru in a poker game and ended up with a squadron of cropdusting aeroplanes. But, having reminisced long enough, I leave these personal experiences for the present, and focus more on how they have changed my thinking and influenced my views, which I include in the following appendix.

Appendix

So What?

I would like to think that these little anecdotes may have been entertaining and even interesting, and while I have had fun putting them down on paper I now feel, as it comes to an end, that something else begs acknowledgement.

Some kind of reply to those readers who put this book down and ask, "So what?" is perhaps in order.

First of all let me say that the experience of digging into the past and trying to remember incidents long gone has not only been fun, but also therapeutic and, at times, disturbing as well as unexpectedly challenging. As these stories came back to me I felt myself becoming the observer, and what I was observing was a stranger with whom I had never spent time before; that stranger was myself. I followed this new acquaintance through a lifetime of anecdotes and while he was getting on with his life I had time to contemplate and learn all kinds of things from his mistakes and experiences. If one acquires wisdom from the mistakes one makes then I should, in theory, be a very wise person. On the other hand, there is perhaps no such thing as a mistake since so-called mistakes also have their place in the bigger picture, and I have to accept that this fits in well with one of my favourite sayings, which comes from Neale Donald Walsch, who likes to say things like, "this is exactly how it is, unless it isn't".

When you come across any kind of paradox, stop and take a second look; there is bound to be a golden thought buried in there somewhere.

Perhaps for me the most significant conclusion to emerge is that everything we see around us is a manifestation of a thought and, at last I have come to understand that for instance, when we look at a bus going by we are looking at source energy, or thought, made manifest. One illustration of this can be appreciated in the creation of an entity like you, reading these words right now. You are made up of fifty trillion cells, but started off as one cell, all on it's own. That one single cell was not endowed with two arms, a head, eyes, legs and a torso, nor did it support any political view, yet thanks to thought, it grew into you, who are able to read this book and do a million miraculous things. You are the end result of thought, which is, like the many important ingredients in the universe, invisible to the ordinary person living on this hertzian plane that we share.

You have so many vitally important components in your makeup that are totally invisible, so if I were to remove all your visible bits and leave you only with your invisible bits, what would you look like? Do you not think that you would become an orb? Would you be visible only on the infrared spectrum?

Invisible thoughts, feelings and emotions introduce us to love, hate, inspiration, fear and also to creativity. These feelings, thoughts and experiences are all part of our significant and all-important self; our invisible self. These are always present, and invisible thoughts plus invisible opinions are being created as you read these words; words that stir up your invisible feelings and will affect your invisible attitudes. These are the attitudes, which cause visible illness and wellness.

So why have I started philosophising in a book, which started off as a collection of anecdotes?

Well, having had the opportunity to observe my quite mundane personal experiences at my leisure it has become plainly obvious to me that THE INVISIBLE WORLD of thoughts, feelings and emotions are not given the recognition in our modern materialistic world, which they might be. And why is this important?

Well let me explain why our invisible selves are all important. This wonderful world that I have explored, enjoyed and at times abused, over the last eighty-three years is, in my opinion, in mortal danger and our survival depends on recognising our place in the overall picture. We are in charge of our thoughts, which create reality, and from where I am standing our future reality looks very unstable. Now that I am aware that the future will be created mostly by my thoughts, and your thoughts, and that we become who we think we are, so I would like to confront you, and challenge you, by asking, "Just who do you think you are anyway?" The answer you give, of course, will help determine who you are going to be and indeed who we are all going to be.

Before signing off, there are a few more thoughts and ideas, which surfaced as the anecdotes developed, but which it felt would be better held back and included in this appendix. I offer them as separate subjects with their own sub-titles and as will be seen, some of them have a bearing on one of the subjects touched on earlier, while others stand on their own.

Scotland versus Lithuania

It was in the mid-1950s that I married into a Lithuanian family. This was one family out of millions who had tried to escape the 'isms' of old Europe. These people had seen enough of Nazi-ism, Commun-ism and Imperial-ism so, like many others, had escaped to South America looking for a new life in the new world.

Life for poor immigrants was usually hard, but South American sunshine and promises of better things to come were beguiling and convincing.

My new father-in-law was called Jonas and he had managed to get a job and build himself a small house for himself and his family, who were foreigners in a foreign land, just like myself.

Jonas had little formal education but a keen, inquisitive mind had gone a long way to self-education, so we were able to enjoy long conversations as he filled me in on life in the Baltic as compared to Scotland or South America.

One interesting discovery during our exchange of national customs and history seemed to be almost uncanny until it became obvious that anybody's experiences of colonialism, no matter where, are going to be similar.

The fact that Lithuania had once been the largest country in Europe came as a surprise to me, and offered no similarities with Scotland. When, however, it became a small country and had not just one large, imperialistic neighbour to contend with, but two, I began to see some points of similarity.

Jonas started off one evening, as we sat in the garden, telling me how challenging it had been when the Russians had dominated his country.

"You know they tried to kill off our national language and replace it with Russian," he told me. "Everything was in Russian, even the radio was all in a foreign language and it caused divisions within families and even fights."

"Tell me," I said. "Was there a death sentence for anyone speaking Lithuanian or wearing Lithuanian clothes?"

"Not actually a death sentence but you sometimes got beat up or arrested," he replied.

"Well," said I, "in my country we were put to death for playing Scottish music, wearing the kilt or even just being suspected of being a Jacobite."

"NO, no, no," pleaded Jonas, "don't make fun of what I say, it is not funny." Then, to satisfy his insatiable curiosity, "What's a Jacobite?"

The story he had to tell became one of division between the generations as the young girls dated the invaders and the young men joined the hated Russian army. He told stories of Lithuanians spying on their own people and working for 'the enemy', almost identical to the story of the Black Watch, which was originally a group who worked for the Hanoverian enemy and spied on fellow Scots; their base, incidentally, is still at Fort George, which is only a few miles along the coast from where I live now.

We spoke of the Native North American peoples who saw their own people work for the army as scouts and trackers, often leading the army to their own people in order to attack them. We agreed that it was great to be away from it all, since putting some distance between the old country and one's self seemed to the lessen the pain. One fundamental difference of course was that before he died he had the satisfaction of seeing sovereignty restored to his country while we in Scotland still peacefully wait. When the subject of the gratuitous cruelty meted out following the battle of Culloden came up, my father-in-law, who had first hand experience of the pro-Nazis in his own country, said, "That sounds more like the way Germans behave, not the English." The large numbers of prisoners taken by Cumberland and then murdered, plus the fact of Scots having been sold on slave markets in the Caribbean and America all seemed to reinforce his view. Even more so when he learned that the Duke of Cumberland, known as the butcher of Culloden, was in fact the son of the German King George II of the house of Hanover and whose family name was Saxe-Coburg-Gotha. These common views and experiences were to help us understand each other and strengthen the bond between us.

The Falklands War

I am sometimes asked about the Falklands and the Falklands War. First, let me say that although, following the war, I was about to travel to these islands as an adviser/project manager for the Falklands Island government, I in fact never actually did the job and I have never set foot on the islands; let me add, to my disappointment.

So the best I can do is to offer my point of view without making any claims as to any expertise on the subject.

I was originally made aware of the Falklands when, as a very young naval draughtsman, I worked for MDF (*Metalurgica y Diques Flotantes*) in Montevideo, Uruguay. The boarding house, in which I lived, was owned by a wonderful Swiss lady who had married an Englishman by the name of Mr Hawkins who, in turn, worked for an English company in Montevideo. It was here that I was to meet many interesting travellers, adventurers and ex-pats, most of them trying to escape post-war Europe. This boarding house was also used by many of the Kelpers – Falkland Islanders - travelling north to Europe, or travelling south to the Falklands. At this time there was a ship by the name of *Fitzroy*, which sailed between the Falklands and Montevideo, bypassing Argentina, and I had the pleasure of meeting some of these largely Scottish or descendants' families and so becoming aware of the existence of the Falklands and its people.

Years later I lived in Buenos Aires, where I worked for a large English company and at that time had a wife and two children. I mention this because I once again became aware of the Falklands every time I looked at my children's schoolbooks. Let me explain.

All children attending school in Argentina during the Peron era were subjected to incessant propaganda regarding Argentinean sovereignty over all the islands in that area, in addition to a large wedge of the Antarctic. The school textbooks and even the exercise books carried photographs of the popular dictator, Juan Peron, and his wife Eva, in addition to maps showing the abovementioned areas as a sovereign part of Argentina. After the fall of Peron the photographs were to disappear but the maps were to persist, as well as Argentina's claim to sovereignty. This was partly a political reaction by Peron to years of a lack of national pride and years of being used by foreign organisations as a pseudo colony without the responsibility of the coloniser. It seemed obvious to me that as generation after generation of children used these books, their subconscious would become imprinted with the 'fact' that the Malvinas/Falklands plus a large slice of Antarctica were, without any doubt, part of Argentina. This awareness must surely have become indelibly engraved in the many generations of school children, since the period of somewhere around the late '40s or early '50s. So, once again, I was made aware of these islands through my children and my many discussions on Falklands' history and sovereignty with my Argentine friends. During these discussions, when emotions would surface, the potential for trouble would become all too evident. In addition to this, in the 1960s and 1970s the Argentine authorities took it to their heads to occasionally hint at confiscating property belonging to British citizens, with the accent on the Patagonian area. The point I am trying to make is that I, like many of my fellow UK citizens in Argentina, had been aware of, and interested in, the Falklands for many years and at times a little worried that the Argentine military may talk themselves into doing something irresponsible.

The British Foreign Office, in spite of being aware of Argentina's stance and in spite of, or perhaps because of, the ever-increasing available intelligence from Buenos Aires, opted to gently reduce London's influence in the South Atlantic. They ever so gradually replaced it with, amongst other things, Argentina supplying the islanders with fuel (which meant that the islanders could buy fuel at the same price as it cost on the mainland), regular Argentine commercial flights between Argentina and the Falklands and stronger ties and mutual understanding through Argentine tourism. Also available was medical care in Argentina for the islanders, free secondary education for all the children in the Falklands who wanted it, and we even saw some Kelpers taking out Argentine nationality. When attempting to appreciate the larger picture it might also be noted that the only runway on the islands before the war was built by Argentina.

My personal opinion is that the decisions taken in London no doubt sent signals to the government in Buenos Aires that the UK might not bother to defend the Falklands.

If this developing situation had been allowed to unfold it may well have allowed a mutually acceptable joint administration or something similar to develop between our two countries. After all the proposed discussions put forward in 1974, 1977 and again in 1980 by London to cover subjects like condominium, sovereignty and leaseback seemed to meet little or no resistance from the people who lived in the islands. All this could, I suspect, have led to a civilised agreement between the UK and Argentina, strengthening our friendship rather than turning us into sworn enemies.

Of course we shall never know, because to the eternal shame of both the British and Argentine governments, two hundred years of commerce, real friendship, inter-marriage, mutual understanding and admiration was bludgeoned, almost to death, when the handful of civilians, eighty marines and one unarmed policeman were attacked by a modern army of ten thousand Argentine soldiers.

It is sometimes quite difficult to sit in today's cushioned, media-fed, plastic Scotland and understand what goes on out there in South America, but perhaps we can explore what just might have induced

General Galtieri to add his name to history's long list of military barbarians.

General Galtieri, who took office in 1981, was the latest in a succession of heads of state who had tried to run Argentina since the military *juntas* took over in 1976. This new, 1981, *junta* included General Galtieri, Brigadier Dozo and Admiral Anaya who it is said was influential in persuading Galtieri to go to war, since it seems that he felt that the UK would never take military action to defend the Falklands.

My contact with the military in Argentina was initially through visiting their Military Academy to play rugby against their super-fit cadets, and later as a guest of the very gentlemanly naval cadets at Rio Santiago, against whom I have rowed and with whom I have lived for a few days at a time at their academy. I also have met many of them socially and for some years counted one high-ranking naval officer as one of my best friends.

My professional insight, however, took place during the years when I worked under enormous pressure and in constant danger and kept in almost daily contact with the Argentine Army Intelligence Service, who kept me informed on terrorist activities and potential trouble.

This contact was established when, between 1963 and 1971, I managed the largest packing house in the world, employing some five thousand people and it was thanks to this liaison that I developed some real, intimate insights and impressions of these military men who – in spite of rigorous training, strict discipline and high academic standards - appeared to do themselves a great disservice by limiting their intellectual potential through the acceptance, and love, of dogmas, which tended to limit most discussions, opinions and debates. I must add something to this that I see as very significant, and it is that these well-fed and very fit men who were trained day and night in the craft of war, were then expected to go through a whole lifetime of playing soldiers but never firing a shot in anger.

More importantly, perhaps, to top this, their social lives were confined largely within their own community of fellow officers and it seemed to me at the time that, within the confines of this narrow, male-dominated and chauvinistic comradeship, the higher an individual moved in rank, the smaller his circle of friends or confidantes became. This, in turn, seemed to engender a certain absence of reality when relating to the world 'out there'. It is said that a captain of a ship is the loneliest man on board, and he finds it difficult to get the feel of what is going on, thanks to his limited circle of contacts. I suspect that Galtieri had got himself into a similar kind of situation and it probably only took a little misguided advice of a few who were close to him to convince him to unleash such criminal stupidity.

Similar circumstances are of course evident on both sides and there is no evidence that I am aware of that, in spite of all the superior American CIA-backed British intelligence and a plethora of contacts between the two countries, anything was ever done by London to avert conflict and this, I must add, is one question where I would be happy to be proven wrong.

I personally had suspected that things could become nasty and took steps to protect several expensive properties and some land that I owned in Argentina. I took steps to avoid confiscation several years before war actually broke out, and I find it hard to believe that my friends and I were better informed than Thatcher and her ministers.

Now, in retrospect, it would seem that following such enormous expense, effort and human sacrifice, all that the people in London have is a second-rate document, which by apparent blunder, accepts the surrender of the Argentine forces, but has had - as I understand it – the word UNCONDITIONAL scored out by the officer who signed the surrender document on behalf of the Argentines.

So who, apart from the arms dealers and the undertakers, benefited from this debacle?

First of all it helped the military *junta* in Buenos Aires by taking people's attention away from the disastrous economic situation at home.

Secondly, it greatly helped Thatcher to win another term of office in 1983, which prior to the war had been far from likely. It also no doubt gave the UK's MOD an opportunity to practice its skills and try out new systems in real combat, although to my simple mind almost a thousand dead and almost two thousand wounded seems an awful human price to pay.

To these figures, of course one should really add the 246 British veterans who have committed suicide following the Argentine surrender, plus the Argentine suicide figures, which I have not yet been able to uncover.

Since going into semi-retirement back home in Scotland I have read *Saddled with Darwin* from which it is apparent that before the invasion of the Falklands, the Americans had listening posts along the Chilean-Argentine border, where they could monitor all Argentine troop movements and communications. This is another little piece of the jigsaw, which strengthens my suspicion that London was much more aware of what was going on within the Argentine military leading up to the invasion than has ever been admitted.

My suspicion was further strengthened after I became acquainted with a very interesting schoolteacher who at one time played rugby for the British Army. While casually talking to him about this part of his varied and interesting life he mentioned that he was allowed time off from his normal duties thanks to his quite considerable rugby skills and only once was he told that he could not have time off to play rugby. He went on to explain that he in fact worked as a cartographer for the army and that for a long time leading up to the Falkland war he and his fellow cartographers had been working fulltime on preparing detailed ordinance survey maps of the Falkland Islands. This work was classed as urgent to the extent that even one of the team could not be allowed to represent the army at a rugby match.

It is also evident that the fascist dictator Pinochet, who ran Chile at the time, was a close friend of Thatcher who went to visit him when he was held under house arrest in London, probably to thank him in person for his help leading up to and during the war. So, looking at these facts I have to suspect that we the public have, unsurprisingly, been fed a version of events that don't tell the true story.

The long, detailed Franks report does little more than confirm that the Argentines want sovereignty over the islands and that the people of the Falklands (supported by the government in London) are not going to change their minds. This is a tremendously retrograde state of affairs if you compare it with the situation prior to the war.

The rights and wrongs surrounding territorial claims are complex and colonialism is difficult to defend. If one were to go far enough down that road one might end up asking, should all the Europeans be expelled from the Americas or Africa?

Should the Falklands, which never had an indigenous people, belong to the incomers or to the continent, which is only four hundred miles away? These and a thousand other questions arise and are backed by strongly held views and emotions as soon as the subject is broached. So far we have only seen ineffective politics being played out, followed by unmentionable barbarism. This leaves us with an uncertain future, which is once again being stirred up by Mrs Kitchener and Mr Campbell who, in my view, are both acting irresponsibly when they trade insults, make covert threats and look more like spoiled children than peacemakers.

Getting on for a thousand years after the Christian Crusaders went to war against the great Muslim civilisation the wound is still open, festering and causing suffering all over the world. This would have been no surprise for that great leader of the Muslims, Saladin, who told his third son, el-Melek-ez-Zaher,

"Do the will of God for that is the way of peace. Beware of bloodshed. Trust not in that for spilt blood never sleeps."

This is all too obviously true when one mentions Wounded Knee, the Battle of the Boyne, Guernica, Culloden or Hiroshima.

Will it be true of this war too that managed to replace international commerce, friendship, mutual admiration and innumerable links between the two countries with death, destruction, alienation and hate? Will the blood spilt in the Falklands never sleep or will a solution be found?

Was all this suffering and trauma avoidable or was it the brainchild of an inflated ego belonging to some pompous ass of a politician, or General, or are we all equally responsible for creating war?

Perhaps we should take a leaf out of Nelson Mandela's book and emulate Mandela's experience by sending all politicians and aspiring politicians to jail for twenty-seven years before taking office. Or perhaps we might take to heart the words of the most qualified military general in my lifetime, General Eisenhower, who also became president of the United States, and said in his famous Cross of Iron speech,

"Every gun that is made, every warship launched, every rocket fired signifies in the final sense a theft from those who hunger and are not fed and those who are cold and not clothed."

General Eisenhower goes on to equate the cost of only one heavy bomber with the construction of thirty brick schools or an electric power plant to supply sixty-thousand people. The money used to build one small destroyer could house eight thousand people, and on and on.

Just contemplate what we could do with the forty billion pounds we spend each year via the MOD. Contemplate the jobs this money could create, the scientific advancement potential, the healthcare and support for the elderly. Why did we waste so much money fighting a war, which I am sure was avoidable?

Now, thirty years later I can only hope and pray that we will never see another government in London using the (still existing) Argentine claim to these islands as an excuse to play politics, or to send our young men and women to fight another war.

It is never too late to heal things, and in my opinion, as long as ordinary Argentines and ordinary Brits are allowed to do what they have already been doing for several hundred years, further conflict can be avoided. I am of course talking about forging trust, friendships and commerce, not via institutionalised pomposity, but at a personal level. It is so often through ordinary people that great things are achieved. If we can see beyond the guns, the politics and the flag waving you and I can make a difference.

To help ground ourselves and make contact with simple reality it may be a useful exercise to contemplate for a moment just who these two confronting armies were. First of all the Argentine Army is made up of officers and NCO's who are full time professionals while the main body of the troops are young conscripts doing their obligatory national service. In my experience these young men have never lacked in patriotism, loyalty or courage when told to do something. The British Army of course is made up of full time professional volunteers and arguably the best army in the world.

The Argentine conscripts come very largely from rural areas and have rarely travelled away from home or ever seen the sea but on being told that they were going to liberate some Argentine islands that were in the hands of the '*ingleses*' I have no doubt that they were willing and ready to do their duty. It has to be said that many would have had no idea where or what the Malvinas were but becoming liberators for the motherland no doubt sounded quite wonderful and boosted their patriotic pride. Once the horror and the killing brought on by this war was finished it would seem that many of these conscripts were quite genuinely surprised to discover that these '*Malvineros*' (as they called the Kelpers) did not want to be liberated, and many of these young conscripts were confused when they discovered that they spoke a foreign language and not a word of Spanish. All this was a far cry from the conquering heroes being festooned with flowers and wine by the grateful liberated residents.

Now on the thirtieth anniversary of the war we have to listen to the old rhetoric where confrontation and hate are paraded once more in Buenos Aires and London. The fact is that the Falklands are more prosperous now than ever before. The economy has grown twenty fold while the prospectors talk of £20 billion worth of oil close to the Falklands and even more to the north of the islands.

Some shrewd economists and prophetic politicians might take the view that where there are such enormous financial possibilities there will be lots of wheeling and dealing, eventually resulting in some kind of Anglo-Argentine deal, which will of course bring us full circle back to collaboration and working for our mutual benefit. This of course, in hindsight, was where we were heading in the late seventies and early '80s before Thatcher and Galtieri.

My final observation has to be that institutionalisation is another way of saying, "forget ordinary people" and "forget all human altruistic endeavours or accomplishments". I say this because, after having looked at this Malvinas/Falklands debacle in some detail, it is obvious to me that the more fundamental aspects of our existence on this planet are not

256

even addressed by any of the religious, political, military or bureaucratic institutions who were involved in this barbaric war. The number of times one diplomat spoke to another diplomat and the views and opinions of politicians that appear in the Franks report are all very interesting, but who or what institute actually addressed the challenge of nurturing the friendship and goodwill built up over centuries between Argentina and the UK? Intermarriage between people of our two nations, the mutual admiration and camaraderie that had developed between individuals and different sporting, social and commercial groups and thousands of personal human friendships were left out in the cold by the numerous involved institutions who were unable or unwilling to prevent the war from taking place, followed by such tragic consequences. I am sure that this situation can be justified by those who were busy planning the military tactics, deciding what to say to the opposing government or working out what kind of threat may frighten the other side into changing its mind, but the fact of the matter is that the people who suffered and those who still suffer today as a result of this stupid war have been sadly let down by all the institutions that were involved.

Darwinism invites competition, confrontation and survival of the fittest and was physically expressed through the abovementioned war. The alternative 'ordinary folk' mentality as postulated by Wallace, was already taking root before the war and could and should in my view be resuscitated and nurtured. This would serve as an example of what can be achieved (in spite of pro-military zealots) between very ordinary people, of which there is a plentiful supply on both sides of this manmade division.

The obvious answer is for ordinary people like you and I to bypass the dominant institutions that have sprung up to run our lives, and do our own thing. We must guide and instruct our political representatives and not be dictated to, by them.

Since finishing this little essay we have witnessed the thirtieth anniversary of this sad little war. Even more sadly we have again been witness to politicians in both countries behaving provocatively, while at the same time we are made aware of decent ordinary people behaving like sane and responsible human beings.

I am referring of course to a number of Falkland veterans from both sides, who have taken the trouble to meet their one time enemies and not only apologise but actually create friendships. There are a number of articles online where one can see videos and commentaries covering some of these encounters. These sincere and at times emotional meetings seem to me to be so distant from the pathetic sabre rattling going on in London and Buenos Aires by what we call our world leaders. Where I have to ask myself, are these leaders trying to lead us this time?

I am beginning to understand that the real conflict is not between the ordinary folk in the UK and Argentina, but between what claim to be the world's leaders, and the extraordinary common folk like you and I the world over who end up fighting wars which are not of our making.

Wallace or Darwin?

When writing about South America the name of Charles Darwin inevitably crops up and so, before moving on, I would like to express a view, not often taken, regarding Darwinism and expressions like the 'survival of the fittest' (coined by Herbert Spencer), 'Natural Selection', 'the law of the jungle' and 'dog eat dog'.

As I have pointed out in earlier chapters, I am not competitive by nature, and it is perhaps this personal trait which attracts me to the idea that the answer is not to 'beat the other guy to the draw', or to be bigger or richer than others. In fact, I have often wondered if Darwin may have got it all wrong when he published *The Origin of Species by means of Natural*

Selection. Not that I claim any great knowledge in this field but I have suspected at times that our collective psyche has been steered in the wrong direction. This commonly held idea that there is not enough to go around and so we must fight for survival has always left me feeling uncomfortable. When our modern New Edge science becomes entangled with that intangible part of who we really are, we discover the very basic fact that everything starts as a thought. It then follows that creating something new cannot be achieved where thought is lacking, and equally true that if we wish to create something (like abundance) it will only follow the thought (of abundance). This is quite contrary to Darwinism's world where it is the lack of abundance that creates competition, winning at any cost then becomes important, and eventually greed becomes incorporated, all in the name of survival. Alfred Russell Wallace suggested in the mid-1800s, at the same time as Charles Darwin was postulating his 'survival of the fittest' theory, that cooperation and sharing are what ensures creativity and survival. Of course there is ample evidence that Wallace, a direct descendant of William Wallace, and who was born in Wales, was the author and founder of the evolutionary theory, which unfortunately has become totally attributed to Darwin. Deeply disturbing as this may be, the real tragedy rests in the tremendously detrimental effect that Darwin's approach and attitude has had on our modern attitudes and our behaviour. Darwin, who was part of the ruling upper class, saw evolution being driven by the struggle to achieve position, distinction and status while Wallace, the commoner, saw a world where we would improve ourselves in order not to be the weakest. In Wallace's view it was the elimination of the weakest and therefore weakness that drove evolution.

So there is the all-important difference. I am of the view that had Wallace's approach dominated our attitudes, rather than Darwin's, there would be much less emphasis on division, competition and survival, but a greater surge toward mutual cooperation and thriving, which is infinitely more inspiring than surviving. I might even go as far as to suggest that this could arguably be the way out of the current situation in which the world finds itself.

On the world stage today we are deeply affected by Darwinism and we play out the fantasy that we have to struggle and compete in order to survive. It is this mentality which justifies the 40 billion pounds (that is forty thousand million) of the people's money being given to the London-based MOD each year instead of it going to science, progress and well being. 'Dog eat dog' is the mantra we are fed through the media, television and glossy magazines. We are deeply influenced by sayings like "don't get angry get even" or "take no prisoners" "reach for the top" "aggressive marketing", "the tough guys always win".

This is a transparently obvious tragedy, but it continues only as long as we go along with it and consume survival-based soap operas, which promote fighting, anger and conflict while we live in ignorance of the existence of wonderful alternatives.

So who benefits from the status quo, and who would be the beneficiaries if we were made aware of a better way of seeing things? Those who sing the mantra DIVIDE AND RULE do not want us to have the knowledge that we are being fooled. Those who run our lives, own the multinational conglomerates and give themselves multimillion-pound bonuses each year do not want us to wake up, kick them into touch and take back our power.

I will stick my neck out a little farther by offering the view that if we follow the modern Newtonian approach to medical care, then we "struggle" to beat disease or we "fight the spread of cancer" or even "attack" the problem of health care, is a by-product of this same mentality. If we were to think of the human body as quantum physics sees it, where the body becomes a collection of high-energy photons, then the reconfiguration of these photons through other approaches may seem more natural than cutting and burning. Rather than promote any one practice I choose to quote from the Christian bible again, which quotes Jesus as saying, when referring to natural healing, "These things I do, you also can do, and greater."

Living in Harmony

With today's modern technology we have a golden opportunity to follow Wallace's model where we communicate and cooperate to create a new mantra in a new world where survival follows naturally.

Our natural state is a state of harmony and wellbeing. Being and working with that inherent goodness which is ours. That is what we really are.

We know that we are being manipulated and programmed to believe that division and conflict is normal.

It is not!

If we can be separated and kept from making friendly and productive connections with others we can be more easily dominated. The old 'divide and conquer' mantra of the empire builders and the supporters of piracy are still alive and well, and still rule our lives.

One small example of this is in my own country where, for centuries, there have been deep divisions and confrontations causing pain and suffering. Scotland is divided between the mainly Protestant loyalists and its Catholics who are made to feel like second-class citizens. When the Saxe-Coburg-Gotha family changed their name to Windsor in 1917, they might have cancelled their long-standing decree banning Catholics from the throne of England. This would have helped removed the cause of some of the ridiculous divisions we still suffer from, so why was it not done? Why was it that following the last major battle on Scottish soil the

Jacobite (Catholic) wounded were stripped of their kilts and shirts on the Wednesday and left naked to lie on the Culloden Moor in the cold and rain until the Friday? Could it have been because they were mostly Catholics? Why did the Duke of Cumberland, the German king's brother, then send his victorious red coats out to butcher those who had managed to survive? The fact that they were 'Catholics' has to be the answer. The ethnic cleansing which then followed as the Hanoverian troops moved through the Highlands killing, burning and even slaughtering the livestock was all justified by the Anglo-German Protestant lust for domination over the Catholics in Scotland. All this, of course, would be better left behind in the dusty annals of history and replaced by forgiveness and the reconstruction of Scottish society were it not made impossible by those who promote the same old attitudes, doctrines and divisions on a daily basis today as I write.

So the question has to be, why is division still promoted and by whom? Do any of the churches make a serious effort to heal the wounds? Is anyone in government big enough to stand up and ask, as the South Africans did, for peace and reconciliation? Can nobody stop the orchestrated division and violence engendered through our multibillion pound professional football debacle? Will we never stop the dominant people from marching through our streets with drums and fifes, provoking and challenging those who are also fellow Scots, but not royalists?

I think that the answer to these questions is that no institution or organisation is likely to make any difference. The solution is in individuals taking responsibility and as much as possible ignoring the institutionalised bodies and bigoted controllers who run our lives. We simply have to take back our power and as far as is practical live independently of those who only want their own power and control.

We can re-establish harmony in our lives if that is what we really want. It's up to the individual. As we create harmony in our own individual lives so we attract other like-minded individuals, who in turn are attracted through the law of physics, which tells us that like attracts like.

Jehovah

While doing some research on Wallace, Darwin, survival and the church- dominated times in which they lived; the name of Jehovah kept surfacing.

This is a very personal - I'm still open to learning - view of religions and gods in general and Jehovah in particular, and it goes like this.

I am convinced that the God who Christians, Jews and Muslims worship and obey is in fact is a very complex and very evolved tyrant who is known as Jehovah. Yes, I am talking about Jehovah of the Old Testament who acts exactly like a tyrant. Now this is a very big statement for a layman like myself, who was mind-conditioned to fear Jehovah from an early age. I now go public and say that I am no longer afraid of offending Jehovah, and do not fear Jehovah as he has instructed and, I might add, that this bold statement, which I now make, has been in the making for at least sixty years.

Over a lifetime I have noted that the confusion and blatant contradiction on which this nasty entity thrives is there for all to see, but it was not until I went to the Ramtha School that I found clear confirmation of my suspicions and the courage to speak my truth regarding the conflicting messages coming to me from the religion I was told that I belonged to, and should never question for fear of being punished. A simple example of this contradiction is the claim that this God called Jehovah is our father who loves and cares for us unconditionally. Now my interpretation of unconditional means without conditions, which in itself is a truly wonderful concept. Who would not look up to and love a father who loves you without conditions and no matter what you get up to? In my religious education I was then directed to read and digest the ten conditions that we must obey and which were handed down to us through Moses; but of course, I had already run into a serious contradiction. These ten conditions were the conditions governing this unconditional arrangement! Of course it gets worse, much worse when we are told that not only must we obey these conditions but that if we fail to do so, this unconditional all-loving father will see to it that we are burnt alive for all eternity! When we add to this the fact that he tells us he is a jealous God and he expects us to fear him, many of us are unfortunately ready to walk away from anything and everything to do with religious or spiritual matters. This is the point where many disillusioned people are prepared to, as New Edge cellular biologist Bruce Lipton would put it, "throw the baby Jesus out with the bathwater". So there you have it: the entity that many look to for compassion, love and forgiveness is perhaps the one who, more than anyone, is turning millions away when it comes to a spiritual life, or at least leaving them confused and bewildered.

The more I look at our world, its people and their beliefs, the more obvious it becomes that this conundrum is far from simple. When looking at the history of Christian beliefs for example, it becomes evident that not everyone always followed the standard Jehovah-based doctrine. An example of this can be seen in Rosslyn chapel near Edinburgh, which is filled, not with saints and angels but with nature, plants and animals. This very touching and beautiful statement in stone, connecting God and nature was of course not acceptable to the Jehovah-worshiping Scottish Kirk, who declared Rosslyn 'a house of idolatry'. Laurence Gardener talks of this in his book, *The Shadow of Solomon* and he goes on to quote the then local minister at one time as saying that, "the alters of Roslene were haille demolishit". This desecration apparently took place in 1572, followed again in 1688 when the Dutch king William of Orange's supporters caused further damage to this totally unique and wonderful building. Then later, in 1954, when, according to Sir Laurence Gardner, a more serious desecration apparently took place at the hands of the London-based Ministry of works who decided to 'clean' the chapel using ammonia and magnesium silica fluoride, leaving it in the state it can be found in today. So we see that even a small building that does not please the Jehovah worshippers is in for a hard time. But again I digress.

The point that I feel strongly about is that a religion, which is based on a loving father/mother figure and includes co-existence between nature and mankind, is simply not compatible with a religious system based on rules and commandments and fear and punishment as dictated by this 'head case' we call Jehovah.

I find comfort when I dwell on the fact that all religions are manmade inventions anyway and that neither Mohammed, nor Buddha, nor Jesus ever had the intention of initiating yet another divisive religion.

Before I move on from Rosslyn chapel I would like to add an insignificant anecdote that my wife and I found intriguing at the time.

When we first met, Susan mistakenly understood that my name was Crowfoot and she still calls me by this name today. I am happy to go along with this and I have developed a habit of signing any notes or even letters to Susan with a little drawing of a crow's foot. When visiting Rosslyn chapel some years ago we went down into the crypt and, being nosy, I looked into a small room which is usually closed to he public and there on the floor were three adjoining cracks making a crow's foot identical to my little signature drawings (see photo).

My wife has been peeping over my shoulder as I write this and has put on my desk a printout of an article by that most distinguished theologian Doctor Míceál Ledwith, which deals with the subject of Jehovah and, unlike my meandering from one subject to another, is written in a professional manner, which is both clear and concise. I considered seeking Doctor Ledwith's permission to print his article but on second thought I am sure that the interested reader can do his or her research without my assistance.

Drugs

As an appendix to my previous observations on Brazil I would like to touch on a serious international subject and challenge that has affected my life and increasingly affects us all.

The subject is mind-altering drugs.

One of my experiences in Brazil while visiting these shanties I mentioned earlier and becoming aware that these people smoked some kind of drug was perhaps an early wake up call for me regarding the growing use of drugs and their potential influence on our future; but whatever the truth was, I managed to ignore it, at least for a time. That is no longer the case, however, and nowadays I never let the opportunity pass if I think that I can, in any way, strengthen the anti-drug movement.

I do not want to go into my personal experiences living with or being close to drug users. This is principally because there is still, for me, some emotion and pain connected to this subject and I also wish to avoid any suggestion of blame or judgement on my part.

Thanks to my personal experience, however, from being in close contact with a few drug addicts I formed my own personal views and opinions, many of which I had confirmed and clarified through the teachings at the Ramtha School. This in turn, led me to delve into quantum physics and New Edge science from which I quote from time to time.

What I first observed in someone using marijuana was, to put it simply, a shocking callousness and a cold disregard for others. I have observed this way of behaving gradually announce itself in small ways like apparent lack of feeling, lack of, once-good, manners plus the capacity to ignore other people's needs or pain. I also have observed the acceptance of casual lying and dishonesty as being a normal part of the common thought structure of these drug users.

I almost instinctively formed these views while I was still unbelievably naive and unaware regarding the drug phenomenon in the world at large.

One amusing early example of my apparent blind spot was when I was living in Buenos Aires and on one occasion was entertaining a visiting American businessman by the name of Victor Ott. When he came home for a meal we got round to talking about and comparing our respective lifestyles. He apparently left the office at four each day and enjoyed a long evening at home, while I seemed to be on call twenty-four hours a day. He told me that every evening when he arrived home his wife would have a joint all ready for him. As he spoke I was visualising this tall skinny American sitting down to a large succulent joint of beef every day, which struck me as rather odd and not at all that healthy. We seemed, however, to be talking at cross-purposes and soon mutually changed the subject.

I was later the victim of some hilarity and ridicule when a couple of friends explained to me that a joint - in drug talk - was a marijuana cigarette.

I simply had never been offered drugs; I did not know the language and was slow to become aware of the extent of their use. I had somehow sailed through life ignorant of one aspect of society that was taking place right under my nose and which was changing our whole world in silent ways, like a creeping sickness, which becomes apparent only when it has become irreversibly established.

While avoiding the temptation to become judgemental I, like most of us, have come across the terrible stories like the 92% of all crime in New York being drug-related. The way drugs are used to create child abuse and child prostitution is quite terrifying. We read of the drug cartels targeting school children while the world's prisons seem to be flooded with drugs. The truth is that our ever increasingly addicted society finances the private armies, the murder squads and political corruption. The guns and aeroplanes used by the drug barons are all financed by those who buy drugs. Since I feel powerless and at a loss to do much about this situation, my curiosity has taken me away from these very obvious outward effects of what I see as the scourge of mankind and offered me an insight into another facet where all things, including addiction, are born. I refer to the quantum field, but let me keep it simple and explain.

Addiction

My wife and I have been students at the Ramtha School and this has invited us to look at the world in different ways while awakening us to many new sources of information and new potentials.

The school has introduced us to a number of 'New Edge' scientists and academics, like Míceál Ledwith, Candace Pert, Joe Dispenza, Rupert Sheldrake, and Bruce Lipton amongst others. These are all courageous and inspiring individuals who have dared to be different and, amongst other achievements, are making us aware of the quantum world in our every day lives.

Joe Dispenza, for example, defines emotional addiction as a situation in which you can't control your emotional state. He points out that emotions are not bad but that, "they colour the richness of our experiences". It is the addiction, he tells us that is the problem and that this addiction is not just psychological, it is also biochemical.

It would seem that the largest part of the information that is going around in our brain is kept in order, NOT by the synaptic connections of the brain cells but by the receptors, all of which are designed to receive specifically designed chemical messengers. This means that an emotion consists of a specific chemical - a neuropeptide - and its receptor. There is a chemical/neuropeptide for each emotion and if the cell is repeatedly bombarded with the same chemical this will increase the number of receptors specific to that particular chemical. If this is done, then when the cell divides, the new daughter cells will have more receptors specific to one particular neuropeptide (chemical) and consequently fewer receptors specific to vitamins, nutrients, fluid exchange and release of toxins and waste products. In addition to this, emotions like love, compassion and associated feelings will also be squeezed out to make room for the emotion (chemical), which has been bombarding the system. So we see that the more we feed our bodies with one emotion (chemical) the more the body has the need for it and makes room for it to the detriment of other emotions like compassion, joy or love.

This is called addiction and one can observe what we call a change of character in our friends or acquaintances, as their cells become limited to fewer and fewer healthy chemicals, or healthy emotions.

The above, of course supports my original personal observations regarding callousness and lack of human feelings exhibited by drug users, while it offers a scientific explanation.

Hope

The other side of this coin offers us hope and solutions as we are told by modern science, in a summary of the Hebbian theory, first introduced by Donald Hebb in 1949, that 'cells that fire together, wire together' and so it is that repetition and association will help develop relationships in the neural net of the brain, creating an identity. An identity may be characterised by slovenliness, unusual habits, lack of interest, or any number of traits that may be seen.

However, we also learn that when the nerve cells do not fire together habitually they lose their long-term relationship.

So every time that we interrupt the thought process that produces a specific chemical response in the body, these connected nerve cells start to break up the long-term relationship. So, interrupting the thought would seem to be a way to reverse addiction.

This process consists of interrupting our thoughts and observing ourselves until we are no longer that body-mind emotional being responding to its environment as though it is on automatic. Through this process we take back our power and release the addiction.

The question then becomes, HOW do we achieve this interruption and observation in practical terms?

The answer lies partly in our subconscious mind and this begins to make sense when, as I mentioned before, we understand that well over 90% of our actions originate, not in our conscious minds but, in our subconscious minds. Bruce Lipton illustrates this beautifully in his DVD called *The Biology of Belief*. At the end of the DVD he invites us to discover several disciplines that are designed to re-programme the subconscious mind. Ramtha's school teaches that drugs such as marijuana are designed to distort neuron activity and always destroy brain cells. I was also taught at the school that this herb was created to alleviate pain in animals, but what kills the pain is the actual dying of the brain cells. So if you are a bit of an escapist and have to use drugs to escape the reality that you have created, then you are free to do so, but at the cost of destroying your wonderful brain. The Creator of all things gave us free will to create whatever we choose without conditions, without commandments, without punishment and without fear. All actions and all our creations do have consequences, however, and so it is up to us to take responsibility for these things that we choose to create.

Creator

Since I have mentioned the Creator, I had better state very briefly that, as I see it, the Creator created you in its likeness and image. This means that you are also a creator, or co-creator, and that you continually create your own reality.

Whatever you are experiencing right now you created it.

I rest my case and trust that you will not suspect me of being another 'head case'.

More on Psychic Phenomena

When writing or talking about subjects like psychic surgery I am often met with polite remarks like, "well I feel very sceptical about that". What these polite friends often want to say is "that's a lot of rubbish" or, "I'm a good Christian and that goes against God's word and is blasphemy", etc.

I now give myself permission to briefly address these seldom expressed, but very understandable, reservations and criticisms.

Perhaps we might like to think back to the days when people approved of burning to death those who claimed that the world was round. Their totally rational argument was that if the world were round then we would fall off of it.

So this perfectly rational thinking dictated that this round earth rubbish could not possibly be true.

We feel safe with our old values and tend to prefer 'the devil we know'. This seems to be why, as science moves into new exciting areas and makes available to us new information and new discoveries, it also has the hideous job of trying to drag a sceptical, fear-ridden army of perfectly rational human beings behind it; this seems to also include some scientists who prefer not to rock the boat or put their heads above the parapet.

It is, however, becoming uncomfortably clear, even to the man and woman in the street like myself, that we are going to have to evolve and move on, or disappear from this little planet of which we are the custodians. I just know that the planet will survive and feel that it would be great if we could be around to witness it.

It is time to confront our own conscious limitations, as well as what we have programmed into our subconscious minds, this is the New Edge challenge we face today.

In spite of he fact that quantum physics invites us out of the dark ages of Newtonian materialism and has on offer a veritable Aladdin's cave of goodies to choose from, we still cling to the old material world, which creates an illusion of being safe.

The psychic connection at long distances, between pets and their owners as demonstrated and recorded by scientist and author Rupert Sheldrake opens us up to the magic of non-locality while the widely accepted energy medicine known as acupuncture are only two simple examples out of thousands which involve the body's energy field. Both of these activities depend on the presence of what I shall call the invisible realm. My wife, who has developed her psychic abilities to a modest degree, informed me on one occasion while we were out walking along the Findhorn river that she wanted to make contact with the invisible realm which she called 'herself in another dimension', something she didn't fully understand on a rational level but something that she wanted to nevertheless experience if possible. As she proceeded to go into a trance, raising her arms up towards the trees and the sky beyond, I felt a compulsion to take a photograph, which I have included in this book for the reader to draw his or her own conclusions.

What is it that is present in a human being, which - although all-important - remains invisible? How about thoughts, or fear, happiness, love, hate? Are inspirations, our deep feelings of joy and sorrow not part of that fundamental invisible realm?

Why do we not recognise the magic of intention and will? Is it because they are not palpable or visible? Does that make them any less important?

Many of us still live within a Newtonian mentality. Our politics, religion and social values are largely governed by Newton's rules and outdated knowledge.

Just contemplate the human body field and its entanglement with the energy fields that flood that so-called empty space called infinity. The fact that these things I mention are part of the invisible realm only goes to accentuate their limitlessness and therefore our own potential limitlessness.

While we continue to stall at the relatively simple idea of psychic surgery we are limiting ourselves, and the minds of future generations, to ignorance and drudgery, rather than moving on to ever-more spectacular achievements. I can hear the accusations that the alternative approach to health care is lacking guarantees, but there is a defining silence when it comes to the multinational drug companies who turn over something like 600 billion dollars a year selling drugs that are supposed to make us healthier. Do you honestly believe that these people who have a monopoly over the world's drugs really want us all to get better and spoil their billions from rolling in? That may sound like cynicism but the evidence supports my views. Bruce Lipton is only one of many authors to point out the fact that in the USA alone three-hundred thousand people die each year from adverse reaction to prescription drugs. It is also true that our GPs are advised and educated by an army of drug company representatives who are employed - at no cost to the GPs - to sell the products that the drug companies want the GP to prescribe and the public to buy. While this situation goes on, the cost of healthcare soars as illness and serious diseases like cancer are on the increase.

Freemasons

My life has been largely guided through my instinctive awareness and it has served me well. Since my early life I have instinctively avoided those who would have me give my power away. I refer of course to religionists, politicians, football promoters, freemasons, and the whole can of devious worms collectively known as 'The Establishment' that needs the support of the unsuspecting masses in order to survive. Many of those who invited me, cajoled me, offered and threatened me to join their 'thing', did it with the very best of intentions and had my best interests at heart, and so my refusal to comply has been seen as bad manners, stupidity, madness, ignorance and worse; as well as sometimes being seen as my bid for personal sovereignty, independence and freedom. So why am I apparently so stubborn? The answer is simply that I have always had an inner knowingness which tells me what to accept and what to reject. I have usually refused initially to join the club, sign on the line or swear allegiance because my instinct has warned me against it. Sometimes I have taken the trouble to learn more about whatever it has been that I have avoided or rejected and without exception have discovered over the years that my rational mind has eventually agreed with my instinct and confirmed that I have done what is ultimately in my best interests.

One example of this process has to do with freemasonry. My grandfather, John Clark by name, was a mason and I believe was the founding master of a Masonic Lodge in my place of birth, namely Greenock. My father and my uncles as well as most of my father's friends were all masons and there was therefore no doubt in their minds that when the time came I would join the brotherhood without question. Not that my opinion was ever sought.

Since my work meant that I spent a lot of time abroad I would repeatedly be told that the next time I came home I would 'go on the square' or that it was all arranged in advance for my next visit. The answers to my questions about the Brotherhood were usually in the vein of, "once you have joined you'll find out". It was too challenging for me to tell my father that it felt 'all wrong' to me, yet painful and disruptive as the situation was to become, I simply could not accept it. The 'join first, then find out what you have become part of' approach was not good enough for me! In spite of these difficulties I managed to survive the pressure without surrendering, but at the same time I privately decided find out what it was all about without giving any of my power to anyone or tarnishing my sovereignty, integrity or independence. This was a lonely, secretive and very private quest, which I shared with nobody, mostly because I feared ridicule or at the very least, being misunderstood.

Whenever it came to looking for answers to the Masonic conundrum it was far from simple and it took me years to work it out to my satisfaction. The answer I came up with is complex but it goes something like this. Basically, in spite of new candidates being advised, when being initiated, that they will be admitted to the mysteries and privileges of ancient freemasonry, they never are. This is simply because the secret information so shrouded in mystery and surrounded by ritual has long since been lost. It has been replaced with ceremonies, lectures pointing members in the direction of spiritual and philosophical enlightenment but quite lacking any practical instruction. I get the impression that there is no interest in research or reference to the New Edge scientific developments, many of which address the very - lost - subjects that would seem to be fundamental to ancient freemasonry. As I understand it, the exact same words are used and repeated time after time in a rigid repetitive form instead of the original progressive and enlightening work experience that was once practiced. The only requirement today seems to be the learning off by heart of the identical script learned by those who came before and those who will come after.

On looking into freemasonry I am able to draw on personal experience, which clearly taught me that in modern day masonry there is without any doubt an old boy's network and the 'you scratch my back and I'll scratch yours' culture goes deep into the workplace, industry and commerce. On the other hand, I was most impressed when a close friend of mine died suddenly and the masons took his wife in hand and looked after her in every detail. In addition to this I have also personally been subjected to the most generous and sincere effort to get me out of my poverty, if I would just do the deed and surrender my sovereignty and become a mason, so I am aware that there are many facets to the organisation and many "good works" being realised.

It can hardly be called a secret society, however, otherwise my investigations would never have borne fruit. Nevertheless it is secretive in its way of doing things and some aspects of learning within the Brotherhood must, according to the rules, be "concealed and never revealed" but as far as secrets are concerned there is, I feel, nothing of substance. There are unquestionably many secrets, which they would prefer not to be made public, such as their involvement in the affairs of the Vatican, made public by Eric Frattini in whose book *The Entity*, tells

276

of five centuries of Vatican espionage detailing the involvement of freemasonry.

At one point, when I believe freemasonry was trying to redefine itself, the emphasis moved to it being a charitable institution, which basically for many people, is what it is today. Having said that - and recognising the many 'good works' being done today - it is also my experience that human nature being what it is, the system can be, and is, abused when deciding on things like who should get a job, a house or a helping hand in 'getting on in the world'. During my fifty years of working life I have been told that "you won't get that job unless you are a mason" and I have seen favouritism in the work place based solely on Masonic membership and in addition to my immediate family I have been invited to become one of the brotherhood "for my own good". This does not mean that all masonry is bad or good, but as far as I am concerned it means that I must explore, contemplate and discover.

More on the Lost Crafts Of Freemasonry

My investigations concerning the tantalising lost secrets of freemasonry, and just what they may be, eventually invites us to simultaneously consider these ancient lost secrets and lost crafts together with recently developed New Edge science.

Could it be that ancient technology, similar to some of our modern scientific capabilities, is what is referred to when we talk about 'the lost secrets' or 'lost crafts'? If we take a look at some of the great buildings of antiquity, which could include the Temple of Solomon, the Pyramids of Egypt, Machu Picchu and the great cathedrals of Europe, could we find evidence of the secret crafts and what the great architects and builders knew that we do not know today? After all what is it that the Jewish tradition is referring to when it talks of Solomon as being a practitioner of divine technology? Might this also be the potential burial ground for the impractical and unrealistic stories regarding thousands of slaves pulling thousands of stone blocks weighing millions of tons up steep ramps to build the pyramids?

If we take a look at what we know as of The Ark of the Covenant, which can be seen in some of the symbolism used in freemasonry we discover what is basically a very heavy gold box. A box, which the experts calculate must have weighed at least one-thousand-two-hundred kilograms. Why would these ancient masons be interested in such an artefact and what purpose could it fulfil? The answer to that question may have something to do with the fact that four men carried this box. Yes, it would seem that four men carried this box weighing well over a ton, or at least it would seem that it was easily moved or transported by only four men.

This in turn invites us to look at New Edge science and the rediscovery of levitation; non-locality phenomena; lasers that cut stone with great precision; and other rediscovered crafts. Craft, of course being a much used, key word when dealing with the history and origins of Masonry.

So perhaps all is not lost since the very ancient capabilities and magical crafts upon which ancient freemasonry was probably built are emerging into the light once more thanks to New Edge science. New Edge science is increasingly uncovering ancient crafts relating to subtle energies, nanotechnology, quantum physics, levitation, lasers and much more. We see biblical mysteries and magic that until now have been the stuff of religion and mythology emerging once again; but this time as twenty-first century New Edge science. So does this mean that science and spirituality can once again dance together hand in hand, confirming, supporting and acknowledging each other?

So, my protracted investigations into freemasonry have not only blown the cover on the fantasy surrounding the secrets of the secret and so added to my understanding but, on a private and personal level while doing so, I have held on to my feeling of personal integrity and justified my lifelong reluctance to be drawn into other people's agendas.

To round off this captivating subject, let me introduce you to an astounding story, which shows how modern freemasonry may be used for unexpected purposes. There was once upon a time a very capable and distinguished gentleman who, after a distinguished career in the military, went on to hold a senior position in the City of London. Thanks to the influential individuals with whom he had come into contact he became intimately connected with events that were being manufactured secretly on behalf of a certain secret group of people. This may begin to sound a little fantastic but it really seems to be perfectly true. What he had become aware of through contact with these people troubled him deeply and he felt a need to tell someone and to expose what he calls this 'band of brothers'. He contacted a highly regarded interviewer by the name of Bill Ryan who, amongst other things, runs an organization called Project Avalon and they spoke at length. The 'whistleblower' explained that this group of people he had met were all British, that there was a bit of aristocracy in the group, some police and military as well as right wing and Conservative party members. Also that the Church of England was totally complicit in everything that is going on and that the group was fundamentally Masonic.

Now I invite you the reader to just speculate for a moment. If someone wanted to start a secret group with a view to starting a new war or to wrest power from a legitimate government or start a revolution, how would they go about it?

First of all they would look for a group and a venue where secrecy is the norm.

They would need a place where secrecy would be seen as something 'only to be expected'. They would want some potential 'foot soldiers' willing to join now and find out later what they had let themselves in for. They would look for a group where everyone has already been carefully vetted. They would be on the lookout for a well established, legitimate and accepted cover, which might for instance be a respected group well known for carrying out good deeds.

Does it sound familiar?

Now let me return to the military gentleman who spoke to Bill Ryan, the interviewer, and let me mention just one of the many things he mentioned. He was talking about a hypothetical scenario where some key figures take over the London government and pointed out that this would not be difficult since in addition to the two-hundred thousand military personnel in the UK there are now, following the twin towers incident, some five-hundred thousand UK security personnel - private armies - who are being given new training and new powers of detention. Add to these figures the police and other agencies and it becomes all too evident that in modern Britain, declaring martial law and installing a police state would be quicker and easier than it has ever been in our history. Why this? Who has surreptitiously created this potential police state? In the USA the military and the police are more high profile and respected than in the UK but we unfortunately seem to be led by what the Americans do.

If you think that this little book of anecdotes is suddenly dealing in fiction I would recommend you look up the complete interview with Bill Ryan, which is called *The Anglo-Saxon Mission Witness Interview Transcript*, and can be found on www.projectavalon.net at the time of writing.

FOOTNOTE

As the writing of this book was coming to an end, I had the pleasure of meeting a lady by the name of Vicky Gunn. We had apparently met a few years earlier but we did not remember each other. Quite unexpectedly Susan and I had to change plans that we had put together to visit Spain, and we ended up staying for a week with Vicky, at her beautiful house in Somerset, in the south of England.

Now this newly found friend turned out, very refreshingly, to be someone we could talk to for hours without repetition or getting bored, as seems ever increasingly, to be our experience regarding our social life. Some of the subjects we find interesting, such as the earth changes, quantum phenomena, what the true reality is behind world events, remote viewing and distant healing to mention but a few, have turned out to be real conversation stoppers with our usual acquaintances; and as a result our social intercourse has been in decline. This was not the case with Vicky, who was very much interested in these subjects.

We discovered, that over the years, Vicky has enhanced her considerable natural healing gifts by studying different healing modalities, while at the same time developing her psychic awareness. This unique lady does not appear to follow any one school of practice, although Matrix Energetics, which is really just a way of being, plays an important part in what she does. Her patients, or clients, seem to come from a cross section of society and include at least one of the world's greatest minds and New Edge scientists, who amongst his many achievements is considered by many to be one of the world's leading cellular biologist. Could one hope for a higher recommendation?

During our visit we inevitably spent time practising various therapies on each other. Vicky, who had no previous knowledge of my background or personal details, asked me on the first day if I was connected with the freemasons. I said that I had no connection whatsoever and that seemed to be the end of it. Several days later this subject came up again, and although Vicky could not remember having mentioned it before, she said that some connection between masonry and myself kept presenting itself to her that day. As we discussed it, it became obvious that she had little or no knowledge regarding the subject of masonry, but she suggested that I was being negatively affected in some way, through some kind of Masonic influence. I briefly explained to her my passing interest in the subject, and how I had become aware of the brotherhood through family members.

Vicky offered to give me her full attention and I ended up lying on a massage bench with Vicky hovering over me with Susan in attendance.

For this session Vicky covered her eyes with a blindfold and seemed to be in a trance-like state, and I - most unexpectedly and uncharacteristically - drifted in and out of conscious awareness.

Vicky said that 'they' had done something to my spine - which has been fractured on two occasions - and that Masonic symbols and my spine seemed to be entangled in some way. She was not clear at first whether these things had been directed specifically at me or inherited through my family bloodline, but it was clear that the intention behind these activities was negative and destructive. The fact that it was my mother's family who were involved in masonry seemed to Vicky, to be in conflict with the influence that she was picking up coming through my paternal family line.

Here were three people who knew nothing about the details of masonry rituals, unexpectedly delving into this complex can of worms with only the words of a psychic as a guide, yet old sceptical me felt fully comfortable with the procedure and fully confident in Vicky's capabilities. At this point I was asked to comment on my father's relationship with the masons, and when I pointed out that he had, at one point, distanced himself from the brotherhood, Vicky declared, 'THAT'S IT!'"

The whole question of masons and masonry had come from my mother's side of the family but I had apparently inherited this negative 'something' from my father, which explained some of the confusion.

Vicky then went on to deal with some jealousy, anger and strong emotions connected with my ex-wife, of many yeas before. This question of my ex-wife seemed to be shrouded in sadness and a kind of stagnation but this was removed and healed before we moved on.

The following hour developed like a bad dream. When Vicky came up with the name Clark (my maternal grandfather and prominent Mason was John Clark), my whole body went into convulsions and muscle spasms. I watched, vaguely alarmed, as Susan got down on her knees while crying out, "Don't do it, please don't do it", and the whole room became steeped a deep overwhelming sadness. Susan says that she was compelled to do this, despite disliking what she calls "melodramatic healing modalities".

I remember only bits of this; since I was not fully conscious all of the time, and it is only with Vicky and Susan's help that I have put these bits of the story together. It was during this very troubled session that Susan saw the 'stick man' hanging by the neck in an inverted triangle and heard the words, "Crawford's father was made the hanged man", which she was later to investigate, with astounding results suggesting that being made the 'hanged man' is an evil Masonic curse used to harm those who do not conform. It should be remembered that none of us had ever had any knowledge or experience of Masonic ritual or habits prior to this.

Vicky put her energies to work healing and clearing these dark energies and during the following days, once we were back to normality, we eventually came to some interesting conclusions and revelations.

One obvious revelation is the fact that whenever I have come across the triad or sacred triangle, it has mysteriously triggered in me, a great frustration. I have in the presence of others, sworn at a totally inoffensive teacher, walked out of sessions and generally refused to go along with any procedure involving triangles, with no rational explanation. Some of the information and teaching at the Ramtha School incorporates the reference to the triangle. This includes the triangular shape of the Christmas tree, the triad as seen by some who belong to religious orders and the use of the triad in the symbolism regarding the seven levels of life or seven heavens as taught by Buddhists and others. I know that my irrational reaction when these things come up has caused some concern from time to time, not least of all to Susan.

I now, thanks to this experience with Vicky, look forward to more peaceful times, but before moving on let me share with you what Susan's investigations have uncovered. This is from Above Top Secret's forum,

http://www.abovetopsecret.com/forum/thread72937/pg1.
I have kept it as is, complete with spelling mistakes:

"Freemasons passing sentance on the public, page 1

Topic started on 13-8-2004 @ 02:23 PM by stancumans

Afterr 20 odd years of persecution, for want of a better word, i actually found out what was going on in my life. I found out that a sentance had been passed on me by the "Mysterious Examiner" and that i was declared a hanged man by freemasons. They don't just go out an lynch you, what's the fun in that? Instead they play with you much like a cat does with a mouse. Ruining every aspect of your life, your health, souring friendships, everything. They pass sentance then use the powers that be to action that sentance. The police, the judicial system are all set against you. I used to get the police knock on my door at 8pm at night ot pictkup money for parking offenses. If you get a job, pressure will be put on your boss to get rid of you no matter how good you are.

I set up this site

www.murderingmasons.co.uk

The method they use is predicatable, if you feel that they are messing with you, please let me know.

Regards

Stan

Oh and please don't think he must of deserved it, i've led a good life and have kindness instilled through every molecule of my body. This was nasty and did not deserve their response."

Note: the website he mentioned above no longer seems to function at the time of writing this.

Royals

During my varied life I have been scheduled a few times to meet members of the Hanoverian royal family. I however, believe in freedom, and I support the Scottish Nationalist movement while I await the day when we in Scotland can trade with and enjoy a healthy, mutually agreed relationship with England, as well as anyone else of our choice. But as long as we are denied that choice, I will not support those who impose their will on how or who we should be. This includes shaking hands with the Anglo-German royal family, who preside over the all-powerful and influential 'Establishment', or indeed in propping them up in any way.

It is normal for the senior management in industry to be introduced to visiting royalty and as chief executive to a small organisation in Shetland and before that as assistant manager in a large organisation in Buenos Aires I was expected to turn up for the visiting royal. I managed to arrange things so that I was not available on both occasions and later, back in my native Scotland, my wife and I, as crew members of a boat being named by a royal avoided having to 'not turn up' by getting on a ship to South Africa just before the occasion. I therefore considered myself to be an accomplished 'royals dodger' until one of them caught me unexpectedly.

At one time I used to exercise some of the horses belonging to the Southdown hunt near Brighton. This hunt was to merge with the Eridge hunt in 1981 and become the Southdown and Eridge Hunt. The only way I could keep my hand in at riding in the UK was by offering this free service and there were always people eager to have their horses exercised. I enjoyed meeting these horsey people and was able to form my own view of fox hunting, and sort out the truth from the fiction. One of the perks of riding these horses, which I did only for my own enjoyment, was that from time to time I would get tickets to the races. These tickets allowed me to attend the race meetings up and down the country and occasionally to meet some well-known people. On one occasion in the company of the daughter of the Lord Mayor of Brighton, who was a keen horsewoman and a good friend, I went to spend the day at the Goodwood races. Our tickets allowed us into the paddock and we were admiring the latest winner when someone poked their elbow into my ribs and said, "A beautiful filly isn't she?" On turning round and looking down, a large flowery hat on top of a wrinkled smiling face looking up and showing brown uneven teeth greeted me. I think I said, "Yeah, nice horse."

My enthusiastic companion for the day tugged my sleeve and whispered, "Talk to her, talk to her, not everyone gets an invitation to chat with the Queen Mother!" I made my excuses and moved on, but out of curiosity kept close to this spritely old woman and observed as Joe Gormley escorted her round the paddock.

Now, I have never had a very high opinion of the royal family, nor do I trust them, but seeing this old woman out for the day with the head of the miners' trades union seriously challenged my thinking and I wondered if it was time for me to reconsider some of my longstanding views and opinions. After all, if the rampant, left wing president of the militant mine workers' union was invited to take the old queen to the races for the day then perhaps I did need to reconsider my views regarding the Hanoverian dynasty. My friend who had been with me during this little encounter, told the story to some of our horsey friends back in Ringmer, near Brighton. They tended to be upper class, right wing, and part of the establishment and I was amused to see that somehow my prestige had moved up a couple of notches in their eyes. Had they known why I had avoided this old woman, it would, I suspect have been a different story.

Almost twenty years went by, Joe Gormley had died in 1993 and the encounter at the races was a distant and insignificant memory when, in 2002, the BBC uncovered some of the truth about Gormley. It transpired that he had been working for the secret services and the police Special Branch, passing on information to them regarding his friends and fellow trades unionists, since the 1970s.

This vile treachery, one must presume, qualified him as a member of the establishment and therefore an acceptable escort for the old queen.

There was a time not so long ago when corrupted traitors and spies were shot, but as is always the case, those who suffered because of this deceitful double dealing, called Gormley a traitor while the Establishment called him a patriot; I called myself a naive fool for not having suspected some kind of establishment skulduggery that day back in the '80s, at the races.

The old woman in the story went on to live for over one hundred years and at the time of her demise was still spending one and three quarters of a million pounds of the public's money each year on herself, while others get three or four thousand a year from the same public purse to live on and just down the road from her residence there were people sleeping in doorways. I am sorely tempted to become judgemental, or is it just discerning? These royals are, without a doubt, authority figures although the power that they wield is quite temporal and illusive since it depends totally on common folk giving them that power by holding street parties when told to, waving little flags when instructed and failing to question the status quo. The day that we start to treat them like the ordinary human beings that they are and go about our lives as though they do not have power, they will in fact cease to exist and the myth will wither and die. Philip and Charles can be pensioned off and the others can get jobs flying helicopters or perhaps someone like Harry would prefer a manual job, while the billions they cost us can be spent on our future generations of children and the older generation. This may look like nonsense right now to some people but my bet is that you will be reminded of what is written here in the not very distant future. Recently, as I have been writing this the queen has had a private audience with the pope of Rome, using Scotland as their venue. What they discussed is of course secret; then Her Royal Majesty visited the Irish Free State, which she and her followers still refuse to allow to reunite with the rest of Ireland; she then had the nerve to lay a wreath in memory of those who died fighting for the union of Ireland and freedom from London and whose deaths have, so far, been in vain. I cannot help but see this as one big fantastic soap opera that it is not played out just for fun but is deadly serious. One day we will no doubt find out what is really going on behind the scenes. I think that they are what my mother would have called 'a bad lot' had she understood the truth. Unfortunately my mother's generation were never made aware that Philip went to nasty Nazi schools or that his sisters who were both members of the Nazi party both married high ranking Nazis, but I'll keep that for my next book.

Ramtha

Having come from a so-called religious background, yet having a tendency to ask questions, I have managed to engender some controversy and even conflict at times. Things that are invisible have always seemed important to me, by which I mean our thoughts, moods, ideas, feelings and emotions. This developed into an interest in absent healing, psychic abilities and other invisible yet powerful realities.

For several years I studied holism, developing a large collection of flip chart diagrams and drawings, which helped me in my lectures and workshops as I took my work to several different countries. I soon became acutely aware that these talks and workshops I was offering were as much about my own development as teaching others. As I was invited to talk on Spanish radio and television, to lecture a large group of medical professionals, and receive invitations to lecture at universities and centres of learning I found myself questioning why I was doing these things. I had to admit that many of my audiences were far more qualified than I was and yet I had the cheek to stand up and teach them. I then saw the big trap looming up ahead. I enjoyed the applause, and secretly enjoyed it when people insisted in calling me professor and doctor. It became increasingly obvious that the dubious status of new age guru was there for me to step into. I quit and went home. The beautiful charts and drawings that had taken me twenty years to develop, I eventually gave to a friend who had shown an interest in them.

All I kept was my unpublished book titled HOLOSAPIENCE written in the early 1990s. Holosapience, as mentioned earlier, being a word that I coined in the mid-1980s to describe the Oneness becoming aware of itself. While working with these ideas and feelings in the '80s and '90s, I had always been aware that transferring them into mere words was always going to reduce them to something less than the original vision or inspiration. For this reason I developed these charts and symbols in the hope that they might be more effective than using a purely verbal approach. Many years after creating the Holosapience symbol I was to learn from one who some believe to be an ascended master how the Creation took place. This was to teach me that the Oneness contemplated itself, looking inwards before creating all that is, so I decided that my Holosapience symbol might be called 'In the beginning' or even 'The Creation' so here we have it again, where the words fall short and are totally insignificant alongside the message.

After I quit as a workshop leader, I spent days walking on the beach and rowing my boat until at last I could look back and appreciate that an interesting experience had come to an end just in time to avoid the alluring opportunity to feed my ego and my vanity as well as my bank balance.

I see this as the kind of thing that Amit Goswami alludes to in *The Visionary Window* in which he talks about the opportunistic element always present within the New Age movement. For me it was a temptation but I knew that going down this road would always feel like a betrayal of the gifts I had been given and I would not be able to live comfortably with myself.

It was not until 2002 that a lifetime of questions and answers were brought together when Susan and I became students at the Ramtha School of Enlightenment. I have to say that in the beginning Susan seemed to find Ramtha totally inspiring, while I found him inspiring, challenging, annoying and frustrating, all at the same time. Part of my frustration, when listening to this incredible master teacher is due to my partial deafness, which was caused by an explosion back in the early '60s, and partly because deep down I do not always want to understand or be part of American English.

With infinite patience the school showed me the bigger picture, bringing together my fragmented concepts, ideas and feelings. Ramtha's teachings made me aware of how I limited my freedom, and he reintroduced me to free will and personal sovereignty, which has been severely damaged in my life's journey, thanks to religion, schooling, fear and social consciousness.

The excuse that I use to justify my slow development at this school, is that I started rather late in life, by which time my whole system had been hardwired with unhelpful influences picked up along the way.

For those of you who do not know this great teacher I will just say that reading the *Life and Teachings of the Masters of the Far East* will help to understand what kind of entity I am talking about. Following this you may or may not want to attend a beginner's retreat or just look at a DVD of the teachings. I am not an authorised teacher nor am I authorised to promote the school so I will just say, that difficult as I have found the school at times, the Ramtha School is the best thing that has ever happened to me in something like eighty years of enquiring and asking questions. I must emphasise that this is neither a religion nor a cult. This school is a place of learning, a place where knowledge and information is made available, and once you have expanded your knowledge it is up to you to use it in the way you see fit. The Ram, as he is also known, himself is a self-sufficient entity and so requires nothing from either you or me. He is not looking for a following as a guru would do, nor is he interested in getting people to 'join the club' as it were, although some people will make a club out of anything. I am aware that our conditioning by religious domination affects our acceptance of anything unusual and, for instance, when we learn at the school that in Greek the word for a knowledgeable person is a Christos, there is an immediate religious connotation, which suggests that maybe we are not just acquiring knowledge but perhaps getting involved in religion. Nothing could be further from the truth for me and the way I attempt to approach what I have learnt there.

Looking Back at Future Events

Groups of people, societies, and whole nations develop characteristics akin to individual personal characters, which tend to endure and transcend from one generation into another. In my own case I was born into a society where ridicule and dogma, mainly driven through religion, is handed down from one generation to another, and yet it somehow managed to survive alongside the great minds, great inventors, statesmen, adventurers and thinkers that Scotland has produced. Nevertheless, in spite of such strong, if subtle, attempts to keep the truth from us and hold us in a state of ignorance, I am aware, like many others on our planet, of many of these very subjects and facts that are being kept from us. One subject I have not addressed is the fact that we are not alone. This is quite obvious to the serious observer. I am also persuaded that we are soon going to become psychologically affected by, and significantly transformed by, the realisation that there are other sentient entities in our midst.

Writing these words of course triggers my subconscious to replay the old tape containing the ridicule and dogma, which has the effect of making us lesser beings, reluctant to seek out our simple truth. I am, however, fortunate to have reached an age and stage where I see ridicule and abuse as the guarantors that one is on the right track and that I have arrived. Arrived at that place where one can understand the price paid by others who dared to say that the world was not flat nor was it the centre of the universe, or more recently, that the Iraq war was immoral and illegal. Without wanting to sound pretentious, I would like these words to perhaps invite the promoters of sarcasm, ridicule and dogma to reconsider before the coming world events overtake them and brush them aside.

The scale and intensity of these world-changing events will be greatly influenced by our social and individual conduct and attitudes. We are more powerful than we have been allowed to understand and this is what Yeshua Ben Joseph meant when he said something like, "These things that I do, you also can do, AND GREATER".

When was the last time you were reminded of that great lesson; or encouraged to be greater than you are? Or perhaps you are so hell bent on that plot in heaven that you do not want to offend the very people who are steering you away from it.

Wouldn't it be just great if the priests and ministers would climb up into their pulpits and shout out this message to their congregations? They could read it directly from the same bible that they use to traumatise the innocent and terrify little children, and they might even - God forbid - be enticed to smile as if they were actually happy in their job. "YOU ALSO CAN DO THESE THINGS AND GREATER!" (Smile-smile-smile!)

I am not saying that all priests or ministers are bad, or that their intention is to terrify little children. What I am saying is that all too often this is the end result; I know because I've been there. An interesting by-product of this is also that many of these traumatised "good" people spend their lives attending churches and doing good deeds out of fear, which of course is the exact opposite of love, which is claimed to be their stock-in-trade.

The reason I am saying these things is not to be clever or to criticise anyone, but to get the reader to think about the alternatives open to us all.

Just think, the ministers could invite the press to report on the change to their once-solemn faces, their new bright outfits and their new outrageous multi-coloured dog collars. In so doing they might inspire the ever-increasing number of absentees from their churches to return and have some fun, just for the hell of it! What have they got to lose, and after all who would dare to challenge the written word of Jesus pronounced from the pulpit? This is what I am talking about here! This is not something that I have invented. Is reading the word of Jesus from the pulpit too far removed from what the priests do these days?

In a world that is going raving mad, it is time for someone to go raving sane, and you never know, others may become infected with the same sanity.

As I write these words [2nd April 2011] the Japanese nation is facing total annihilation. In spite of this evolving and disastrous scenario, the media, the government and those in public office just pretend, to the public at least, that they know what they are doing and have everything under control.

I hear you say yes I agree, but what can I do about it? My personal belief is that we can only change things by changing our individual attitudes. The more people acknowledge what our attitudes have already created, and decide to change attitudes, then the better will be our chances of survival. This, by the way, is borne out by New Edge quantum physics when they talk about the entanglement of our individual morphic fields and the far-reaching effect of our thoughts.

We are more powerful than the people who create divisions and run our lives want us to understand. We are one unified consciousness capable of anything that we may choose. The churches, politicians, the military and the multinational corporations, the drug companies and arms dealers cannot exist without the power and the money they take from us as individuals. Once we understand what is going on we can ignore their propaganda, and end their tyranny. I think it is safe to say that there is already evidence of a global consciousness shift when we hear - in spite of an effort to cover it up as well as taking advantage of it politically - of the millions of people protesting in the Arab world, in Spain, Italy and in the USA.

The loud cry of FREEDOM rings out across Scotland as never before, and the continent of South America, dominated for years by a series of dictators at last begins to shake off the heavy hand of American appointed heads of state as individual countries claim the right to handle their own affairs.

Once we wake up to how powerful we actually are, we will be seeing what has been called 'the last waltz of the tyrants'.

The taking back of our enormous power, of course comes accompanied by responsibilities but I feel that it is the only hope we humans have of survival. Perhaps we should keep in mind that the best things are accomplished in a light heart, then just trust and go for it.

Love each other and learn to enjoy the experience, but don't try too hard.

Memoirs of a Maverick

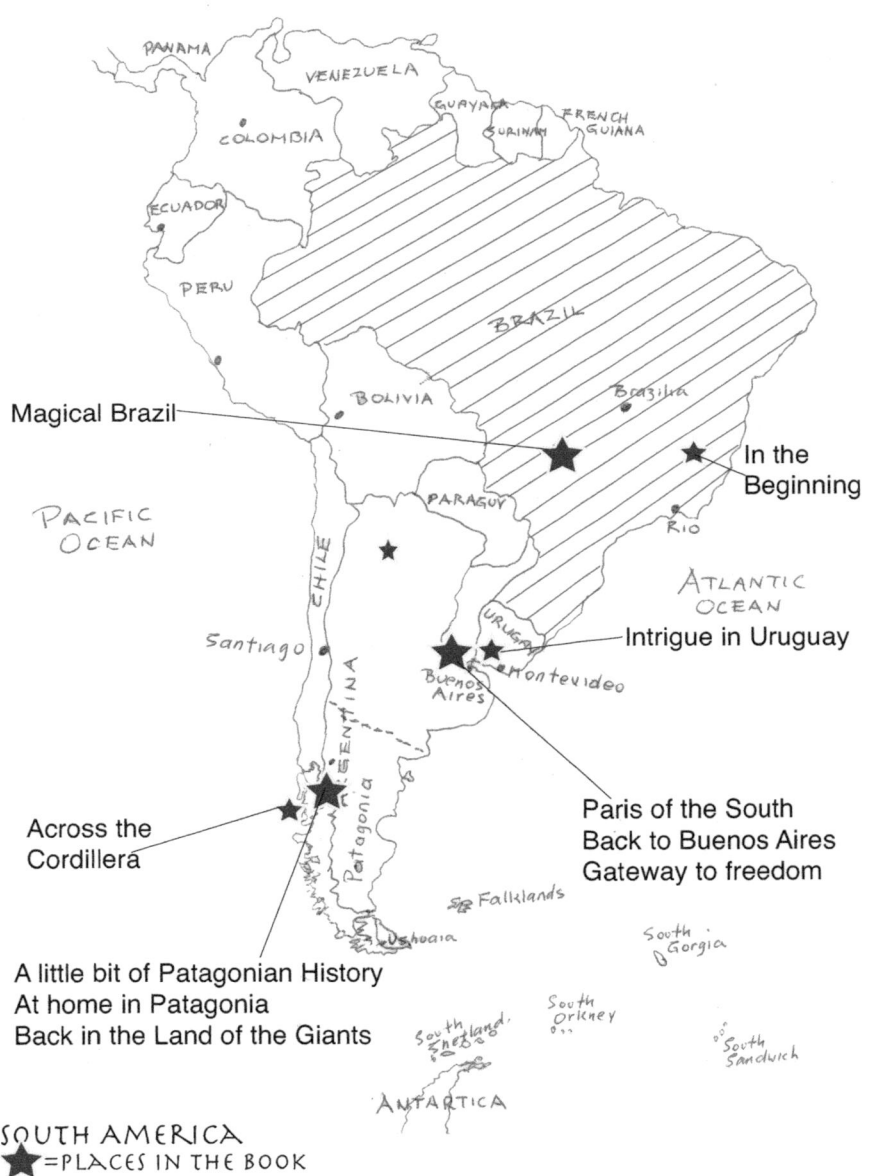

SOUTH AMERICA
★ =PLACES IN THE BOOK

SOUTH POLE

A MAP OF SOUTH AMERICA SHOWING ARGENTINE TERRITORY
(SIMILAR TO THE MAP FOUND IN ARGENTINE SCHOOLBOOKS IN THE
1960S.)

Tigre Boat Club gets a move on

Following the Tigre Boat Club's recent annual general meeting, at which Mr C. Kemp was elected president, Mr T.S. Carstairs vice-president and Mr J. Saragosi treasurer, over a 100 people sat down to an "asado" to officiallyinaugurate the club's three new barbecue grills.

That was the excuse – but it was more significant than that. They were sitting on what, for many years, was just a plot of waste-land, sometimes used as a car park, at the back of the club. Now part is laid out as a garden, while most of the space is taken by the new swimming pool – 18 x 8 meters, with a double filtering system – which is already in use, but will be officially inaugurated shortly at another party.

This is by no means all that is being done by a club which has "stood still" for far too long. The club house is to be remodelled – it has already been re-decorated and looks very different inside – and efforts are being made to aquire a piece of adjacent land for further expansion and also an island situated where there is less river traffic than on the Lujan and from where members could go out rowing without taking their life into their own hands.

The club hopes to get a lot of its former members back and, of course, also new members, as a result of improvements already carried out and to speed up further developments. As far as boats and other facilities are concerned, statistics show that it is one of the Tigre clubs with most to offer per member.

Its current membership drive is aimed chiefly at members of the British and American communities, but all nationalities are welcome to join its very cosmopolitan membership. (E.W.)

This page: Buenos Aires Herald, 1971.

Page 302: Letter following my resignation as President of the Tigre Boat Club.
Page 303: Brighton Argos, circa 1987.

T. E. 749, TIGRE 0071

TIGRE BOAT CLUB

VICTORICA 156

TIGRE, F.C.N.G.B.M.

March 27, 1972.

Mr. Crawford Kemp,
President,
Tigre Boat Club.

Dear Mr. Kemp,

On behalf of the Committee, I am writing regarding your letter of March 19 asking for the acceptance of your resignation as President of our Club.

We of the Committee feel that your continuing to occupy the position of President is important to the Club. However, we are sure you will want certain conditions established.

The purpose of this letter then, is to ask you to fix the terms under which you would be willing to continue to head the Club.

Yours sincerely,

David Edmonds, Secretary.

301

when conventional medicine fails?

Doctor Feel good...

by Jan Jacques

FEELING tired and run down? Perhaps you can't imagine where all that energy you once had has gone. Don't think you're alone. Crawford Kemp has no shortage of women patients who have the same complaint.

But the first step of his treatment is not to prescribe a tonic — but to hand out a questionnaire.

He calls himself a holistic doctor and doesn't confine himself to just a few of the main alternative remedies. He uses four or five together.

Crawford, who is based in Brighton, says: "In order to treat the person, and not just the symptom, you've got to know about

their lifestyles, past illnesses and attitudes.

"There is no point in prescribing a cure if the cause of the problem is going to go undetected.

"I get an incredible amount of women in the 35 to 45 age bracket who complain of having no energy.

"You quickly find out that they're holding down a job and looking after their families.

"It's a sort of juggling act and many don't have time to eat properly. They expect to run on all four cylinders at 10am when they haven't had a meal since 6pm the previous day.

"It's not a prescription they

need, but a change of lifestyle. That's where I can help."

Crawford declares himself a firm believer in the theory that "a change in habits and mental attitudes can work wonders for your health.

"Most people have lost their way and need a nudge in the right direction," he says.

He's a jovial Scotsman who insists most of his patients were sceptics when they came to see him.

"Some come because they are sick of being prescribed painkillers by their doctor for an ailment that doesn't seem to be healing, or medication for nerves that aren't improving, or because what they

have is said to be incurable.

"By using the questionnaire and a few other methods, I can see pointers to what is causing the problem. And then I tackle the cause."

Patients pay £20 for a session which can take anywhere from one to three hours. He has a surgery in Valley Drive.

Among the methods he uses are reflexology, which works on the principle that certain parts of the soles of the feet represent different parts of the body.

For instance, a slight tenderness when the instep is pressed may indicate a kidney weakness.

He also uses homeopathy, a

sort of massage called Shiatsu, and pays great attention to the lines of energy we all have flowing through our body called Meridians.

He is keen on good nutrition and the effects of herbs, and also deals with the Bach Flower remedies which are said to help heal anything from stomach upsets to migraine.

He loves to keep up to date with the latest natural therapy discoveries and says: "Why confine yourself to one or two when they can all work wonderfully together."

Crawford's telephone number is (0273) 560021.

Acknowledgements

These little stories in *I Did It My Way* belong to the people and places of which I have written. So, as I acknowledge all of the different places and people that have contributed to these many and varied anecdotes, I would like to express a big thank you to all whom, so far, have accompanied me along the way. Thank you too, to all my friends who have encouraged me while writing the book.

To my good friend Carol Argyris, I'll always be in your debt for your forthright and honest opinions that managed to bring me back into line. When I have been tempted to get up on my soapbox and pontificate you have stopped me as only a good friend could, thank you Carol.

Most importantly, just saying thank you to my wonderful wife Susan falls far short of what I feel.

Without you this little project would not have been born. You are my inspiration and my support. When I felt like giving up you gently persuaded me to keep at it. Then, when I decided that I had written enough, you became my editor and then book designer. A thousand thanks for your faith in me, and I love you.

Glossary

Bolas – also known as *boleadoras*, they are a throwing weapon made of weighted balls on the ends of interconnected cords, designed to capture animals by entangling their legs. They are most famously used by the South American *gauchos*.

Campo – literally field, but also refers to open countryside

Chacra – a small farm

Chuspa – tobacco pouch from skin of ostrich neck

Charqui – jerked meat, biltong

Chulengo – young guanaco

Comissária – police station

Comissário – rank of police commissar

Estancia – large rural estate, used in the same way as we use the word ranch in English

Faena – slaughter

Galletas de campo – hard tack bread/biscuit eaten when out on the vast *estancias*

Guanaco – beautiful animal found in the southern part of South America, sometimes known as the 'camel deer' or 'Spanish sheep'; related to the llama of the north

Gauchos – there are several conflicting ideas concerning the origin of the term; it may derive from the Mapuche *cauchu* (vagabond) or from the Quechua *huachu* (orphan). Originally the *gauchos* were nomadic people who roamed the South American pampas and were a mix of indigenous and colonial groups. The *gauchos* developed their own distinct way of life and won respect for their toughness, and skills, especially when they fought in the armies that defeated the Spanish colonial regime. Excellent horsemen, they eventually started working for the owners or *patrons* of the vast *estancias*, making them loosely equivalent to the North American 'cowboy'. Argentine writers have celebrated the *gauchos*, and *gaucho* literature is an important part of the Latin American cultural tradition.

Gendarmeria – a military force charged with police duties among civilian populations. Members of such a force are typically called "gendarmes".

Junta – usually means a military junta, or a government led by a committee of military leaders. Sometimes a military *junta* becomes a military dictatorship.

Mapuche – group of indigenous inhabitants of south-central Chile and southwestern Argentina

Mallín – [*pronounced mah-zheen*] flat valley bottom

Mapundungun – the language of Mapuche people

Marcachifles – roving merchants

Mate – prepared from steeping dried leaves of yerba maté *(llex paraguariensis)*, mate is a traditional and popular South American infused drink. It is sipped through a metal straw, called a *bombilla* in Argentina, from a hollow calabash gourd.

Mayordomo – overseer, ranch manager

Nineo – a kind of tumbleweed

Notro tree – also known as Chilean firetree, the Notro tree *(Embothrium coccineum)*, is a small evergreen tree that grows in the temperate forests of Chile and Argentina and deep red flowers. It is a striking sight.

Pichi – armadillo

Pudu pudu – small deer, which range throughout the lower Andes of Chile and southwest Argentina.

Quillango – soft, waterproof poncho made from guanaco hide

Rebenque – heavy duty riding crop

Recado – a *gaucho* saddle, which consists of many parts

Subte – an abbreviation commonly used for *subterraneo*, or underground railway

Tolderia – campsite

Uinca – Mapundungun for white man

Bibliography

E. Lucas Bridges, *The Uttermost Parts of the Earth*, Readers Union Edition, Hodder & Stoughton, 1951

Joe Dispenza, *Evolve your Brain*, Health Communications, Inc, 2007, ISBN 978-7573-0480-4

Eric Frattini, *The Entity: Five Centuries of Secret Vatican Espionage*, St. Martin's Press, 2004, ISBN 978-0-312-375942

Laurence Gardner, *The Shadow of Solomon: The Lost Secret of the Freemasons Revealed*, HarperElement, 2005, ISBN 0 00721660 2

Toby Green, *Saddled with Darwin: A journey through South America*, Weidenfeld & Nicolson, 1999, ISBN 0-297-81901-1

Amit Goswami, *The Visionary Window: A Quantum Physicists Guide to Enlightenment*, The Theosophical Publishing House, 2000, ISBN 0-8356-0793-3

Miceal Ledwith, www.hamburgeruniverse.com, which contains an excellent archive of articles

Bruce Lipton, PhD and Steve Bhaerman, *Spontaneous Evolution*, Hay House UK, Ltd, 2009, ISBN 978-1-419-2580-2

John O'Donahue, *Anam Cara*, Transworld Publishers, 1997, ISBN 0593 042018

Candace Pert, PhD, *Molecules of Emotion*, Simon & Schuster, 1997, ISBN 0-671-03397-2

Ramtha, *The Last Waltz of the Tyrants: The Prophecy Revisted*, JZK Publishing, 2009, ISBN 978-157873-1176

Bill Ryan, Project Avalon, *The Anglo-Saxon Mission: the Third World War and the Inheritance of the New World transcript*, February 2010, www.projectavalon.net

Stan, Masons passing sentence on the public, Above Top Secret's forum, http://www.abovetopsecret.com/forum/thread72937/pg1

Juan Carlos Walther, *La Conquista del Desierto*, Editorial Universitaria de Buenos Aires, 1970

"*Eternity*" - Music & Lyrics by Dougie MacLean. Published by Limetree Arts and Music (PRS & MCPS UK)

"*Those Were the Days*" is a song credited to Gene Raskin, who put English lyrics to the Russian song "Dorogoi dlinnoyu" literally "By the long road", written by Boris Fomin (1900–1948) with words by the poet Konstantin Podrevskii. I referred to Mary Hopkin's recording of 1968.

I DID IT MY WAY